MW01679744

PERSPECTIVES ON AMERICAN EDUCATION

Thomas E. Deering
Augusta State University

KENDALL/HUNT PUBLISHING COMPANY
4050 Westmark Drive Dubuque, Iowa 52002

On the cover:
Apple image © JupiterImages Corporation
Book images © Comstock

ISBN 978-0-7575-2662-6

Printed in the United States of America
10 9 8 7 6

DEDICATION

As always, I dedicate this book to my wife, Carol, and my son, Ian, the two most important people in my life.

TABLE OF CONTENTS

ACKNOWLEDGMENTS

Without the assistance of friends and colleagues, this book would never have seen the light of day. Each contributing author has my heartfelt thanks. A special word of appreciation goes to Steven Jones and Jerry Whitworth. Both Steve and Jerry are contributors to this effort, but more importantly, they have been colleagues and friends of mine for many years. Over those years, and through countless conversations during which we solved the problems of the world, they have helped me think more clearly about education and teaching. Of course technology is playing an ever greater role in the writing, editing, and publishing process. Without the help of Bill Gray I could not have used this great tool in the production of this book. He knows how much I appreciate his assistance. Finally, I thank the staff at Kendall/Hunt for their patience and professionalism.

INTRODUCTION

In 1636, shortly after their arrival in Massachusetts Bay, the Puritans established Harvard College, the first institution of higher education in what has become the United States. Just eleven years later in 1647, the Puritans of Massachusetts Bay passed the Old Deluder Satan Act, which required every town with at least 50 families to pay a man to teach the town's children how to read and write. The law was designed to ensure that all children could read the bible and use its truths as a bulwark against the evils of the devil. Throughout our colonial period a variety of schools were established to ensure children's intellectual and moral development. Dame Schools were fairly informal schools held in a housewife's or widow's home. Children were taught basic reading, writing, and religion. Latin Grammar Schools a provided formal classical education designed to prepare young men for college. Unlike the Latin Grammar School, the English Grammar School offered young men a practical rather than a classical education. During the eighteenth-century the colonies become more established and began to play a substantial role in England's economy. In response to these economic changes private academies began to offer young men a curriculum designed to prepare them for a career in business. By the mid-nineteenth- century many of these academies became private and exclusive college preparation schools. A common feature of most schools during the colonial and early nationalist periods was that they were controlled by religious or charitable organizations. Even those which were not still had a very heavy emphasis on moral development, and often times used the bible as a textbook.

Of course, much has changed since those earlier times. Dame schools are a thing of the past. Young children now receive their basic early education in primary schools staffed by college graduates who also possess a state-issued teaching certificate. College preparation schools, close relatives of the Latin Grammar schools, are fairly not wide spread and mostly private. English Grammar Schools have evolved into one of the tracks of the modern comprehensive high school. And although church controlled K-12 schools continue to provide a solid academic curriculum for many students, more than 90% of America's youth now attend public schools. Dramatic changes have taken place in higher education too. Many of the colonial colleges, among them Harvard, Princeton, and Yale, have developed into some of the best research universities in the world. Finally, no longer does one apprentice or "read" to become a doctor or lawyer. Instead, it takes many years of formal schooling, and in the case of medical doctors, years of specialized training, before they are "board certified." Like the world's best research universities, some of the premier medical and law schools are in the United States.

Along with the changes in structure and mission, control of education has shifted, too. K-12 education is no longer left up to the local communities. It is now a state responsibility and is funded primarily by state resources. Instead of the "hit and miss" school attendance of the past, states now mandate children attend school until at least their early teens. This usually means until 16 years of age. Mandating school attendance has helped produce an American high school graduation rate of approximately 75%. Another major change in education involves school credits and curriculum. By the start of the 20th century both had become fairly standardized throughout the nation. This standardization, together with landmark court cases regarding the education of minorities and those with special needs, has ensured that every child now receives an education that is more similar than it is different. This standardization also makes transferring from one school to another easier, facilitates the application process for those applying to post-secondary institutions, and is seen as an affirmation of America's concept of equal opportunity for all.

As education has become more systematic and standardized, the role of educators has followed suit. Teaching is now a career, not a way for widows to earn a little money or a means of income for the young minister waiting for his first congregation. Teachers today are required to have a college degree, specialized training, and be certificated by the state. Learning theory, child and adolescent development, and psychology now dominate teacher preparation programs. During a teacher's thirty plus year career, he or she will experience many changes in teaching strategies and methods, and state requirements of all sorts. To keep up with the ever-changing nature of their job, teachers must continue to learn through university courses, seminars, and professional development opportunities, while at the same time states and accrediting agencies are requiring teachers to become more knowledgeable in their academic content area.

Yes, American schools of today are a far cry from those of our colonial ancestors. In many important ways schools today are also very different from schools of the early part of the last century. But with all of the changes (you can decide if they are good or not) some things have remained the same. Budgets are still tight. Physical education and the arts are again under assault because many see these disciplines as frills that we can't afford in these tough financial times. As has been the case throughout our history, teacher salaries lag behind those of other professions, and attracting good candidates has become a major challenge for school boards. Moreover, almost 50% of teachers leave the profession within the first five years of their careers. Low salaries, recruitment, and retention are perennial problems that show no sign of being resolved any time soon.

Even with these and other serious problems facing our education system, history is on our side. For more than three hundred years, through wars, economic depressions, political turnover, and great changes in the nation's social fabric, Americans have believed in the power of education, and they continue to be committed to providing the best education possible for their children. Fortunately, as has been the case since the earliest days of this nation, America is blessed with talented and dedicated teachers. This nation's teachers spend an exorbitant amount of time, energy, and even their own money to assist students in becoming the best educated, most complete human beings they can be.

This book is a collection of original essays by just such professionals. Each contributor is a veteran teacher who is convinced that there is no career more important to the health and well-being of the nation than teaching. All the contributors have spent countless hours thinking critically about American education. Their studying, reading, thinking, and questioning have led them to the same conclusion -- the American educational system is far better than its critics claim, and we as a nation should be proud of what the system has helped us accomplish. They are convinced, however, that the system can and must improve. Our drop-out rate is too high, and large numbers of high school graduates are not prepared for higher education, nor do they posses the skills needed to compete in an increasingly competitive job market. These problems are compounded because America lacks a comprehensive, high quality vocational/technical school system. While we have some exceptional K-12 schools, many urban and rural districts are unable to provide the education available to children in the wealthier suburban areas. Most of the authors in this collection see American education as too test-driven and too caught up in the "science" of teaching. Many think the American egalitarian spirit has been bastardized to mean equal outcome instead of equal opportunity. Each contributor to this collection has spent years in the classroom trying to coax the very best out of students. Each has written thoughtfully and carefully about a specific aspect of American education. Each has a hope, which is also mine: we want you to be as committed to the education of America's youth as those teachers who have gone before you.

These essays cover issues from the earliest grades through higher education. Classroom management, students with special needs, character education, and the negative influence sports has on higher education are just a sample of the questions and issues addressed. Practicing teachers as well as those preparing to become teachers should find something interesting in the collection.

As you make your way through this book, the authors ask that you, the reader, take your task seriously: read, think carefully about what each author has to say, balance what they say with what others have said and with your own experiences, come to class prepared to discuss in an organized and logical fashion, and challenge the authors, your classmates, and yourself. This is what you as a teacher should expect of your students, and this is what the authors ask and expect of you. The authors have provided guiding questions at the beginning of each reading to help you find your way. At the end of each selection there are several questions designed to stimulate class discussion. Classroom discussion is an excellent way to hone your position and challenge your classmates. There are also multiple choice questions for each reading. These can be used as short quizzes to ensure that students understand the material they have read and discussed. If you read these essays with the same dedication the authors have demonstrated in writing them, you will learn much, and even enjoy the experience. Good luck!

CONTRIBUTORS

Steve Broidy teaches educational foundations and human development at Wittenberg University. His Ph.D. is from The Ohio State University. Steve's current research interests include the role of sensibility in ethics, and the ethics of teaching.

Tom Brown is an assistant professor of elementary education at Kennesaw State University. He is a former high school teacher and his Ph.D. is from Georgia State University. Tom's areas of interest include exploratory science, student voice, and brain-based learning.

Thomas D. Cavenagh, JD is Professor of Business Law and Conflict Resolution and Chair of the Department of Management & Marketing at North Central College in Naperville, Illinois. In addition, he is the founder of and directs the North Central College Dispute Resolution Center. Tom graduated from Trinity College with a B.A. in religion and philosophy. His J.D. is from DePaul University College of Law.

Debra J. Coffey is an Assistant Professor of Elementary and Early Childhood Education at Kennesaw State University. She is a former elementary school teacher. Her doctorate from the University of Tennessee is in Literacy, Language, and ESL Education, and her areas of interest include tutorial strategies and teacher education.

Thomas E. Deering is the Dean of the College of Education at Augusta State University. He is a former secondary school teacher and school principal. Tom's Ph.D. from the University of Missouri-Columbia is in Foundations of Education, and his areas of interest include philosophy of education and teacher education.

J. Gordon Eisenman is the Chair of the Department of Teacher Education at Augusta State University and an Associate Professor of Early Childhood Education. He is a former elementary teacher with interests in classroom management. Gordon's EdD. is from the University of Georgia in Early Childhood Education.

Samuel B. Hardy, III is an Assistant Professor with Augusta State University in the Department of Educational Leadership, Counseling, and Special Education. His Ed.D in Curriculum and Instruction is from the University of South Carolina. He is a CPA and comes to the field of higher education after a 25 year career with a commercial bank. Sam's areas of interest include school finance and school administration.

John D. Hoge is a Associate Professor of Social Science Education in the College of Education at The University of Georgia. He is a former elementary school teacher. His Ph.D. from Florida State University is in Social Science Education and his areas of interests include early childhood social studies and civic education.

Charles E. Jenks is Associate Professor of Social Science Education in the College of Education at Augusta State University. He is a former middle school and high school teacher. His Ed.D. from The University of Georgia is in Social Science Education. His areas of interest include teacher education and the history of American education.

Steven P. Jones is an Associate Professor in the School of Teacher Education at Missouri State University. He is a former high school English teacher and directs the Academy for Educational Studies at MSU. His Ph.D. from the University of Chicago is in Curriculum and Instruction and his areas of interest are philosophy of education and teacher education.

David Jerner Martin is professor of science education in the Department of Elementary and Early Childhood Education at Kennesaw State University. He was a teacher of science and mathematics for 18 years at the elementary, middle grades, and high school levels. He has his Ph.D. in science education from Georgia State University. His primary area of interest is process-oriented constructivist inquiry science teaching.

Gwen McAlpine is an Associate Professor of Elementary Education at Kennesaw State University in Georgia. She is a former secondary school English teacher and community college instructor. Gwen's Ed.D. from the University of Virginia is in English education and her areas of interest include diversity, global education, and literacy.

Eric C. Sheffield is currently an Assistant Professor in Missouri State University's School of Teacher Education. He spent the fourteen years prior to his arrival at Missouri State teaching high school English in north central Florida. His completed his Ph.D. at the University of Florida in Foundations of Education. His research interests include service-learning, philosophy of education, democratic education, and educational policy.

Barry R. Thompson is an Associate Professor of Science Education at Augusta State University. He is a former secondary school science teacher. Barry's Ph.D. in science education is from the University of Virginia. His areas of interest include science pedagogy and environmental science.

Mark L. Warner is the Associate Dean of Undergraduate Studies in the Bagwell College of Education at Kennesaw State University. He is a former elementary and middle grades teacher and school principal. His Ed.D from Appalachian State University is in Educational Leadership with a major concentration in curriculum design. Mark's areas of interest include problem-based learning and technology in education.

Jerry E. Whitworth is Chair of the Department of Education at Abilene Christian University. He is a former general and special education teacher and Director of Special Education. He received his bachelors from the University of Kansas and his doctorate from the University of Missouri. Jerry's research interests are in teaching at-risk students and the inclusion of students with disabilities in the general classroom.

Judi H. Wilson is an Assistant Professor in Teacher Education at Augusta State University. She is a former teacher, and school and district administrator. Judi's Ed.D. in Educational Administration is from Georgia Southern University and her areas of interest include teacher education and the teaching of language arts.

**Curriculum Revision, Program Development, and New Initiatives:
Beyond the Rhetoric of Improving Teacher Quality**

Mark Warner and Debra Coffey

Guiding Questions

1. Briefly describe an ideal school community.
2. In your description of the school community (Professional Development School Network) how is teacher education involved?
3. How would you establish the relationship between the school and the community?
4. How might you inspire cooperation and collaboration among all stakeholders to share the vision for your Professional Development School Network (PDSN)?

Curriculum Revision, Program Development, and New initiatives: Beyond the Rhetoric of Improving Teacher Quality

Mark Warner and Debra Coffey

Introduction

A brief history of attempts to improve the overall terrain of education reveals a great quest for educational reform. Storms of reform have lashed our education coastlines for decades. Though the storms have brought about some changes, most have been weathered well, and our schooling landscape remains relatively unaltered. As citizens occupying this territory we have endured various attempts at restructuring school organization such as curriculum revision and waves of assessment. According to Dewey (1938), educators have the distinct role of creating present experiences that live fruitfully and creatively in subsequent experiences. With this end in mind, we need educators who are qualified to facilitate this educational goal. Consequently, improving teacher quality is the most promising initiative on the horizon for positively impacting the learning of today's students. Effective schools employ highly qualified teachers as their most compelling educational resource. These teachers are leaders who hold a central position to bind schools and communities together to advance the quality of life for those communities (York-Barr & Duke, 2004). Teacher educators agree that the phrase "highly qualified" is often misleading. It is not exclusively content area expertise, nor is it merely demonstrating a profound understanding of what constitutes effective teaching methods within one's area of expertise. Highly qualified teachers are leaders who transform teaching and learning in a school that ties the school and community together (Crowther, Kagan, Ferguson, & Hann, 2002). This collaborative effort for the benefit of individual students has the potential to transform our educational landscape by releasing the untapped potential of individuals working for the good of everyone involved.

Therefore, this chapter takes the view that improving teacher quality means increasing teacher engagement in community building, and it is predominantly written to contribute to essential dialogue about the role of teacher preparation in community involvement. Teacher preparation programs must retool and enable teacher candidates to view themselves as community leaders who actively participate in community building. Perhaps the most authentic vehicle available to accomplish the task of community building is to broaden our perception of the role that Professional Development Schools play in developing teacher leaders. This may be accomplished by devoting more energy to designing a portion of teacher preparation curriculum around community building. This chapter stresses the need to stretch beyond the traditional boundary lines of school partnerships. Most school partnerships focus only on collaboration between university and school faculty. Here we explore the idea that principals, teachers, university coordinators, community leaders, and parents all participate in teacher preparation. If we take the view that teachers are not institutionally isolated from, but rather actively involved in the resurrection of community, then our programs need to equip our prospective and in-service teachers with the knowledge, skills, and dispositions to be able to carry out their mission as community leaders through active involvement in the community.

Topics Covered in this Chapter

With this in mind, we will begin our journey by first examining a typical *teacher preparation department's mission statement.* Then we will examine elements of this typical undergraduate teacher preparation program to determine if it is in compliance with the recommendations and outcomes found in the *National Standards*. Next we will unpack some interview-based conversations with teacher education faculty members willing to voice their opinions about what's worth keeping in a program, what needs improvement, and areas for further investigation. Finally, we will investigate *new ideas, other proven programs, and a synthesis of possibilities* to improve our role as leaders in our extended community.

A Case Study

Mission Statement

According to our sample Mission Statement, Grandview College's Early Childhood Teacher Preparation Department is committed to excellence in teaching, service, and scholarship. Through collaboration with university colleagues, school district personnel, community groups, and accrediting agencies, the department strives for the preparation of professionals to work with children and youth in the 21st century. The primary mission of the department is to prepare educators to facilitate learning of multiple content using pedagogies developmentally appropriate for early childhood general education and life-span special education (pre-kindergarten through grade five). Through a collaborative, integrative approach, the department prepares individuals to function professionally in multiple settings in general education (P-5) and life-span special education within the context of a multicultural, pluralistic, and technological social community. How does Grandview's mission statement stack up with the recommendations and outcomes found in the National Standards?

National Association for the Education of Young Children (NAEYC) Position Paper—Where Grandview Stands

Recently, one of the national organizations that generate standards for teachers who educate young children (NAEYC, 2003) posed three inspiring questions: (1) What should children be taught? (2) How would we know if they are developing well and learning what we want them to learn? (3) How could we decide whether programs for children are doing a good job? According to the National Association for the Education of Young Children (NAYEC), answers to these questions are the focal point of a position statement that tenders a hardy set of recommendations regarding early childhood curriculum, child assessment, and program evaluation. The NAEYC take the position that policy makers, the early childhood profession, and other stakeholders in young children's lives have a shared responsibility to:

- *Construct comprehensive systems of curriculum, assessment, and program evaluation* guided by sound early childhood practices, effective early learning standards and program standards
- *Build a set of core values* including: belief in civic and democratic values; commitment to ethical behavior on behalf of children; use of important goals as guides to action; coordinated systems; support for children as individuals and members of families, cultures, and communities; partnerships with families; respect for evidence; and shared accountability
- *Implement curriculum* that is thoughtfully planned, challenging, engaging, developmentally appropriate, culturally and linguistically responsive, comprehensive, and likely to promote positive outcomes for all young children
- *Make ethical, appropriate, valid, and reliable assessment a central part* of all early childhood programs. To assess young children's strengths, progress, and needs, use assessment methods that are developmentally appropriate, culturally and linguistically responsive, tied to children's daily activities, supported by professional development, inclusive of families, and connected to specific, beneficial purposes. These purposes include: (1) making sound decisions about teaching and learning, (2) identifying significant concerns that may require focused intervention for individual children, and (3) helping programs improve their educational and developmental interventions.
- *Regularly engage in program evaluation* guided by program goals using varied, appropriate, conceptually and technically sound evidence to determine the extent to which programs meet the expected standards of quality and to examine intended as well as unintended results
- *Provide the support, professional development, and other resources* to allow staff in early childhood programs to implement high-quality curriculum, assessment, and program evaluation practices and to connect those practices with well-defined early learning standards and program standards

Program Compliance with NAEYC Position Chapter

Grandview College's course catalog for Elementary and Early Childhood Education includes course descriptions in their undergraduate program of study that align with the most current research findings. For example, the course description for Teaching Reading in the Early Grades states that a primary emphasis of the course is developing strategies for teaching reading and writing skills that are contextualized in children's literature. Furthermore, the course description advocates an emphasis on multicultural perspectives and the use of technology to facilitate and reinforce instruction. Another example, Teaching Social Studies in Early Childhood Education, describes the course as one in which emphasis is placed on developing an integrated approach to social studies and on developing inquiry processes. It is apparent that these courses, as well as others in the program of study, are deliberately and purposefully correlated to the recommendations found in the NAEYC position statement.

Conversations with Grandview Faculty

Grandview faculty members who were responsible for developing the current program of study for teacher preparation have reached consensus regarding a vision for their teacher preparation program. When asked to reflect upon further curriculum revision, program development, and new initiatives that would meet the needs of their service area, these same faculty members considered deeper issues. After several interactive small group discussions, faculty members impassioned conversations resonated around developing a more systematic vehicle for cultivating school partnerships, selecting cooperating teachers, involving school principals, strengthening university and school faculty relationships, and establishing learning communities. We will now take a moment to listen to what they had to say.

School Partnerships and Cooperating Teachers

Many participants agreed that school partnerships needed to be more pronounced, less arbitrary, and more integrated into the overall plan of the local school. Faculty members pointed out that many of the cooperating teachers involved in the teacher preparation program simply volunteered for these potentially influential roles and that there was no formal application and selection process designed to employ high quality cooperating teachers. These teacher educators echoed the negative effects on teacher candidates who are placed with mediocre cooperating teachers who reinforce the folkways of teaching (Buchman, 1987). Education faculty members are all too conscious of the corpus of research (Kagan, 1992) that indicates how pre-service teachers' attitudes and beliefs about teaching and learning are hardy and highly resistant to change. Most teacher candidates believe that they already know how to teach since they have already served a 13-year apprenticeship in their own schooling (Lortie, 1975). Unfortunately most teacher candidates have been successful at regurgitating information and therefore persist to maintain the status quo. Additionally, this same research regretfully reveals that pre-service teachers tend to filter away teacher education course content in deference to their prior beliefs about teaching and learning (Pajares, 1993). To make matters worse, poorly arranged and unarticulated field experiences reinforce the often unvoiced complaints held by pre-service teachers that teacher education course work is nothing more than "fluff" and furthermore "out of touch" with the real world of teaching. Moreover, teacher candidates working with and befriending so-called cooperating teachers, who do not trust university faculty, further vilify college course work and thus exacerbate this problem. These teacher candidates are thrown into a socialization process that is skeptical and disrespectful toward any current attempts to make changes in timeworn curriculum, outdated instruction, and multiple choice assessment of learning. These negative experiences galvanize pre-service teachers' beliefs that they already know how to teach, and they continue to teach like their ancestors.

As an alternative, teacher educators are much more concerned about working collaboratively with undergraduate teacher candidates. Teacher educators desire to create action research units of instruction for children that are designed to impact the learning of these students. Suggestions for research topics might center on studying the impact of culturally relevant, evidence based curriculum on student performance. Other areas of concern might include the influence of inquiry on student motivation and subsequent academic achievement as well as the effects of engaging multiple intelligences to measure and evaluate student performance. These vibrant proposals amount to stimulating opportunities for teacher candidates, lab teachers, and university faculty. In this context, all participants have an opportunity to study the craft of teaching and experience a powerful means to break the inertia of pedestrian classroom teaching.

Involving School Principals

During this phase of the discussion, faculty members collectively observed that individual school principals were not fully vested in the idea of school partnerships. Most principals only have a tacit awareness of their school's involvement and participation in the teacher preparation program. One faculty member declared, "Our school partnerships are merely tolerated, not celebrated." Education faculty members reified their own understandings about creating a climate of mutual trust and respect in their relationship with the local schools. They agreed that they needed to provide more opportunities to communicate the department's vision of quality collaborative partnerships that strive for the preparation of professionals to educate children in the 21st century.

University and School Faculty Relationships

Further conversations centered on the need for a more deliberate, systematic approach for collaborative program delivery. Teacher education professors shared their concerns about reducing the fears that still reside in the hearts of classroom school teachers regarding university faculty. Some of the questions spawned by this dialogue include: (1) How do we level the playing field for all participants in order to prepare quality teachers for tomorrow's classrooms? (2) Is there a forum that enables classroom teachers to communicate their expertise and voice their perceptions about what's right and what's wrong with teacher preparation? (3) What's lacking in the overall ownership and accountability of what constitutes teacher preparation and professional development? These are some of the questions that need to be addressed if university-based teacher education units are to begin an honest dialogue. Hopefully this dialogue will be orchestrated to remove any fears, anxieties, or resentments aimed at teacher educator efforts so that we can improve the quality of teacher preparation.

Learning Communities

Another conversation emerged giving strong consideration to the idea of schools being centers for community learning. Questions were raised such as: (1) How can we better serve after-school programs and utilize this captive and essential audience to engender the development of community in our schools? (2) How do we meet and engage parents? (3) To what extent is it the College of Education's responsibility to facilitate the development of a learning community that nurtures the idea that schools can once again belong to the public?

Summary

Given all of the concerns brought to the discussion table, we are now ready to investigate ideas and approaches to increase overall teacher quality in our nation's schools. In this investigation, we will consider (1) the framework of Professional Development School Networks, (2) some proven programs in various regions of the United States that have successfully developed schools as centers for community learning, and (3) a synthesis of possibilities to engage parents and the community. Our definition of community includes business partners, private and publicly funded enterprises, and local government agencies who are committed to an educational perspective that promotes free, responsible choices in a culture dedicated to the well-being of all human beings.

Investigation of New Ideas and Other Proven Programs

Professional Development Schools and Teacher Leadership

Professional Development Schools owe their genesis to the idea (Schlechty, 1997) that teaching is not a service delivery profession, like doctors or lawyers. It is a leadership profession. Teachers must assess their own success through others rather than directly through their own performance. Teachers are not surgeons, and they should not be viewed as actors. They are leaders, and what they do should be understood in terms of theories of leadership. The concept of teacher leadership (York-Barr & Duke, 2004) suggests that teachers rightly and importantly hold a central position in the ways schools operate and in the core functions of teaching and learning. Effective teacher leaders improve the teaching and learning in our nation's schools, and the result is increased achievement for every student.

An expanded view of teacher leadership (Crowther, Kaagen, Ferguson, & Hann, 2002) is described as action that transforms teaching and learning in a school, that ties school and community together on behalf of learning, and that advances social sustainability and quality of life for a community. However, the following caveat (Yarger & Lee, 1994) reveals, "in the absence of conceptual frameworks for guiding program development and evaluation, teacher leadership programs will continue to be sporadic, idiosyncratic events." (p. 235)

Teacher leadership (York-Barr & Duke, 2004) is practiced through a variety of formal and informal positions, roles, and channels of communication in the daily work of schools. Sometimes teachers serve in formal leadership positions, such as union representatives, department heads, curriculum specialists, mentors, or members of a site-based management team. At other times leadership is demonstrated in informal ways, such as coaching peers to resolve instructional problems, encouraging parent participation, working with colleagues in small groups and teams, modeling reflective practice, or articulating a vision for improvement. Given the significant impact that teacher leadership has on the overall success of teaching and learning in a school community and warnings regarding its sporadic, idiosyncratic nature, Professional Development School Networks were designed to empower teacher leaders.

Key Components of Professional Development Schools

A Professional Development School Network (PDSN) is usually a university/school system enterprise with the following purposes: (1) create a sustainable network of schools through which the schools collaborate fully with the university to prepare new teachers; (2) support teaching practices that promote and assist all students achieving to high standards, and (3) nourish teaching excellence through experienced teachers' and university faculty members' continued professional development. The PDSN (Gendernalik-Cooper, Eisenman, Thornton, & Warner, 2000) endeavors to cultivate an association of vigorous learning communities. These communities are characterized by a strong articulation of academic and field experience components of the educator preparation curriculum. The entire teacher preparation culture shares a commitment to educational excellence.

Work in the PDSN is organized around the four functions of PDS as described in the NCATE Draft Standards for PDS: (1) educator preparation, (2) student learning and achievement, (3) professional development, and (4) communities of inquiry to improve teaching and learning. The PDSN coordinates the curriculum, including course work and field work, along with assessments of candidate performance with national content and developmental standards. Similarly, the PDSN adopts the guiding principles of the National Board of Professional Teaching Standards for defining and reviewing both "master teacher" and university coordinator expectations. Student learning and achievement are framed within the state content standards and appropriate national content standards. These efforts to align the PDSN work to these national standards facilitate agreement of purposes and actions across functions.

Throughout the PDSN implementation process, considerable participant time and energy is invested in cultivating shared understandings of the purposes and standards. These considerations include: (1) what they look like in the highly complex reality of practice, (2) how they resonate with other institutional purposes and standards, and (3) how well or poorly they serve to inform assessment and accountability expectations. This investment is deepened and enriched by collaboration across school and university boundaries. Master teachers, in particular, become increasingly knowledgeable and articulate in relating their practices and their own professional development agendas to these purposes and standards.

One of the primary goals of the PDSN is considerable role maturation among all members involved in the initiative. Master teachers are expected to become increasingly comfortable and confident in their role, enriching their repertoires to effectively and consistently model best practices and to appropriately guide and evaluate pre-service teachers' performances. Simultaneously, they assume much greater prominence in defining and enacting the expectations for the master teacher selection and renewal process. Master teachers are also the primary designers of PDS initiatives such as summer enrichment programs for marginalized students and contextualized Problem Based Learning (PBL) projects. It is important to note that these types of initiatives might never materialize without the development of the PDSN.

The university faculty role as liaison in the PDSN is critical to the success of the initiative. Communication links with PDS Building Coordinators and master teachers deepen and widen as university faculty invest valuable time and energy cultivating evocative relationships with members of the public school learning community. Mutually supportive practice is evident in joint teaching and scholarly projects that are undertaken by individual faculty members and master teachers. Collaboration between university coordinators and building coordinators regarding lab and apprentice placements is central to empowering teachers in meaningful decision-making. Faculty members regularly seek master teacher input into course and program change ideas. In turn they are increasingly sought out by master teachers for assistance and guidance in school-based initiatives. Faculty's scholarly agendas increasingly encompass, utilize or resonate with the PDSN.

Since the inception of the PDSN, it is expected that university coordinators and building coordinators will assume primary responsibility for field experience and apprenticeship placements of pre-service teachers. Since these faculty know the students well and the building coordinators know their colleagues and commitments, this process is intended to eliminate poor matches or inappropriate assignments. When issues do arise within this context, they should be quickly evident and resolved to mutual satisfaction. Student complaints about field experience placements should disappear. The role of the cooperating lab teacher, involved in course-related field experiences, becomes the focus of considerable attention by building and university coordinators. As changes in the educator preparation programs increasingly focus on assessing performance in order to help youngsters achieve academically, the pivotal nature of the lab teacher's role is heightened.

Faculty members' advising role is similarly deepened and matured within the PDSN. Faculty members provide high quality advisement throughout the program as they work with the same students from the beginning of the program through program completion. This arrangement facilitates opportunities for effectively introducing students to the program. Then faculty guide students through the PDS structure and placement rotations from expectations for performance in classes and field experiences to the portfolio assignment through which students will document both progress and achievement in relation to standards found in the college of education's conceptual framework. This advisory role reflects faculty commitment to program excellence and documentation of program effectiveness in educator preparation.

The opportunity to schedule teacher preparation programs and field experiences in the middle of each semester, when on-campus classes are suspended and students and faculty are in the PDSs, fosters collaboration between university faculty and PDS lab/master teachers. Each semester parallel instruments are used to assess the performance of master teachers, building coordinators, and university coordinators in their collaborative roles with each other and apprentice students. As appropriate, items on these instruments are keyed to the NBPTS guiding principles. These assessment instruments are completed by all participants each semester and submitted to the PDS director. These data figure into annual evaluation of university faculty. The data on master teachers and building coordinators are shared through the university coordinators with the building coordinators and master teachers for any appropriate performance improvements.

This multifaceted evaluation system affords participants a continual stream of data and documentation reflective of the inherent complexity of the PDSN. Through a formal review of the compiled data over several years, participants can formulate a priority agenda for PDSN goals that clarify the distinct mission of PDSs. The emphasis on excellence in teaching practices, participation of teachers in decision making aimed toward improving student achievement, and increased understanding and participation of PDS administrators are all central features of the PDSN.

In all these ways, primary outcomes for the PDSN extend and deepen participation of faculty, administrators and students from all participating institutions. Additionally, it is hoped that collaborative efforts on behalf of these parties will catalyze complementary initiatives. Included among these are (1) Teacher Leadership projects; (2) Problem Based Learning (PBL) projects; (3) various after school and Summer Enrichment Academies; (4) Advanced Academy for Future Teachers project which is, in part, linking PDS and non-PDS schools to cultivate interest in and preparation for teaching careers among high school students; (5) Impacting Student Learning projects which bring teacher education faculty together with PDS master teachers and student teachers to design program components for documenting teachers' impact on student learning and achievement across subject areas and grade levels; (6) Induction of Beginning Teachers and Initiatives which provide a comprehensive model of support, assistance, and professional development for newly minted teachers.

Beyond the PDS Model—Limitations of the PDS

Despite the sustainable academic accomplishments noted, many PDSNs find it challenging to fully engage the interest of all school principals and capture the interest and commitment of community leaders, businesses, and parents. This may happen because the community considers the school a social institution that functions outside the boundaries of other institutional mechanisms that constitute a democracy (Dewey, 1938; Sarason, 1991). When key players abdicate their key responsibilities, they place many children at risk of failure. As noted by Cochran-Smith (2004), "the dire circumstances of children living in poverty are not going to change because teachers teach better. The challenges of urban teaching are the result of systemic deficiencies that individual teachers cannot alter—complex school bureaucracies, the isolation of schools from communities they are supposed to serve, and the large numbers of students whose families have neither the resources nor the will to support school values. By ignoring structural inequalities and differential power relations, the Teaching Commission (2004) and others with a single focus on fixing society by enhancing teacher quality place enormous and unrealistic responsibility on individual teachers." (p. 199)

In light of this stinging indictment, we will now consider how Colleges of Education might rise above these challenges and leverage their teacher educator vantage point to cultivate a disposition, within both undergraduate and graduate teacher candidates. This vantage point embraces a vision of educating children for life by developing strategies that include community leaders, businesses, and parents in the overall educational process. Additionally, we will consider how we can support existing programs that seek to educate parents and encourage their quality participation in the education enterprise. Therefore, in this section of the chapter we will (1) investigate developing schools as centers for community learning, (2) explore principles of public engagement, and (3) examine some currently funded programs that engage parents and the community in schools.

Developing Schools as Centers for Community Learning—
A Potential Enterprise for Service to the Community

Cultivating a genuine appetite for assisting fellow citizens replaces the thinly veiled indifference encountered in the usual garden variety of standard teacher preparation courses of study (Warner, 2004). Teacher candidates are a captive audience often strategically positioned in local schools with the potential to activate centers for community learning. What might a program designed to facilitate the birthing of centers of community learning look like? More importantly what knowledge and skills need to be acquired and what dispositions need to be developed to initiate and sustain the kind of grassroots program of study that might eventuate in helping the public reclaim its schools? Currently, most teacher preparation programs of study focus on enabling in-service teachers to develop units of instruction that demonstrate higher educators' conception of best practices in curriculum, instruction, and authentic assessment couched in the language of the most recent reform agenda. No contemporary teacher educator would argue against the highly charged rhetoric that eschews traditional models of teaching. The real question is, what is the distinction between change that comes from the reform mill and change that is likely to result in the lasting betterment of schools?

According to Oaks, Quartz, Ryan, & Lipton (2000), "the reforms from the reform mill are usually generated as top down innovations. Are teacher educators so enthusiastic about the reformation of teaching that they are blind to the perceptions of their students? Consequently, reforms often obscure rather than elucidate the conflicting demands and needs of all constituencies, both within and outside the school. By silencing or ignoring those who do not agree, do not understand, or remain unconvinced that the new idea is more worth trying than a competing one, the reforms fail to gain the necessary community backing and wholehearted support of those who need to implement them. 'We are always changing, but we are not sure why we are changing,' laments one teacher. A principal says of her faculty, 'We just have so many things going on that you almost get to the point where you just want to quit. The sad thing is that clearly outstanding people are the ones who get close to burnout'...The challenges that they take on are so involved that they require multiple hours of outside work." (p. 194)

Larry Cuban (2000) points out that those innovations having the best chance of sticking are those that have the constituencies that grow around them. Furthermore, Cuban argues that another factor contributing to the success of a particular reform seems to be the ways the reform reflects a deep rooted social concern for democracy, for equity, or for preparing students to lead fulfilling adult lives. How does one marshal the commitment to make schools places where teaching and learning are the primary purposes? We need schools that are better for teachers, students, and communities. Why not engage students, who have already counted the cost of the time and energy it takes to earn a degree, as teacher leader initiates in order to establish authentic centers of community learning? In this promising scenario, professors might have to stretch their muscles away from that which is pedagogically familiar and invite outside community leaders into classroom discussions regarding ways to find and solve the real world of problems indigenous to the schools. The list of community leaders needs to go beyond educational experts and include politicians, corporate executives, civic organization executives, engineers, private business owners, and parents.

Graduate and undergraduate teacher education programs are in a historic position to create forums and enjoy extended classroom conversations filled with opportunities to develop action plans that stand a chance of building lasting relationships dedicated to the cause of improving the quality of families and the lives of individual children. Well-known author and early childhood educator, Vivian Paley (1979) has expressed her disappointment and regret that she waited so long to understand that she had it in her power to make school like a family, a place where one enjoys the casual interaction with those who are learning to love each other. Paley has apologetically stated that we keep the families out of schools and there is no reason to. Our jobs as educators are better when everyone is involved. We are on the wrong track if we feel we can educate children without their families.

Proposed Course of Study

Institutions face a loss of legitimacy when those who created them no longer believe that the institutions are their agents, acting on their behalf. What do site-based management programs, vouchers, charter schools, home schools, private schools, and state takeovers of "bankrupt" systems have in common? They all concern the control of education. There are evidently a great many people who no longer believe that public schools are their agents, who don't believe that public schools are responsive to their concerns. They are creating their own schools, trying to take back their schools, or putting someone in charge who will make schools respond to their priorities. Given these conditions, whether publicly spoken or unsaid, teacher preparation programs are in a promising position to prepare teacher leaders to assist with a public reclamation of schools. Teacher preparation courses need to carve out space for students to develop and implement strategies for this vital enterprise.

Course descriptions need to include such phrases as "gaining public support" and community building. Restoring legitimacy to the public school system will require rewriting the compact with the public, which will in return require a public that can define its interests. The usual techniques are not going to revalidate the compact with the public. What passes for "public support" today does not constitute a true public—a diverse array of citizens constantly joining together to decide on and advance their shared interests, the interests of the community as a whole. Campaigns to engage the public are often hindered because there is often no public waiting to be engaged, to provide legitimacy, or to rewrite the compact with the schools (Mathews, 1997). Given that situation, school reform has to be recast as "public building." The focus has to be on the community rather than the schools. In other words, certain things have to happen in our communities before we can see the improvement in our schools. It is unlikely that schools will change unless communities change and citizens become an effective public by increasing their capacity to band together and act together. Teacher preparation programs can respond to this urgent need by developing curriculum that will enable its graduates to acquire the knowledge, skills, and dispositions necessary to participate as role models in this community building process.

Most of all, making choices together identifies the shared or interconnected purposes that join people as a public. The fate of any community is determined by the choices people make or refuse to make. So community building is, in its most basic form, doing "choice work." How do we learn to build a genuine community? One of the more obvious ways is for people to start making choices together about the kinds of communities they want, choices that define the public's interest. Making common choices with consideration and reflection cultivates a sense of public responsibility. We feel more responsible for what we have chosen than for what has been chosen for us. Choices also make public action possible. We cannot work together until we decide on our common goals. Most of all, making choices together identifies the shared or interconnected purposes that join people as a community. Schools find their charters, their purposes, and ultimately their support in choice work.

Educators, as citizens, have to make common cause with other citizens. What exactly does choice work teach? Choice work is a quintessential public activity. It is careful deliberation with others about a range of options or ways of approaching difficult issues, such as how a community can support troubled families. Deliberative forums do not necessarily result in consensus on one particular action. That isn't their objective, yet they can produce an agenda for a range of actions tied together by a shared sense of purpose and direction. A proposed course syllabus focusing on community building might include the following principles of public engagement (Wadsworth, 1997):

1. *Listening involves understanding public concerns as expressed in people's own language.* Rather than start the conversation with experts' views or solutions, the experts should start by understanding the views of others.
2. *Create an ongoing process.* Engaging the public takes time and requires consistency and patience. Trust and credibility are not earned easily or quickly.

3. *Go beyond the usual suspects.* The process requires a constituency that is broader and more inclusive than those with whom leaders and experts are accustomed to working.
4. *Provide choices.* The core of engaging the public on education is helping people to grapple with their conflicting values as they weigh such alternatives for improving the schools as traditional versus innovative teaching methods or various types of assessments. Creative approaches can expose the public to options they can understand, analyze effectively, and ultimately embrace.
5. *Deal with obstacles.* Allow sufficient time and opportunity for the public to work through obstacles. Anything less arouses suspicion and costs time in the long run. Assist in helping to make the distinction between hot issues and emotional ones.
6. *Avoid Jargon.* Be willing to participate in thoughtful, nonpartisan discussion in which answers to questions are provided calmly and credibly.
7. *Communicate productively.* Frame issues in a way that allows for deliberation.

Promoting Community Involvement in Schools

Teacher preparation course work must also promote curriculum content that reinforces the notion that parental and community involvement contributes to improvements in student achievement. Increased student achievement in traditionally low performing areas may also influence higher quality teachers to remain teaching in these areas. In an article on teacher effectiveness, Carey (2004) identifies a recent study (Freeman, Scafidi, & Sjoquist, 2002) from Georgia illustrating that teachers who moved to new schools within a district went to schools with higher levels of student achievement and with lower proportions of students in poverty. If we are concerned about teacher job market decisions that negatively impact our underserved children, then we need to develop strategies that promote and engender compassionate service through exploring opportunities to build communities that attract quality teachers. Quality teachers are more likely to remain in a school environment where all constituents demonstrate an active concern for the well-being of its children.

Another study (Shirley, 1997) has confirmed this view. According to the study, the efforts of community members to create a health clinic at an elementary school in Austin, Texas, played a role in raising students test scores over a two-year period. Similarly, attempts to reach out to parents in a middle school in Fort Worth, Texas contributed to an increase in test scores, from 20th (last place) to 3rd among all middle schools. Likewise, a community-wide campaign to improve traffic safety outside an elementary school in El Paso, Texas, helped to increase the percentage of fourth graders who passed state mandated tests from 27% to 61% in reading and 21% to 51% in math. These developments are a direct result of dedication to developing a constituency of parents, community leaders, and educators working together to improve student achievement in low-income communities. With support from the Texas Education Agency and state funds, schools bring together members of community based organizations, parents, and school staff to improve their schools and neighborhoods. If increased test scores is an index of success, then community based, school initiatives demonstrate that the power of involvement for improving learning may come from a number of different sources. Beyond changes in curriculum or improvements in self esteem, meaningful community involvement sets in motion a chain of events that transforms the culture of the school and often, the community that school serves. Furthermore, common patterns among schools that engage the community suggest that public involvement contributes to improvement in: (1) the physical conditions, resources, and constituencies that support learning, (2) the attitudes and expectations of parents, teachers, and students, and (3) the depth and quality of the learning experiences in which parents, teachers, and students participate. Ultimately, success will be measured not by higher test scores, but by the extent to which communities transform the conditions, expectations, and learning opportunities for their students.

In addition to initiatives that energize community involvement that indirectly influences academic achievement, individual parental engagement makes a direct significant difference on measures of student performance (Wang, Haertel, & Walberg, 1993). What constitutes parental engagement, and how does it operate to increase student achievement?

Parental Engagement that Makes a Difference

The influence of parental engagement is evident in the lives of many teachers. Typically, teachers experience success in school. They relate stories and reveal that the origins of their success were in no small way attributable to the hours their devoted parents spent reading with them, playing games with them, answering questions, and asking them questions. Even though their parents often did not realize the full significance of these activities, they were usually committed to a type of child/parent relationship that is espoused and lauded by current brain researchers (Wolfe & Brandt, 1998). In many ways teachers were nurtured to love learning as they enjoyed their parents' devotion and guidance while they prepared for school. If you are reading this chapter, there is a strong likelihood that you share in this experience.

Our sophisticated culture privileges success in school. Success in school is a predictor of material success in life and all of the other benefits that accrue from this success. As long as we continue to privilege success in schooling as a significant portion of our capital assets, we must all also realize that failure has its own set of accrued consequences as well—drugs, teen pregnancy, crime, poverty, depression, fear, anxiety, and a litany of other neuroses.

If we know that what transpires at home between parents and young children is critical and highly correlated to the success of children in school and ultimately in life, then why are we not devoting more of our time, talent, energy, and dollars to educating parents about the significance of academic study at home? Our alleged concerns about increasing student achievement have precipitated the expenditure of millions of dollars on improving curriculum, generating ideas and conducting research regarding best instructional practices and student achievement on tests. However, we are overlooking perhaps the most organic, potentially cost effective resource available to improve student achievement. Research indicates (Wang et al., 1993) that parental involvement at home is even more significant than parental involvement in school on measures of student achievement. Why are we not focusing more energy on engaging the public in the educational rearing of its children? From where does this disconnected thinking originate? Is there an underlying belief among teacher candidates and their veteran colleagues that parents are inept when it comes to enhancing or even initiating academics in the home? Do teachers have an awareness that most of their oral and written communication as well as their body language experienced by parents, distances them from ever being able to convince parents that working with their children is more beneficial than lying on the couch channel surfing?

Researchers (Finn, 1993 & Tracy, 1995) have identified three types of parental engagement at home that are consistently associated with school performance: (1) actively organizing and managing the child's time, (2) helping with homework, and (3) discussing school matters with the child. Additionally, studies (Finn, 1998) have shown a positive relationship between a literacy laden home and students' school performance. Even when these literacy resources are in short supply, reading to a child and having the child read to a parent are crucial activities for the development of literacy. Unfortunately, many households, especially low income or minority homes have few books that are appropriate and interesting to children. Children from these homes arrive at school with surprisingly little experience with books. Concurrently, many parents lack the skills to guide their children's reading or schoolwork. Some school sponsored programs have been highly successful at improving these situations by providing books for children to take home twice a week. Other programs such as Even Start have proactive components to recruit parents, improve their literacy skills, and develop a regular structure for home-based literacy. This helps parents overcome obstacles to literacy activities in the home and to convince them that their children can become successful readers. These parental engagement behaviors are important for young children. Early behavior that is dysfunctional tends to be sustained and to increase over the years. Although the research evidence on parental participation in school is mixed, the evidence about parental engagement at home is persuasive. Disengagement is incapacitating. Steinberg (1996) found that children whose parents are disengaged, who fail to provide guidance or structure in the family setting, have the poorest developmental patterns. They often lack psychological maturity, social competence, and self esteem. The problems encountered by these youngsters, in school and out, multiply throughout the school years. Our knowledge of how negative relationships in the home impact student success in school makes us culpable if we do not consider how we can assist teacher candidates in planning and implementing interventions that counteract this negative influence.

Models of Parental and Community Involvement in Schools

Are there current models on the American educational landscape that are pioneering the cause of parental and community involvement? New American Schools is a promising business-led, nonpartisan, nonprofit organization designed to offer key stakeholders the tools and external assistance needed to facilitate and sustain both student and adult learning.

New American Schools (NAS)

New American Schools (NAS) is a leading provider of professional services and investment in K-12 education. New American Schools (http://www.naschools.org) is committed to helping all students succeed by shaping, supporting, and sustaining system-wide innovation and improvement in learning. To achieve its mission, New American Schools works on efforts that promote choice, entrepreneurship, equity, quality, and sustainability. NAS advocates policies that advance these values while they partner with high-quality education providers to make best-in-class services available on a national scale. As a business-led, nonpartisan, nonprofit organization, NAS and its strategic partners give support to state departments of education, school districts, charter authorizers, and networks of schools. Their task is to help them design, implement, and align the essential components of a comprehensive school improvement strategy. The following paragraphs provide a synopsis of information from the website of New American Schools. These examples are representative of NAS involvement in establishing community-based schools.

The Accelerated Schools Project (ASP)

The Accelerated Schools Project (ASP) centers on values and three core principles that support powerful learning experiences for all students. The values of (1) equity, (2) participation, (3) communication and collaboration, (4) community spirit, (5) school as the center of expertise, (6) risk taking, (7) reflection, (8) experimentation and discovery, and (9) trust mesh with three principles that guide the school's work. The three principles are empowerment with responsibility, unity of purpose, and building on strengths. When put into action, they unite the school and lead to a positive and collaborative school culture where everyone works toward the common goal of increasing student learning. The ASP school's journey begins when the entire school community, staff, parents, students, and the broader community forge a vision for their dream school and carry out inquiry on central challenges they must overcome to achieve their vision. Members of groups called cadres learn to use a method of inquiry to identify root causes for the school's challenges and to identify solutions which are the best match for the school's unique context. The core of the project is acceleration through powerful learning. This approach discourages the use of remedial practices that slow down and mechanize learning for struggling learners. It offers them and all students interesting and motivating instructional experiences that are authentic, inclusive, learner-centered, interactive, and continuously built around the instructional practices typically reserved for the gifted and talented population. ASP schools have reported success in the following ground breaking areas:(1) significant decreases in discipline referrals to the school principal; (2) increases in school attendance and decreases in grade retention; (3) reduction in school suspensions; (4) increases in parental involvement including partnerships with the local university to develop and provide training facilities for students to practice Accelerated School strategies; (5) increases in the number of students participating in extracurricular activities and in the amount of family/community involvement in school programs; and (6) teachers and parents exercising greater decision-making power, including the establishment of a parent resource center. The resource center serves as a place where parents can spend time reading books and parenting magazines or watching educational videos. Parent coordinators organize "coffees" for parents to come and spend time networking with each other and school faculty. More information about ASP schools can be found at this website: http://www.naschools.org/contentViewer.asp?highlightID=57&catID=87.

Co-nect

Co-nect concentrates on helping low performing schools raise test scores through alignment of curriculum, instruction, assessment, and educational resources with state learning standards. Co-nect consultants work with teams of teachers to devise data-driven goals for improving student achievement in literacy, mathematics, science and other core subject areas. Co-nect has worked in 30 states, 85 districts (including the 10 largest districts in the country), and over 300 schools. Independent studies document Co-nect's success in forging improvements in student achievement, school climate, and instructional practices in Title I schools. Co-nect schools have documented that (1) implementation of Project Based Learning (PBL) involving a collaborative approach, has provided a seamless link between curriculum and resource integration resulting in higher test scores; (2) incorporation of technology into projects, investigations, and every aspect of everyday school life has improved student achievement; and (3) differentiation of student instruction driven by work on projects and research conducted on the Internet increases content mastery growing from its relationship to real world applications.

Different Ways of Knowing

Different Ways of Knowing is an adaptable, research-based, and field-validated approach to school improvement for K-12 schools. Numerous independent research studies consistently show its effectiveness in improving achievement in low-performing schools. The core premise of the model is that all children are capable of high-level learning provided that classroom instruction draws on a wide range of intelligences. This multi-year professional development program is based on the model's six practices for high-achieving schools: (1) planning curriculum, instruction, and assessment using standards linked to "big ideas;" (2) facilitating teaching and learning that support student inquiry and self-directed learning; (3) teaching strategies that expert learners use in reading, writing, and mathematical thinking to close the achievement gap; (4) integrating the visual, performing, literary, and media arts in all content areas; (5) engaging families and communities as partners in student learning; and (6) developing leadership for results inside a learning community. Through on-site coaching, professional development workshops, and summer institutes, the program provides strategies and tools that are customized for schools and districts to dramatically increase achievement for all student groups.

Turning Points

Turning Points is a design for comprehensive middle school reform coordinated by the Center for Collaborative Education (CCE) in Boston, Massachusetts. The design is driven by one overarching goal—ensuring success for every student. Turning Points seeks to create high-performing schools through teacher collaboration and data-based inquiry. Member schools are provided with intensive on-site coaching and professional development. Turning Points help middle schools create challenging, caring, and equitable learning communities that meet the needs of young adolescents as they reach the "turning point" between childhood and adulthood. In no other period of education can one find such a wide range of cognitive, physical, and social development among students. Cognitively, middle school learners are moving from thinking concretely to reasoning about abstract concepts. Young adolescents are making choices that have long-term consequences for their education and well-being. The challenge for middle schools is to engage young adolescents in significant learning and prepare them for the independence and responsibility necessary for becoming lifelong learners, citizens, workers, and family members (Wiles & Bondi, 2003). By fostering collaboration among faculty and focusing sustained professional conversation on student work, student learning, and teaching practice, Turning Points helps middle schools to achieve the challenging, but all-important vision of ensuring success for every student.

The Bernstein Center

The Bernstein Center approach to education places the arts at the center of learning across all the disciplines. It prepares teachers to use the arts and the creative process to strengthen teaching and learning by providing a system to organize curriculum through units of study and assess student performance based on content and performance standards. Through the Artful Learning approach, participants are immersed in its four components: experience, inquire, create, and reflect. Like Leonard Bernstein, both students and teachers explore their learning environment using the lens of the artist, the mentorship of the teacher, and the discipline of the scholar. Artful Learning was inspired by Leonard Bernstein's vision that music and the arts could be used to improve a child's academic achievement and instill a love of learning. Artful Learning uses powerful arts-infused curriculum units developed by teachers to engage and excite children. The Artful Learning Framework—Experience, Inquire, Create and Reflect—encourages and supports best teaching practices and improves the way students, and teachers, learn. Teachers are assisted in the Artful Learning Model to become proficient in reliably producing engagement by students. This engagement, done with arts-based skills, which are grounded in classroom research, builds a joy in learning that leads to a love of learning. Classrooms systematically employ key, proven approaches to strengthen understanding, retention, transfer, and application.

The Bernstein Model serves all students, especially marginalized students, but it also successfully challenges average and currently high achieving students. It addresses traditional standards for basic skills and addresses the "basics of the future" including learning to learn, learning to love learning, creativity, problem-solving, and the character education and relationship skills for successful citizenship and employment.

Expeditionary Learning Outward Bound

Expeditionary Learning Outward Bound is a proven model for comprehensive school reform for elementary, middle and high schools that emphasizes learning by doing, character growth, teamwork and literacy. Teachers connect rigorous academic learning, aligned with standards, to adventure, service, and character development. Through school-based and national professional development, teachers learn how to teach reading, writing, science, math, the arts, and other subjects through a challenging set of connected, real-world projects called Learning Expeditions. It calls on schools to build a culture of high academic and social standards by designing Learning Expeditions aligned with district and state standards, grouping students heterogeneously, and supporting all students to achieve beyond their expectations. In Expeditionary Learning schools, students spend most of their day engaged in learning expeditions, which are hands-on, six-to-eight week long studies of a single topic such as water quality, the Civil Rights Movement, or the scientific revolution. Teachers work in teams to design their own learning expeditions that align with district and state standards. Block scheduling and common planning time make it possible for students to go into the community for fieldwork and service. To create a culture of support and high standards, schools mainstream all students, schedule time for advisories and morning circles, and ask teachers to stay with the same group of students for two years or more.

The Urban Learning Centers (ULC)

The Urban Learning Centers (ULC) is organized around three essential components:

- *Rethinking Education* (Teaching and Learning) is designed to ensure that all students are taught in a community of learners using effective educational practices.
- *Restructuring Schools* (Governance and Management) engages learning community members in decision-making and ensures that the Learning Center can improve and evolve. Urban Learning Centers also incorporates the extensive use of advanced technology as an essential element for implementation of the design.
- *Rebuilding Community* (Learning Supports) establishes new strategies to overcome barriers to student by addressing the health and well being of students and their families.

Operating at one site, or across a K-12 family of schools, the Urban Learning Centers design envisions the school as a safe, active hub of community life. The Urban Learning Centers goal is for every student to acquire fluency and comprehension, the communication skills necessary to listen carefully, speak articulately, and write effectively. They also emphasize activities to build an understanding of fundamental mathematics concepts and their application. Every student is expected to obtain a solid understanding of the basic subjects of history, geography, science, mathematics, and English, as well as a second language and the arts. Students are also expected to develop critical thinking and problem solving abilities, understand and be able to use new technologies, and be prepared for success in college and the workforce.

Concluding Remarks

This chapter is predominantly written to generate essential dialogue about the role of teacher preparation in community involvement and to propose a way in which this problem might be addressed from the teacher educator's vantage point. A teacher educator's responsibility is not solely to change pre-service teachers' flawed beliefs and misconceptions about teaching and learning. It is not enough to merely develop numerous strategies (Brooks and Brooks 1998) and interventions that enable teacher candidates to interact positively with children. It is also imperative that teacher educators wholeheartedly assist in the empowerment of transformed teachers. These teacher leaders will become change agents who significantly impact and rehabilitate the community to help reclaim its schools.

Teacher preparation programs need to reevaluate their distinct missions to determine whether or not they provide adequate time to prepare teacher candidates to educate parents. Questions need to be raised in the context of teacher preparation course work. Does the community feel welcome or invited to participate in the well-being of its schools? Do public schools really belong to the public? Many public schools are in grave danger of losing their credibility because they have failed to petition for the public to participate in contributing to the soul of the school. If we care about what happens to children, then why don't we aggressively approach parents as primary movers and shakers in the education process? How can we as teacher educators participate in abating this problem? Can we continue to look the other way and pretend that it is not our place to be involved?

Perhaps the most authentic vehicle available to accomplish the task before us is to hybridize the role of the Professional Development School by devoting more energy to designing a portion of our curriculum around community building. We need to stretch beyond the traditional boundary lines of school partnerships that only chiefly encourage and endorse collaboration between university and school faculty. We need to explore the idea that principals, teachers, university coordinators, community leaders, and parents all participate in teacher preparation. If we take the view that teachers are not institutionally isolated from, but rather actively involved in the resurrection of community, then our programs need to equip our prospective and in-service teachers with the knowledge, skills, and dispositions to be able to carry out their mission.

Finally, our program quality is best measured by the overall successes our graduates experience with young children achieving to higher standards in our local schools. Criteria that measure this kind of effectiveness naturally include increased test scores on norm referenced tests. However, as educators who understand the notion that

Schlechty, P. (1997). *Inventing better schools: An action plan for educational reform.* San Francisco: Jossey-Bass.

Shirley, D. (1997). *Laboratories of democracy: community organizing for school reform.* Austin: University of Texas Press.

Steinberg, L. (1996). *Beyond the classroom.* New York: Simon and Schuster.

Teaching Commission. (2004). *Teaching at risk: A call to action.* New York: Teaching Commission.

Tracey, D.H. (1995). Children practicing reading at home: What we know about how parents help. In L.M. Morrow (Ed.), *Family literacy: Connections in schools and communities.* College Park, MD: International Reading Association.

Wadsworth, D. (1997). Building a strategy for successful public engagement. *Phi Delta Kappan, 78*(10), 749-752.

Wang, M.C., Haertel, G.D., and Walberg, H.J. (1993). Toward a knowledge base for school learning. *Review of Educational Research, 63*(3), 249-294.

Warner, M. (2004). An emergent problem-based course for prospective middle grades teachers. *Middle School Journal, 35*(4), 33-41.

Wolfe, P. and Brandt, R. (1998). What do we know from brain research? *Educational Leadership, 56*(3), 8-13.

Yarger, S.J., & Lee, O. (1994). The development and sustenance of instructional leadership. In D.R. Walling (Ed.), *Teachers as leaders: Perspectives on the professional development of teachers* (pp. 223-237). Bloomington, IN: Phi Delta Kappa Educational Foundation.

York-Barr, J., & Duke, K. (2004). What do we know about teacher leadership? Findings from two decades of scholarship. *Review of Educational Research, 74*(3), 255-316.

Reflection and Service-Learning in Higher Education:
Some Philosophical Underpinnings to Transforming Service into Learning

Eric C. Sheffield

Guiding Questions:

What is service-learning?

What is a weakness of the service-learning pedagogy?

What brings about true reflective thinking and how is that thinking structured?

How can service-learning educators teach students to be reflective thinkers?

**Reflection and Service-Learning in Higher Education:
Some Philosophical Underpinnings to Transforming Service into Learning**

Eric C. Sheffield

Service-Learning, the Briefer Course and a Problem

I begin this discussion with a very brief description of service-learning for those readers who may be unfamiliar with it: service-learning is a pedagogy wherein students apply knowledge and skills learned in a university course of study (for our present purpose, though the same might be said of K-12 class work as well) to community problems that they, the students (with instructor guidance), find both socially important and academically appropriate to the course--appropriate in that the academic connection to the community problem and its possible solutions is a reasonable one. In so doing, course-based content knowledge and understanding can be expanded and deepened, a disposition to and capacity for reflective thinking grown, interaction among disparate community "strangers" encouraged, and service, as an essential democratic practice, incorporated into the regular modus operandi (habit) of the service-learning participants.

Though the service-learning pedagogy looks simple enough, it is not and its complicated structure makes service-learning, though incredibly worthwhile, difficult to practice successfully. This is especially so in colleges and universities where the typical semester course lasts no more than several months--certainly not enough time to either understand service-learning nor practice it with much, if any, real understanding. In fact, as I will ultimately argue here, I believe that service-learning courses at traditional, "semester-schedule" colleges and universities must be developed so that there exists either a prerequisite course on the theoretical structure of service-learning that emphasizes how and why service-learning can be educationally sound, or that service-learning courses be sufficiently long (two semesters, at the very least) to provide the time needed to explore the nature of service-learning as a pedagogy that is, above and beyond anything else that it might be, a transformative pedagogy of reflection.

Unfortunately, many service-learning projects fail to reach their full potential because service-learning's sophisticated theoretical underpinnings are ignored and consequently its practice is poorly implemented. The misunderstanding and/or ignorance regarding the philosophical bases of service-learning is particularly dangerous in colleges of education where we hope to encourage potentially powerful transformative pedagogies and yet often fail to fully teach their underlying structures. This lack of theoretical understanding on the part of pre-service teachers spreads rather than contains the very disease that might well destroy service learning's potential as a sound pedagogy: bad practice based on bad or incomplete theory. Those of us in colleges of education who champion such critical pedagogical endeavors do well to first understand those underlying theories ourselves and then to clearly and thoroughly "teach" them to our students. The need for a full semester course extension and/or the development of a full semester course that exclusively examines service-learning's complicated theoretical structure can be seen by closely examining just one of its numerous components: reflection.

<u>The Practical Reflective Disconnect</u>

Janet Eyler expresses quite clearly the central importance of reflection to a service-learning project when she argues that

> Reflection is the hyphen in service-learning; it is the process that helps students connect what they observe and experience in the community with their academic study. In a reflective service-learning class, students are engaged in worthwhile activity in the community, observe, make sense of their observations, ask new questions, relate what they are observing to what they are studying in class, form theories and plans of action, and try out their ideas (2001, p. 35).

Service-learning advocates such as Eyler have long understood that reflection is *the* component that transforms the interaction of academics and service into a deep and abiding understanding of both (Chickering 1977, pp. 12-18; Honnett and Poulsen, 1989; Mintz and Hesser, 1997). As Eyler says it, "In practice it is critical reflection that provides the transformative link between the action of serving and the ideas and understanding of learning" (1996, p. 14). Clearly, understanding reflection, and practicing it accordingly, is essential to successful service-learning particularly at colleges and universities.

What happens all too often in service-learning projects, however, is the *understanding* that reflection is paramount to success and, at the same time, a disinclination to teach reflective theory or, even, to incorporate structured reflective practice into the project design (Eyler 2001; Duley 1981; Boud, Keough, and Walker 1985; Eyler, Giles and Schmiede 1996; Tool and Tool 1995; Mabach, 1994). This disconnection between understanding and practice on this matter seems to have a two-fold cause. Firstly, as Boud, Keough, and Walker argue,

> The activity of reflection is so familiar that, as teachers or trainers, we often overlook it in formal learning settings, and make assumptions about the fact that not only is it occurring, but it is occurring effectively for everyone in the group. It is easy to neglect as it is something which we cannot directly observe and which is unique to each learner (1985, p. 8).

Secondly, because we come into the world able to reflect on a limited, instinctual level we educators often assume our students simply do it both regularly and successfully:

> The basic reflective and puzzling techniques that help us make sense of everyday life form the core of the very same

techniques that enable students to derive meaningful learning from the experience of service; [however,] it is the critical questioning of why things are and the attempt to fully understand the root causes of observable events and behaviors [that must be taught]. This depth of critical reflection grows out of the instinctual reflective process but must be cultivated purposefully as a habit of the mind (Eyler, Giles, and Schmiede 1996, p. 14).

If service-learning practice is to be successful, reflection--as well as the various other components of service-learning--must be clearly understood, modeled, taught, and practiced. In the case of university/college students (particularly future/practicing public school teachers) the complicated structure of reflective thought has to be examined in detail if it is to be successfully incorporated into a service-learning project. That examination can be initially undertaken by looking at the theoretical structure provided by John Dewey.

The Features of Deweyan Reflection

Dewey argued that thinking could be understood in several different ways. It is first discernable as conscious thought that, try as we may, we cannot stop. It is this type of thought that William James described as the "flights and perchings" of consciousness (1892, p. 27). Thought also is found in fancy and imagination. Story making falls into this second category and is characterized not by the quest for knowledge or problem solution, but as an emotive expression that has as its goal an interesting plot or surprising climax. A third kind of thought Dewey called belief. Belief is the type of thought that is built up through "tradition, instruction, [and] imitation" (1933, p. 7). Belief is based on "prejudgments," not on examinations of evidence. Finally, Dewey talked of formal, scientific thinking. It is this formal, problem-oriented, thought that he called "reflective thought." Reflective thought is "active, persistent, and careful consideration of any belief or supposed form of knowledge in the light of the grounds that support it and the further conclusions to which it tends" (1933, p. 5). It is reflective thinking that Dewey was most concerned with, and it is reflective thinking that brings service-learning projects and academic, classroom skills together to create learning.

Dewey theorized that reflective thought has specific features that can be understood by disentangling them conceptually from the actual process:

> So much for the general features of a reflective experience. They are (i) perplexity, confusion, doubt, due to the fact that one is implicated in an incomplete situation whose full character is not yet determined; (ii) a conjectural anticipation--a tentative interpretation of the given elements, attributing to them a tendency to effect certain consequences; (iii) a careful survey (examination, inspection, exploration, analysis) of all attainable consideration which will define and clarify the problem in hand; (iv) a

consequent elaboration of the tentative hypothesis to make it more precise and more consistent, because squaring with a wider range of facts; (v) taking one stand upon the projected hypothesis as a plan of action which is applied to the existing state of affairs: doing something overtly to bring about the anticipated result, and thereby testing the hypothesis (1944, p. 153).

It is essential to point out here that Dewey's conceptual outline of reflection is not a regulated, four- or five-step program, or stop and go cycle that leads to reflective perfection. Numerous writers who support service-learning particularly, and experiential learning generally, seem to forget that Dewey's discussion is a means to understand what is in reality an intricate process (Fry and Kolb 1998, pp. 79-92). To "view" the process is to see complicated meanderings from problem, to hypothesis, to past experience, to testing, and back and forth. That means that individual students may be at different reflective "places," doing somewhat different things, at different times. Though this makes a teacher's work even more complicated, it is the nature of reflective thought.

"Felt Problems" as Catalysts to Reflection

In Dewey's construction, reflective thought comes about because an experience causes a "state of doubt, hesitation, perplexity, mental difficulty" in individual students (1933, p. 12). In reflective practice and, therefore, in service-learning, student interest and purpose are essential. This becomes acutely clear when one examines how reflective thought is initiated. Reflective thought begins only when a truly felt problem (one vitally important enough to cause perplexing uneasiness) is "discovered," "found," "stumbled upon," or "lead to." If a problem does not come out of student experience, if it is fabricated by another, or is not genuinely felt by the student, there will be no catalyst to reflection. And without reflection, no contextual connections are made between classroom learning and the experience itself: learning/growth does not occur.

For service-learning practice to be successful, the emotive nature of problems, both as catalysts and aims of reflection, must be understood as well. The realization of a problem comes about as a "feeling" that something is amiss. In an article defending Dewey's view of emotion in problem discovery, Robert Sherman reminds his readers that

> The fact of the matter is that we do have such feelings. (Though we may suppress them and not recognize that they are a motive to thought.) We are *surprised* or *intrigued* or *revolted* or *elated* by experiences. We *like* the recommendations that one essayist has, or *dislike* the proposals put forward by some legislator. Our "guts" are tense, our heads ache, we pace the floor, and our voices rise. These all are indications that we have an "interest" in the matters at hand. Alas, instead of using these as a motive to thought, to exploit the interests, we suppress the feelings; we believe they are in competition with thought and always should be judged the loser (Sherman 1985, p. 7).

This affective character of the reflective process is precisely what Dewey meant when he described the initiating stage of thought as "a felt difficulty":

> The difficulty may be *felt* with sufficient definiteness as to set the mind at once speculating upon its probable solution, or an undefined *uneasiness* and *shock* may come first, leading only later to definite attempt to find out what is the matter (Dewey 1997, p. 72).

Service-learning participants must understand that projects, to be successful, can come only from a direct emotional attachment to the service problem. In this way, the service itself, through reflective connection to academic study, can accomplish educationally sound aims. Without that emotional attachment, there is no problem to be solved and no context for the application of academic, course-acquired knowledge and skill.

Not only does the affective realization of a problem initiate thought, it also necessarily drives the entire reflective process. Because the initiator of thought is a perplexity, or incompleteness in experience, the goal of reflection is the closing of that uneasiness, a reconstruction of the experience that brings wholeness to it once again. As Dewey argued, "The two limits of every unit of thinking are a perplexed, troubled, or confused situation at the beginning and a cleared-up, unified, resolved situation at the close" (Dewey 1997, p. 106).

In bringing academic skills learned in a university course to the service project, purposeful activity in the form of knowledge and skills are brought to a genuinely felt problem in a student's experience. In this way, the particular knowledge and skills are practiced, honed, and critiqued for success and adjustment within the service project activity. The service project experience and academic learning are bound together intimately through reflection by asking and answering such questions as "what can be done together, using the knowledge/skills learned in this course of study, to solve this important community problem?" The result can be the reinforcement in experience of academic learning as well as the formation of participatory, democratic habits.

The Mediation of a "Felt Problem"

As an emotional, affective activity, problem detection is no more a reflective feature than the instinctual, involuntary reactions of beasts. If humans simply felt and immediately reacted, we would be as other creatures on earth, acting simply on instinct. However, the second, third, and fourth of Dewey's "features of reflective thought" replace instinctual reaction with thoughtful mediation:

> To be genuinely thoughtful, we must be willing to sustain and protract that state of doubt which is the stimulus to thorough

> inquiry, so as not to accept an idea or make positive assertion of a belief until justifying reasons have been found (1997, p. 16).

This reflective patience is a crucial feature of reflection and it is essential that students, as well as other community members, participating in a service-learning project understand its importance to the reflective process. The mediating feature of reflection is where reasoning proper occurs and where answers to the question, "what can we do to solve this community problem?" are initially considered. Avoidance of snap, or unreasoned, or reactionary attempts to solve problems is, in fact, the hallmark of good reflective thinking.

While mediating a problem, plans for problem solution are turned over in the mind, discussed, and hypotheses are formed:

> The object of thinking is to help reach a conclusion, to project a possible termination on the basis of what is already given. Certain other facts about thinking accompany this feature. Since the situation in which thinking occurs is a doubtful one, thinking is a process of inquiry, of looking into things, of investigating (Dewey 1916, p. 152).

The ultimate goal of problem mediation is to develop an hypothesis that, once applied, will bring a reconstruction of the problematic situation to make it complete and satisfying once again. That is, mediation as a reflective feature provides the time and consideration to develop academic solutions that can be applied to the community problem.

Reflection After Mediation: Hypothesis Testing

Testing hypotheses involves two important steps. Initially, hypotheses are formulated and go through a "mental testing." Through this mental testing, possible consequences are considered for each plan and those that are found lacking in one way or another, are discarded. Once one hypotheses or plan is chosen, it must go through a second, decisive stage of testing. This second stage of testing the hypotheses is accomplished through application to the project problem and makes experience both the means and aim of service-learning education. That is, to be educative, service-learning must begin and end with student experience. If it does not, then the purposeful nature of student interest will not drive learning. This process necessitates that hypotheses or ideas about how best to solve a felt problem be tested in experience. In describing this feature of reflection, Dewey explained that the;

> concluding and conclusive step is some kind of experimental corroboration, or verification, of the conjectural idea. Reasoning shows that if the idea be adopted, certain consequences follow. So far the conclusion is hypothetical or conditional. If we look and find the characteristic traits called for by rival alternatives to be lacking, the tendency to believe, to accept, is almost irresistible. If

> it is found that the experimental results agree with the theoretical, or rationally deduced, results, and if there is reason believe that only the conditions in question would yield such results, the confirmation is so strong as to induce a conclusion (1933, p. 114).

In the particular case of service-learning, reasoned "guesses" about how to transform the community problem are applied and then evaluated for their success or failure. The community problem is then reevaluated and the process continues until reconstruction brings back the initially lost equilibrium. The hypothesis-testing feature of reflective thought shows those involved in the project exactly how their hypotheses worked out. Learning in and by experience occurs in testing these reasoned hypotheses and academic skills learned in theory become experientially real--including lessons learned about reflection itself.

Reflection: A Continual Component of Service-Learning Projects

As Eyler says and Dewey implied, reflection must be a continual component of any service-learning project. Reflection, as explained by Dewey, is an unending cycling from experience to mediation to testing to experience that cannot be ignored before, during, or after a service project. Eyler, Giles, and Schmiede make clear that "reflection should maintain an especially coherent continuity over the course of each [service] event or experience. Continuous reflection includes reflection before the experience, during the experience and after the experience" (1996, p. 17). James and Pamela Tool write that "although the literal definition of reflection means 'looking backward,' reflection occurs at every phase of the service-learning cycle: reflection to prepare for service, reflection during action, and reflection upon action" (1995, p. 102). Exactly how reflection can and should be maintained before, during, and after service projects is a crucial issue to the success of service-learning--one that often is ignored or left only for post-service activities.

Reflection Before Practice: "Preflection"

According to Diane Falk, "preflection" is the reflective preparation that occurs before the actual service project begins (1995, p. 23). Keogh, Boud, and Walker point out that during preflection, "students start to explore what is required of them, what are the demands of the field setting and the resources which they themselves have to bring" (1985, p. 9). Preflection provides the opportunity for students to imagine what the experience will be like and to express concerns related to the project (Falk 1995, p. 23). It is a concept that reminds service-learning educators that reflection must be continual and adds to Dewey's analysis of reflection by indicating the preparation needed, both emotionally and cognitively, to engage in problem-solving service.

However, preparatory reflection as described above is missing an essential Deweyan element: student involvement in project choice. As I argued above, for students to involve themselves in a project whole-heartedly and with purpose and, therefore, interest, the project absolutely must come out of the felt interests of those students. The feeling of a crucial community problem is the catalyst to reflection and, therefore, must genuinely be "felt" for substantial learning to occur. That felt interest must be part of the "preflective" stage of project reflection. Combining Deweyan felt interest with the preparatory character of preflection, makes it a complete and helpful notion to reflective theory and, therefore, to service-learning practice. As James and Pamela Toole make clear,

> Reflection *before* service may seem a contradiction, but we commonly reflect on and use prior knowledge and experience when we plan and design any project. In preparing for service work, students recollect, propose, hypothesize, build models, predict and make judgments. Students reflect when they choose a service project (*What do we wish were different in our community?*); when they clarify project goals and action plans (*What do we want to see happen?*); and when they prepare for the service itself (*How do we feel about participating in this project?*) (1985, p. 105).

Dewey was also adamant that reflection, as described here, does not imply leaving students--even university students--to their own means hoping that they stumble upon a problem of interest (1938, p. 71). Instead, the preflective/affective stage of reflection entails a reformulation of the professor's role that is far from traditional. Instead of being a purveyor of already established knowledge or a teller of problems, a university professor working under the service-learning pedagogy must be a guide who leads students to realize problematic situations. The leading of students to problems in experience is not an easy task. The service-learning instructor might use traditional modes of teaching (the reading of great works and contemporary literature, for example) as well as more non-traditional practices, including going into one's community to see firsthand what is happening. In either case, the problem must be owned by the participants for the project to evolve successfully.

In addition to project choice and interest, preflection must be a time for project preparation. Once students discover a problem, the reflective process is in full swing. The process will naturally incorporate previous experience and, more importantly, indicate lack of previous experience. This will be particularly true when students meet community "strangers"--those fellow citizens who have first-hand knowledge of the "felt" problem (Radest 1993). The preflective stage, as is pointed out above, must include expressions of emotions and clarifying of assumptions about the problem and about those citizens who regularly experience that problem. It will involve some guessing as to outcomes, roles, and further problems. Preflection will, in short, be the catalyst or, as Dewey says, "The steadying and guiding factor" for the project (1997, p. 72).

Reflection During Service

Reflection is an ongoing process and though "preflection" is essential to project implementation, much, if not most, reflective thought in service-learning occurs during the project work. Reflection during the project drives academic learning as the hypotheses developed for solving the project problem are tested, adjusted through further data gathering, re-applied, and re-tested. Reflection provides the opportunity for learning by bringing the service problem and the university together in the context of the project. Applying classroom learning in the project context "teaches" academic understanding well beyond traditional classroom settings because the students use classroom-constructed knowledge and skills to solve real problems. Students, side by side with community members who have a stake in the service problem, make project decisions. Students operating in the project context create knowledge and sharpen academic skills as they attempt to solve present and future community problems. The project context also leads to better reflective skills as students make project decisions and test those decisions for success or failure.

Reflection, as understood in this discussion, will bind students and community members, classroom learning and experience only if it is structured with both cognitive and affective goals in mind. Boud, Keough and Walker argue that

> Reflection as we have described it is pursued with intent. It is not idle meanderings or daydreaming, but purposive activity directed towards a goal. This is not to say that it may not be helpful to have periods of reverie and mediation associated with conscious reflection, but in themselves these activities are not what we are referring to when we discuss goal-directed critical reflection.
>
> The reflective process is a complex one in which both feelings and cognition are closely interrelated and interactive. Negative feelings, particularly about oneself, can form major barriers towards learning. They can distort perceptions, lead to false interpretations of events, and can undermine the will to persist. Positive feelings and emotions can greatly enhance the learning process; they can keep the learner on the task and can provide a stimulus for new learning. The affective dimension has to be taken into account when we are engaged in our own learning activities, and when we are assisting others in this process (1985, p. 11).

I want to emphasize here one additional aspect of reflection that is particularly forgotten or misunderstood in service-learning projects: reflection has a public side as well as the commonly understood private side. Reflection is certainly private in that it comes out of personal experience, involves personal thought, and ends in personal action; however, as a process whose end goal is the solution of a public (in the case of service-learning) as well as a personally felt problem, it must involve reflective dialogue with those who find themselves most intimately connected to the particular community problem and it must involve a communal application of the problem solution. Reflection is in these ways a community activity and it is only through reflective public discussion--discussion among all community members effected by the problem--that individuals in a community can connect or reconnect with one another in cooperative, and, therefore, more insightful ways to meet the project problem with viable, democratic solutions. This public aspect of reflection is in some ways synonymous with Amy Gutmann's conception of reasonable public dialogue/debate and as such, celebrates critical public disagreement as well as public agreement just so long as the debate is reflective, inclusive and nonrepressive (1987, pp. 7-23). It is also in public reflection that can be found the important community action component that advocates of service-learning believe can become a regular participatory habit of students who work within the service-learning pedagogy. The public aspect of reflection is also one that is, unfortunately, often ignored in service-learning projects (Maybach 1994). There simply is not space here to give a full accounting of why service-learning projects so often lack this essential public dialogue. Suffice it to say here that it is a complicated issue more often related to the concept of service being relied upon rather than the concept of reflection and is another clear indication that a prerequisite course on service-learning theory is necessary.

Post Project Reflection: A Continuation, Not a Culmination

Reflection means "looking back," so it is most commonly practiced when projects are over. As James and Pamela Tool remark, "In the aftermath of a project, students therefore need to formally reflect in order to evaluate the project, assess their own development, look for generalizations to guide future decision making and find 'new applications' for what they have learned" (1995, p. 107). In the case of American universities, reflection more often than not is seen as an end to the particular project and as a culmination of a semester course. Certainly it is crucial that reflective discourse carry into the post-project period. However, seeing post-project reflection as the final act in the project context is clearly a misunderstanding of Deweyan reflective features. Instead of the project ending when the service-learning course ends, reflective practice (when understood correctly) requires that the project problem be re-examined by all stakeholders, together. In this way, democratic interaction and evaluation is practiced and encouraged, and project success is evaluated through continuing reflection.

The reflective post-project examination will determine the successes and failures of the problem solutions. The post-project evaluation will also indicate future and related problems with the project context or similar contexts. Project activities must, therefore, be constructed and implemented based on the idea that the project is over only when a satisfactory reconstruction of, or solution to, the problem has been achieved. Until that time, the project will continue in new and different ways, with new and different insights, and maybe new and different students. Post-project reflection is simply another case of stepping back from the situation to see the degree to which project activities have solved the initial problem. It is a time for bringing together both project impact and learning with an eye to future similar experiences. As to time constraints, it is post project reflection that also calls for courses to be tailored to the longer period of time needed to understand service-learning, carry out a project, and evaluate that project.

On an individual basis, Deweyan reflective theory asks each student involved in the project to continue reflecting on the problem after the project is completed. In like fashion, the service-learning pedagogy asks that students take both the general reflective skills and the knowledge of the particular community problem with them to other, future community destinations. In this way, reflective thinking generally and the problem situation particularly will enhance their lives after the particular project is completed. Service-learning, when done well, will create continuity through opening new and related experiences from those of the past, and in so doing will insure continued student growth.

Unfortunately, as I indicated above, reflection is often the weakest aspect of a service-learning project when it should, in fact, be the strongest. At times reflection and celebration have seemingly become one in the same as reflection is reduced to simply some "fun" activities that allow students to look back with (albeit) well-deserved pride and joy at what their service project has accomplished (Learn and Serve Florida 2002). Celebration can be an important aspect of any service-learning project, but it is not necessarily reflective. Additionally, I agree with Rahima Wade that there is a common and understandable tendency among service-learning advocates to engage in more action-oriented cheerleading than in open-minded critical reflection on our practices (1997, p. 13). Evidence of this can be found in simply looking to the numerous volumes that have been published listing reflective activities (rather than examining its meaning) (Hiott, Jackson and Winecoff 1998; Honnett and Poulsen 1989). Suggested activities in these volumes are wide and varied in structure. Group discussion, role-playing, writing, acting, presenting, and debating activities all might lead to good reflective practice.

These kinds of activities, however, do not, in and of themselves, satisfy the reflective requirement suggested here for service-learning education. The success of each such activity will be found in whether or not it leads the student to reflecting in a manner that is similar to that described by Dewey. Does the activity lead students to see a problem in their experience? Does the activity make students step back from a problem to plan a solution? Does the activity get students to apply their academic learning to possible solutions? Does the activity lead students to test that plan in the problem situation? Does the activity bring students to a reevaluation of the problem situation and those similar to it? Does the activity involve dialogue among all stakeholders? Does the activity encourage further reflection? Regardless of what the reflective activity specifically entails, if it is not structured in such a way to answer the above questions in the affirmative, then it is not reflective in nature and should probably be eliminated from a service-learning project; of course, and this is the crucial point, the evaluation of the activity cannot be accomplished by anyone who does not understand the underlying structure of reflective thought.

Service-Learning Theory: Sound Practice Through Sound Understanding

As I hope I have made clear, the reflective process is a far cry from a purely instinctual process that we college and university professors can rightly assume our students to understand and practice well—though certainly some do better than others. Because reflection is an essential component to a viable service-learning project, I believe that its underlying structure must be thoroughly examined by our students so that sound theory, rather than vagaries and ignorance, direct practice. I believe just as strongly, and for much the same reason, that understanding the history of service-learning, the concept of service, experiential learning theory, and the democratic demands on service-learning, is equally paramount to its success as a transformative pedagogy and should, in fact, be the core concepts around which a prerequisite course for service-learning students (and future teachers) is developed. In this way, we might be much more confident that the rather complicated service-learning pedagogy will truly "sink-in" with our students.

Of course, it's one thing to abstractly discuss and then assert the need for yet another education course, and quite another to actively defend that need by actually developing the course and trying it out. Leaving the discussion in that shadowy realm of "what if" is precisely the kind of inaction that leads practitioners to doubt and even dismiss foundational thinking of the sort found here and is certainly antithetical to the reflection called for in a service-learning project. I am, it seems to me, duty bound to at least briefly outline a course that examines service-learning history, theory, and practice and will use the remainder of this discussion to do just that.

Service-Learning 101: Pedagogical Theory and Practice

As you look over this course outline, I ask that you keep the following in mind: First, I have not implemented it. I plan to do so in the very near future, but can provide no feedback as to its actual success at this time—it is an hypothesis yet untested. Secondly, I teach in a college of education and so although this is a course that would be a prerequisite elective for other university wide courses that carry the service-learning "tag," it would also fit well into a college of education curriculum where future teachers would have the opportunity to study its theoretical and practical structure and would hopefully incorporate it into their future public school classrooms. Finally, I am not an administrator and so I use the "101" course number somewhat in jest. This course would in fact be far beyond simply an introductory course—its nature is that of a higher-level foundations/epistemology/philosophy of education course and its course title would certainly have to reflect that degree of depth.

A typical university semester course runs approximately 16 weeks and at least initially I would simply divide the course into equal sections to cover the history of service-learning, the concept of service, experiential learning theory, reflection, and service-learning as a form of democratic education. I would also build in a course-ending "mini" service project so that we could apply our theoretical work in a very Deweyan, hypothesis-testing manner to see how we did and as a way to pull the different theoretical discussions together to form a complete picture of the service-learning pedagogy. Much of this course would be built around reading and discussion and as such I would make the course similar to a graduate level seminar. This format would give us about two weeks on each topic, additional time for a mini project, and importantly, some unstructured time to adjust to the particular needs of the students (some sections, I imagine, will need more time working out the nature of service, for example, and so course/time adjustments will be needed).

Because I believe that understanding the history of an idea is essential to understanding its contemporary state of affairs, I would spend some time tracing through the very interesting educational events/movements that brought service-learning to where it is today. Admittedly, there are few histories of service-learning (in fact, none that I know of that could be described as comprehensive) and so studying its historical evolution would be a matter of pulling pieces from various texts together to give a clear picture of its development as a pedagogy. Service, experiential learning, and reflection are the core educational concepts that drive service-learning's practice and as such each must be closely examined for understanding—there exists a myriad of possible texts that could be called on for that purpose. Finally, service-learning must answer the demand that it be a viable form of democratic education and so an analysis of what a democratic form of education must entail and then an examination of service-learning as such is, I believe, crucial to understanding and defending its practice within our system of public education.

The following is a suggested list of possible readings for each section of the Service-Learning 101 course of study:

<u>The History of Service-Learning Education</u>

For the history section, I suggest a packet of readings that contains:

ACTION. 1972. *High School Student Volunteers*. Washington, D.C.: National Center for Service Learning.

Conderman, B. and Patryla, B. 1996. Service Learning: The Past, Present, and the Promise. *Kappa Delta Pi Record* 32 (4): 122-125.

Giles, D. and Eyler, J. 1994. The Theoretical Roots of Service-Learning in John Dewey: Toward a Theory of Service-Learning. *Michigan Journal of Community Service Learning* 1 (Fall): 77-85.

Hepburn, M. 1997. Service Learning in Civic Education: A Concept with Long, Sturdy Roots. *Theory Into Practice* 36 (3): 136-142.

Hill, D. 1997. Death of a Dream: Service Learning 1994-2010: An Historical Analysis by One of the Dreamers. Service Learning 2000 Center, Stanford University.

James, W. 1910. The Moral Equivalent of War. *International Conciliation No.27*. New York: Carnegie Endowment for International Peace.

And, selected portions of

Hanna, P. *Youth Serves the Community*. New York: D. Appleton-Century Company.

Stanton, T., Giles, D. and Cruz, N. eds. 1999. *Service-Learning: A Movement's Pioneers Reflect on Its Origins, Practice, and Future*. San Francisco: Jossey Bass.

A Few Alternatives:

Adams, A. and Reynolds, S. 1981. The Long Conversation: Tracing the Roots of the Past. <u>Journal of Experiential Education</u> (Spring): 21-28.

Cooley, R. and House, G. 1930. *School Acres: An Adventure in Rural Education*. New Haven: Yale University Press.

Eberly, D. *National service: A Promise to Keep*. 1988. Rochester, NY: J. Alden Books.

Hatcher, J. 1997. The Moral Dimensions of John Dewey's Philosophy: Implications for undergraduate Education. *The Michigan Journal of Community Service Learning* 4 (Fall): 50-58.

Kilpatrick, W.H. 1922. *The Project Method: The Use of the Purposeful Act in the Educative Process*. New York: Teachers College, Columbia University.

Merrill, P.H. 1981. *Roosevelt's Forest Army: A History of the Civilian Conservation Corps, 1933-1942*. Montpelier, Vt.: P.H. Merrill.

Pollock, S. 1997. *Three Decades of Service–Learning in Higher Education (1966–1996): The Contested Emergence of an Organizational Field*. Stanford, CA: Stanford University Press.

<u>Service</u>

I recommend the following text:

Radest, H. 1993. *Community Service: Encounter with Strangers*. Westport, Ct.: Praeger.

Some alternatives:

Bellah, R., et. al. 1985. *Habits of the Heart*. Berkeley, CA: University of California Press.

Coles, R. *The Call of Service*. Boston, MA: Houghton Mifflin Company.

Dass, R. *Compassion in Action: Setting Out on the Path of Service*. 1992. New York: Bell Tower.

Tocqueville, A. *Democracy In America*. 1956 [1835]. New York: The New American Library.

<u>Experiential Learning</u>

Though there exist numerous resources on experiential education (including *the Journal of Experiential Education*), I would rely primarily on portions of the following:

Bacon, F. 1901 [1605]. *Advancement of Learning*. New York: P.F. Collier and Son.

Chickering, A.W. 1977. *Experience and Learning: An Introduction to Experiential Learning*. New Rochelle, NY: Change Magazine Press.

Dewey, J. 1931. *The Way out of Educational Confusion*. Westport, Connecticut: Greenwood Press.

Kolb, D. 1984. *Experiential Learning: Experience as the Source of Learning and Development*. Englewood Cliffs, NJ: Prentice-Hall.

There are, of course, many of other texts/articles that would work equally well including these additional Dewey titles:

Dewey, J. 1938. *Experience and Education*. New York: Macmillan Co.

Dewey, J. 1944 [1916]. *Democracy and Education: An Introduction to the Philosophy of Education*. New York: MacMillan Co.
Dewey, J. 1966. *Lectures in the Philosophy of Education 1899*. New York: Random House.

Reflection

Dewey's treatment of reflection is a classic

Dewey, J. 1933. *How We Think: A Restatement of the Relation of Reflective Thinking to the Educative Process*. Boston: D. C. Heath and Company.

Additionally, any of the articles mentioned in the above discussion of reflection and listed here on the references list would be appropriate for this section..

Service-Learning as a form of Democratic Education

I would select excerpts from the following texts/articles on democratic forms of education:

Boyte, H.C. c1989. *Commonwealth: A Return to Citizen Politics*. New York: Collier Macmillan.
Dewey, J. 1944 [1916]. *Democracy and Education: An Introduction to the Philosophy of Education*. New York: MacMillan Co.
Gutmann, A. 1987. *Democratic Education*. Princeton, New Jersey: Princeton University Press.
Harkavy, I. and Benson, L. 1998. De-Platonizing and Democratizing Education as the Bases of Service Learning. *New Directions for Teaching and Learning* 73 (Spring): 11-15.
Lisman, C. D. 1980. *Toward a Civil Society*. Westport, CT: Greenwood Publishing.
Putnam, R. 1995. Bowling Alone: America's Declining Social Capital. *Journal of Democracy* 6 (January): 65-78.

Conclusion

As an advocate of the service-learning pedagogy, I am concerned about its future—a future that I believe depends on the degree to which we examine and understand its practice as firmly grounded in reasonable foundational thinking. Misunderstanding and ignorance of that foundation leads (as is usually the case) to bad practice and certainly bad practice might well lead to the demise of service-learning. I suggest that to insure sound practice based on sound understanding requires colleges of education at universities that utilize service-learning to require a course on service-learning theory and practice—a prerequisite for anyone wanting to participate in a course that carries the service-learning "tag." Alternatively, initial service-learning coursework might be extended to at least two semesters so that an examination of service-learning theory could take place as part of the coursework. In either case, the above course outline is provided simply as a starting point for what I believe can be a valuable, rigorous, and ultimately an essential part of protecting and growing the service-learning pedagogy of reflection—a sophisticated pedagogy that can lead to sophisticated construction of socially important knowledge.

References

Boud, D, Keough, R. and Walker, D. 1985. What is reflection in Learning? in *Reflection: Turning Experience into Learning* edited by David Boud, Rosemary Keough, and David Walker. London: Kogan Page Ltd.

Chickering, A.W. 1977. *Experience and Learning: An Introduction to Experiential Learning*. New Rochelle, NY: Change Magazine Press.

Dewey, J. 1933. *How We Think: A Restatement of the Relation of Reflective Thinking to the Educative Process*. Boston: D. C. Heath and Company.

Dewey, J. 1938. *Experience and Education*. New York: Macmillan Co.

Dewey, J. 1944 [1916]. *Democracy and Education: An Introduction to the Philosophy of Education*. New York: MacMillan Co.

Dewey, J. 1997 [1910]. *How We Think*. Ontario Canada: Dover Publications.

Eyler, J. 2001. Creating Your Reflection Map. *New Directions For Higher Education* 114 (Summer): 35-42.

Eyler, J., Giles Jr., D. and Schmeide, A. 1996. *A Practitioner's Guide to Reflection in Service-Learning* (Nashville TN: Vanderbilt University.

Falk, D. 1995. Preflection: A Strategy for Enhancing Reflection. *NSEE Quarterly* 13 (Winter): 21-23.

Gutmann, A. 1987. *Democratic Education*. Princeton, New Jersey: Princeton University Press.

Hiott, B. C., Lyday, W.J. and Winecoff. H.L. 1998. *Service Learning Handbook for Teacher Educators and Practitioners*. Columbia, SC: University of South Carolina.

Honnet, E.P. and Poulsen. S.J. 1989. *Principles of Good Practice in Combining Service and Learning*. Racine WI: Johnson Foundation.

James, W. 1985 [1892]. *Psychology: The Briefer Course*. Notre Dame, Indiana: University of Notre Dame.

Kendall, J. 1990. Combining Service and Learning: an Introduction. Chapter One of *Combining Service and Learning: A Resource Book for Community and Public Service* ed., Jane C. Kendall and Associates. Raleigh, N.C.: National Society for Internships and Experiential Education.

Learn and Serve Florida, *2002 Request for Proposals*.

Maybach, C.E. 1994. *Second Year Evaluation of Three Components of Colorado Campus Compact*. Denver, CO: Colorado Campus Compact.

Mintz, S.D. and Hesser, G. 1997. *Principles of Good Practice in Service-Learning in Service Learning in Higher Education: Concepts and Practices*, edited by Barbara Jacoby. San Francisco: Jossey-Bass.

Sherman, R. R. 1985. Philosophy With Guts. *Journal of Thought* 20 (Summer): 3-11

Toole, J. and Toole, P. 1995. Reflection as a Tool for Turning Service Experiences into Learning Experiences in *Enriching the Curriculum through Service Learning*, edited by James Tool. San Francisco: Jossey Bass.

Teacher Professionalism and a Teaching Ethic
Steve Broidy

Guiding Questions:

1. What are the connections and distinctions among these related terms: profession, (de)professionalization, professionalism?
2. In what ways is teacher professionalism fundamentally an "ethical" matter?
3. Why is exhibiting professionalism crucial to the success of individual teachers and to the field of teaching?
4. How does an "ethic of kindness" provide for the sort of teaching ethic that allows teachers to exhibit "real" professionalism?

Teacher Professionalism and a Teaching Ethic
Steve Broidy

Though it has been tending in that direction for nearly half a century, American schooling has recently taken an even sharper turn toward centralization of control. Moreover, the instruments of that control, such as the No Child Left Behind Act, are widely perceived by educators to be coercive and even punitive toward them.

This perception has caused many teachers and teacher organizations to fear that one consequence of this central control will be the de-professionalizing of teaching. Such fears are moving philosophers of education and other writers to once again consider some of the conceptual and cultural features of teacher professionalism.

There is an old and fairly futile philosophical debate concerning the parameters of 'profession'. At one time, the urgency of that conceptual discussion was fed by the rising aspirations of educators to a new status in the broad community. Today, as educators witness increasing centralization of authority for educational decision-making, and increasing measures of educator accountability to centralized authorities, they fear that the modest gains in status and reward that have accompanied their general acceptance as professionals will be lost. While those fears may be justified, it is not de-professionalization in the sense of the occupation losing status that poses the challenge most crucial to teachers' work. In these changing conditions, it is the consequences for teacher *professionalism* that may prove to be most important, both to effective teaching and to the future value of teachers' work.

Is teaching being de-professionalized? In *some* senses of that awkward and ambiguous term, de-professionalization of teaching is occurring: Depending on how the issue is interpreted, the situation at this moment seems to be that 1) the idea of teaching as a profession is rapidly losing credibility; 2) the professionalization of teaching, in the sense of formalizing and systemizing features of induction and practice, is in some ways under challenge, and in other ways continues apace; but 3) it remains to be seen in what ways and to what extent elements of teacher professionalism will be affected by the shift to centralization and the obsession with accountability that mark today's educational climate.

In fact, this paper argues for re-formulating educators' concerns: it is in recognizing and emphasizing the essentially ethical nature of teacher professionalism that educators will find the means for affirming their status in society. To argue a position for what should be recognized as teacher professionalism is only in part to make a conceptual point. It is also to demonstrate the special value of the expertise that educators can bring to bear on the various challenges individuals and communities rely on them to meet.

I will argue here for the importance of a crucial aspect of that valuable expertise. I hope to establish that in the special relationship between educators and their clients--students, parents, and the larger community--educators' skills must include the ability to establish and maintain a unique balance between justice and care (I call it an "ethic of kindness") that is fundamentally democratic, because it acknowledges and serves the often conflicting educational aims/ideals that Americans hold to. The very notion of "serving the welfare" of students, within the circles of community that encompass them, depends in part on recognizing and acknowledging those conflicting ideals, and finding ways to balance them with teachers' own ideals.

Current trends in educational control threaten educators' ability to exercise that set of skills effectively; and that, I argue, is the variety of de-professionalization that educators and indeed the broad community should fear. If educators lose the opportunity to acknowledge and serve a range of hopes that they and other Americans have for education, one irony for education reform may be that, though we may leave no child behind in attaining the academic knowledge for which reformers hunger, we may lose the other and larger aims that knowledge is one tool for attaining.

On the other hand, it is also ironic that in highlighting their unique opportunities to establish and build upon an ethical basis for their work, educators may find their most effective leverage in defending their professional status. Drawing public attention to the reasons for and the uses of what I will call a "teaching ethic" helps to counter the reductionist thinking of NCLB and other initiatives. It serves to remind the community of the larger and more valuable purposes that teaching serves. Teaching, we may demonstrate, is much more than technical activity in the service of some distant politician's agenda or a bureaucracy's system.

Especially in a period of professional uncertainty for teachers, it is important for teachers to focus their efforts on concerns that are central to their work and enduring in nature. In focusing upon features of teacher professionalism that are crucially and perhaps constitutively bound up with ethical issues I will argue that in a very fundamental sense of 'professionalism' , one that is broad enough to encompass many occupations, teachers' professionalism can successfully resist the challenges of centralization and the public obsession with accountability.

Professions, Professionalization, and De-professionalization

As noted already, when educators worry that de-professionalization is underway, they are sometimes expressing the fear that teaching as an occupation is being stripped of features that make it recognizable to the community as a profession (see Yinga & Nolan, 2003). Without supposing that "profession' has clear conceptual boundaries separating the term from many near relations (occupation, vocation, etc) teachers' concerns about the loss of hard-earned status may still be taken seriously. The value that teachers have assigned to these features of occupational status is often expressed as a desire that teaching be recognized as a "profession". Taking these concerns as a starting point, it's not hard to notice or to anticipate the loss to teaching of some features that teachers value highly, or of features they aspire to and would hate to lose if they actually possessed them. In the wake of increasingly sophisticated state and national systems of standards, NCLB, and a climate favoring strict accountability, teachers, collectively, certainly have less autonomy and control over practice, for example in curriculum--and teachers value such control as a feature of recognizable professions. Arguably, they also have less opportunity for initiative in creating or adopting programs of instruction, for sequencing instruction (Loh, 2003), and even for developing the pedagogy for delivering instruction. Moreover, teachers do not seem to be leading participants in the discussions that result in the setting of goals for schooling. That discussion has been appropriated by state and federal government, and by the politicians and policy-makers that populate parts of government and the private sector. Increasing accountability measures convey to the public that the services of teachers to the public are not, in Wilensky's term, "uniquely trustworthy". (cited in Quinn, 2003) All of these features are both highly valued by teachers and frequently cited as necessary to recognizing a 'profession',

Moreover, teachers do not have direct control over the preparation and conditions that lead to entry into teaching, as do some "professions"; nor do they possess, as a group, formal powers to sanction teachers for misconduct in practice. States have been unwilling to allow this, and in current circumstances are even less likely to consider it in the future. Add to this a decline in the already tenuous social and economic status of teaching and it makes sense to speak of the de-professionalizing of teaching. (Though we should notice that this is a picture of 'profession' that is institutional. There are other constructions, including some that are cognitively oriented (Richardson, 1999, p. 67), or frankly cynical (Bledsoe, p. 32).

From another perspective, if 'professionalization' means making the work of practitioners more systematic and regular, more transparent to practitioners and to clients, and more closely and formally self-supervising, then the professionalizing of teaching is an old and a continuing trend. NCLB calls for more "highly qualified" teachers, which would at least seem to be an impetus to more professionalization. Even so, current initiatives by local districts and by state and federal government have created a variety of entry points for new teachers--a trend that at least temporarily makes teaching less systematic and transparent. And though the current political climate has put pressure on teachers to conform ever more closely to practices that are tied to a standards-based curriculum, many view this trend to standardizing teaching as technicization, as opposed to professionalization. (Loh, 2003; Manzo, 2003)

Professionalism

In the face of other sorts of de-professionalization, it is not clear whether teaching is also being de-professionalized in the important sense of teachers abandoning the commitments and practices which clients, peers, and critics most value in teachers' work, i.e. teachers' professionalism. Answering that question depends first on having a clear idea of what teacher professionalism, in practice, includes; and secondly on regarding the question from the differing perspectives of clients, peers, and critics.

In order to construct an account of that sense of 'teacher professionalism' I want to argue is most central to teachers' work, it is useful to review the features of the term that most often appear in educators' own discussions. Teacher professionalism may involve any number of features, and in speaking of professionalism, observers typically focus on some subset. Connie Monroe (2001), in reviewing the literature on teacher professionalism, summarized the features she found in that literature in 22 categories, which she further condensed to ten:

1) *Collegiality;* focusing on teamwork, mentoring, and community
2) *Power and autonomy*, focusing on freedom within a framework, creating freedom, balancing autonomy and conformity, and dealing with the "intensification" of demands
3) *Feeling a "call to teach"*, i.e. counting a conscious decision to teach as vocational
4) *Child-centered thought and action*
5) *Sense of purpose*, involving a sense of service, and commitment to long-term or continuing aims
6) *Expertise and judgement:* in many roles and situations being able to apply special knowledge and solve problems successfully
7) *Commitment of time and effort, and endurance devoted to teaching and to education*
8) *Growth throughout a career*
9) *Identification with teachers, their organizations and communities, and with education generally*
10) *Standards*; both personal and those set by authorities (p 10; cf. Sockett, 1993)

We might usefully make this list still more compact, in order to focus more manageably on the issues before us. In general, Monroe's categories describe a) *teacher competence*--#6, clearly; but also #'s 1, 2, 9, and perhaps 10; b) *continuing efforts to improve practice*--#'s 7 and 8; and c) what we might call an *ethical perspective on practice*--#'s 3, 4, 5, and possibly 10.

Professionalism and the Ethical Perspective

While most discussions of teacher professionalism focus on elements of teacher competence, I want to argue that the most fundamental category is that of ethical perspective, *because it provides a rationale for acquiring a concern with the others, and for describing the parameters of the others.* A commitment to long-term aims—to educational ideals that guide our actions--and conscious, deliberate use of that priority in decision-making make it important to attend to all those matters that are instrumental to honoring that commitment. In this light, concerns with expertise and judgment, standards, a work ethic, and professional growth are grounded in the importance of these matters to addressing long-term aims/ideals. The same may be said for concerns with the nature of children and working successfully with them, with building and functioning within a professional community, and with working well in systems and institutions.

In other words, the competence and continuous improvement facets of teacher professionalism are shaped by a commitment to a long-term conception of the welfare of children and other clients. It is at least confusing, and probably entirely arbitrary, to try to describe the skills teachers should acquire, the standards they should live up to, the kinds of improvement they should seek, etc. without reference to their role in addressing the ideals—or as Neil Postman (1996) put it--the "gods" they cherish. In this country, we rarely engage in large-scale efforts to articulate such educational ideas; much less do we attempt to achieve a level of consensus about them. Therefore, though NCLB and other "reforms' such as complex state systems of standards and their elaborating systems may be internally coherent, they are ultimately arbitrary (see Broidy, 1999, for a more complete argument to this position).

In any case, when teachers form a commitment to long-term teaching aims and work continuously and competently to address them, we recognize professionalism in such teachers' work—as long as we honor the long-term aims to which such teachers are committed.

Critics, clients, and peers may evaluate teachers' professionalism in any of the three (or ten) categories above. Some writers have argued, though, that clients have a tendency to see teacher professionalism primarily in competent choices and concern for client welfare; whereas peers tend to see professionalism in the *process* of on-the-job choosing; and critics tend to see professionalism in compliance with larger agendas (Stronach, 2002 p. 110-11). Their peculiar interests, then, condition the perspective from which they consider the degree of teacher professionalism displayed.

Even if these generalizations are warranted, however, they reflect the centrality of active commitment to long-term aims in teacher professionalism. The competence of teacher choices and actions can be assessed only, among other things, in light of the ends toward which those choices are made and actions taken. The factors that make peers admire or dismiss teachers' decision-making methods are many, but they are all ultimately referenced to the manner in which methods connect with desired outcomes. And critics' agendas, whether continuing or merely current, are themselves justifiable in terms of their relation to long-term "goods".

Are current conditions serving to de-professionalize teachers in the sense of compromising their ability to act with professionalism? Some writers argue that the centralization movement in education has pre-empted teachers' ability to choose *what* competencies and methods of improvement to pursue (McClure, p. 67). To the extent that this is true, this claim also implies a co-optation of teachers' free commitment to the ethical perspective that gives meaning to their actions. If teachers' on-the-job choices are rigidly constrained, as they are when teachers are forced to teach to state (and perhaps national) tests not of their making; when the range of subjects taught is narrowed, and the pedagogical options constrained, the chances that teachers can successfully address their long-term aims can be greatly lessened.

But centralization of long-term aims can also occur directly and in that case teacher professionalism in terms of competencies and continuous improvement can, in their turn, be affected—sometimes in subtle but important ways. There are many instructive examples of what happens to the competence and improvements facets of professionalism when the ethical perspectives of teachers are co-opted. In *The Twisted Muse: Musicians and Their Music in the Third Reich (1997)*, Michael Kater tells the stories of several world-class musicians and conductors who prospered under Nazi rule. Kater demonstrates that, once these musicians lost the guidance of their own musical ideals, under the coercive and punitive oversight of the Nazis, their competencies, while not diminished, were greatly limited in the scope of their application, and their commitment to improving the conditions of their practice became narrowed to a concern to please their overseers (ch. 2).

Especially in the context of centralization of educational means and ends, however, if teachers work to reconstruct teacher professionalism from a foundation of attention to educational ideals and the practice that would address them, they can begin to make progress toward community recognition of the value of their professionalism--and perhaps also make progress toward the status to which they aspire.

Teacher Professionalism and Professional Ethics

That there are many features of teacher professionalism, and many perspectives and interests that help to focus attention on various of those features, insure that teachers' actions and choices are always debatable. They are not any less debatable in a political climate that values high levels of teacher accountability. Even extraordinary levels of teacher professionalism will not eliminate criticism of teachers' decisions and actions.

One important source of this continuing critique comes from the fact that there are a number of educational ideals that retain legitimacy in our society. Among these, briefly, are the ideals of 1) developing individuals and communities that approach the full realization of human potential; 2) developing autonomous individuals who are able to address their own unique aims; 3) perfecting (or as some would have it, introducing) democratic practices; and 4) maintaining/increasing the material success of individuals and of our society in a challenging world. Though most Americans have absorbed a range of ethical perspectives on education, they tend to differ on which educational ideal deserves first priority. The curious fact that Americans rarely engage in public discussions of such long-term aims, or attempt even on a local level to reach consensus on the subject, adds to the likelihood that what teachers do will always find a critic.

Though the federal and state governments currently give priority to economic prosperity and hegemony as the main educational project, that priority does not diminish the importance of the variety of alternatives that citizens hold dear. And since many people (and groups) are teachers' clients, teachers must acknowledge their aims and account for them in the context of teachers' own ideals.

To whom are teachers accountable? Though government at several levels has established itself (though in the name of the community) as the supervisor of teacher accountability, government is just one of a number of teacher client (and not the most crucial one, I will argue later). It is the essential challenge of teacher professionalism in a democratic society to acknowledge and balance the claims of many clients, and to formulate long-term teaching aims that, whatever their priorities, give due regard to the many legitimate claims to service that teaching's clients put forward.

It is in this challenge that we may see the connection between what is central to teacher professionalism and teacher professional ethics. As David Carr (2000) puts it

> "The need for a high degree of ethical sensitivity on the part of educational professionals arises precisely from the essentially contested character of the educational enterprise: the fact that there is much debate and controversy about the point and purpose of education, and about what in the nature of human flourishing it should be concerned to promote."(p. 19)

That "ethical sensitivity" includes formulating and working toward long-term aims that a teacher personally values, while acknowledging the welfare claims/ideals of a range of clients. It also requires informed, skillful, self-conscious, and reflective professional choices. That is:

1. It requires knowledge of the aims that clients value, of client needs in given situations, and of the effects of instructional and other professional practices on the welfare of clients.
2. It requires that instructional, interpersonal, institutional, and other abilities be chosen and deployed in a manner that effectively addresses the needs and agendas of clients affected by teachers' decisions and actions.
3. It requires teachers to be continuously aware of their own ideals/long-term aims and to make professional decisions deliberately, with these aims in mind.
4. It requires continuing assessment of professional choices past, current, and future, in the light of teaching aims—those of the teacher and those of the teacher's clients.

This way of viewing teacher professionalism, it should be apparent, subsumes most if not all of the usual features of professionalism under the vision of teaching as what Carr calls a "moral project" (p. 29). It puts the attributes, knowledge and skills, decisions and practices of teachers in the service of a teacher's own ideal of human welfare; and in the service of clients' visions of their own and others' welfare. What sort of teaching ethic can help teachers deal with this complexity of purpose? Not a simple one, it seems.

A Teaching Ethic of Kindness

If what is central to teacher professionalism is active engagement with long-term aims, in all aspects of teaching, and if that engagement is attempted in a context that includes serious acknowledgement of the welfare claims and ideals of many sorts of clients, then professional ethics is a complex task. Nevertheless, there is at least a clear starting point for many of the professional decisions teachers make, and therefore a useful starting point for assessing teacher professionalism.

Teachers teach students. That is, teachers' decisions and actions are typically most directly concerned with instructing a particular student or group of students (R.S. Peters, quoted in Carr p.17). Though teachers also make professional decisions that affect the welfare of colleagues, parents, or people in the broader community; most teaching decisions and actions are directed at student learning. Moreover, teachers teach students to some purpose. The aims that teachers commit to and work toward may focus on various constructions of individual or community welfare, but *it is in the service of those aims that they instruct students, when they are acting professionally*. It is also this feature of instruction, in its context of competing aims and client welfare claims that makes teachers' decisions and actions ultimately ethical ones.

Therefore, it is a "teaching ethic"—an ethic fundamentally concerned with the relations of teachers with students--that is most fundamental for teachers; though these relations have a broader set of connections and contexts. What is required are decisions that help students to learn, in a context in which a teacher knowledgeably, skillfully, self-consciously, and reflectively addresses aims the teacher values--while acknowledging the welfare claims of those affected by teachers' decisions and actions.

Although a teaching ethic that displays such professionalism is directly concerned with the individual students and groups of students in a teacher's charge, it cannot be single-mindedly absorbed in the self-defined educational and other needs and desires of individual students. Nor can it be entirely concerned with some broad notion of a just distribution of teacher services and commitments among all possible clients. Because teachers teach individual students directly, their weighted obligation is to the welfare of those students. But teachers teach those students in the context of teaching other students and groups of students; and teachers' decisions and actions directed at students can also affect the welfare of other, more indirect clients such as colleagues, parents, and community agencies. Moreover, a teacher's construction of the welfare of particular students is informed not only by the immediate situation and students' own views of their needs, but by the shorter and longer term aims that actively guide a teacher's instruction.

It is not strictly caring, nor strictly justice that is the focus of a teaching ethics, then. It is a concern to meet the learning needs (and other needs connected to these) of individual students in the context of teachers' aims and of the welfare of others affected by teacher decisions. A professional ethic, on this view, has a three part focus: a more heavily weighted focus on the welfare of a student, but also a focus on the welfare of other students and other people affected by professional decisions; and on the aims of the teacher.

Perhaps surprisingly, an approach to ethical professional decision-making and action that emphasizes what I construct as "kindness" is a good candidate to meet the complex demands on a teaching ethic described above. Elsewhere (Broidy, 1997), I have argued at length that kind actions are those in which

1. relationally, the one acting kindly (K) toward some recipient of that kindness (R) is in a position to affect some need of R which, left unaddressed, would actually

cause harm to R; while at the same time K is aware that his/her actions may also affect the welfare of others and the achievement of the teacher's aims; i.e. K takes a multiple perspective on relationship.

2. intentionally, K wants to act in such a way that R's need is met, and intends, in addressing that need, to show respect for R's position (a feature that distinguishes kind acts from condescending ones). Also, K's actions are voluntary and discretionary; in other words, kind acts are not coerced, and they are not merely conventional. They are intended to deal with the unique situation each opportunity to act kindly provides. Even if the action corresponds to a conventional response, the multiple perspectives K needs to take in each instance demands a unique set of intentions each time. Kindness is not courtesy or good manners.

3. emotionally, K has empathy and sympathy with R--even in the case that K does not approve of R or R's position.

4. regarding knowledge and belief, K understands R's situation and need, K has the ability to meet that need, and K has both the ability to take and the belief in the importance of taking multiple perspectives from which to choose how to act toward R.

This analysis, if correct, shows kindness to be a suitably and relevantly complex concept. It requires commitment to meeting a student's need in the company of those of other clients and of the teacher's own situation. It requires a level of social-cognitive ability--empathy, insight into student need, and respect for the student's position. It requires knowledge of how to help, and skill in helping. It requires the ability to help a student with the welfare of others affected by the action in mind; and it requires that "helping" the student be understood in the context of the teacher's own vision of the desired ends of teaching that student. An action that the teacher sees as leading away from the long-term welfare of that student individually or in the community (depending upon the ideals to which the teacher is committed) will not be recognized by the teacher as kind.

A teaching ethic of kindness, by extension, involves certain perceptions, priorities, and privileged reasons. In such an ethic, teachers are *disposed* to see teaching decisions as involving the multiple perspectives described above; to giving priority to meeting student needs within the framework of those multiple perspectives, and to developing arguments for action that heavily weight student needs within that framework. A teaching ethic of kindness is one that is uniquely suited to the central demands of teacher professionalism. It provides a practical foundation for teachers' competencies and agendas for improving practice.

Resisting De-Professionalization of Teaching

In a period when whatever professional standing and privileges teaching enjoyed or aspired to seem likely to be lost in considerable measure, it may be small comfort to teachers to hear an argument for how they may increase the level of their professionalism. Moreover, if what is lost to teaching as a 'profession" includes the practical authority to influence the long-term aims toward which teaching may dedicate its efforts, it would seem that a great deal of the argument I have presented is rendered moot.

On the contrary: The aims of education in the United States have, in general, always been contested ground. Even the long-running Common School consensus that helped to build and maintain from the bottom up a system of public schools in this country was founded on political appeals to groups with a wide range of interests and long-term aims for education. When teachers have acted professionally, they have acknowledged this push and pull and incorporated it into their professional decision-making, as a corollary to their own professional hopes, dreams, and ideals. There is an old saying that educational reforms are defeated at the classroom door. It is fairer to say that, in acting professionally, teachers are bound to at least partially modify and re-prioritize the agendas of others. To fail to try to do this, or to fail to accomplish it would be a failure of teachers' professionalism. Resisting de-professionalization, in this important sense, is a matter of acquiring the commitment, skills, and judgment to work for what teachers value.

In that resistance, I suspect, lies the key to the advancement of teaching in every respect, including that of public standing.

Parents and Classroom Climate: The Missing Piece for Learning
Gordon Eisenman and Judi Wilson

Guiding questions:

1. What is the purpose of classroom management?
2. How does the climate of the classroom contribute to or detract from learning?
3. What is the role of parent involvement in classroom management?
4. How can teachers increase communication between the home and school?

Parents and Classroom Climate: The Missing Pieces for Learning
Gordon Eisenman and Judi Wilson

Management exists to make sure students are able to learn. Quality classroom management prevents interruptions to learning and teaches students how to control their own behavior. The job of teaching consists of planning, teaching, assessing, and student learning with classroom management the glue that holds them all together.

Management is different than discipline. It is much more comprehensive. Discipline is what teachers do to reward or punish behavior that has occurred. Behavior refers to everything people do, good or bad, right or wrong helpful or useless, productive or wasteful. Desirable school behavior is that in which students show self-control, responsibility and consideration and respect for others. It usually involves cooperation and helpfulness. This definition of good classroom behavior is quite different from the traditional definition, which often connotes obeying, acquiescing, keeping quiet, following directions, and doing as expected (Charles, 2005).

Misbehavior is behavior that is inappropriate for the setting or situation in which it occurs. Classroom misbehavior is any behavior that, through intent or thoughtlessness, interferes with teaching or learning. Management is everything involved in making sure that learning occurs. Management is primarily concerned with learning. It is proactive rather than reactive. The teacher's main concern changes from student obedience to student responsibility. The teacher's attitude shifts from turning to punishment and reward as the first option to looking at the causes and reasons for behavior: from short term solutions to long term problem solving

Teachers and schools exist to help students learn. All other possible tasks, jobs, and foci should take a back seat to learning. All that we do in school can be judged by its impact on learning. If a pedagogical strategy, program or assignment does not add to learning it should not be done. If the approach adds to learning it is probably a good idea.

Management is no different from any other aspect of teaching. All possible management strategies or theories can be judged based on the impact on learning. If a management strategy increases learning is a sound strategy, but if the management practice detracts from or decreases learning it should not be used. As an example we can look at the classic teaching text, "Sideways Stories From the Wayside School." In the first chapter the students are confronted by (teacher's name). The management strategy that the teacher employs involves turning students who misbehave into apples to be eaten later. By some theories of management the strategy is successful. The instances of misbehavior stop completely. However, when we put (teacher) practice to the learning test it fails miserably. While all students left in the class would not misbehave, they also will not learn.

Learning is always a personal matter to the student (Ginott, 1971). There is a significant body of research that indicates that academic achievement and students' behavior are influenced by the quality of the teacher-student relationship (Welhage, Rutter, Smith, Lesko & Fernanadez, 1989; Phelan, Davidson, & Cao, 1992). Joan Lipsitz (1984) found that successful schools provide a warm, personal learning environment. Students want, and perform better academically for teachers who are warm and friendly, positive, and caring.

Traditional Management Focus

Most teachers see only two possibilities when it comes to management. One is total control and the other is total chaos. Many teachers believe that if they do not exercise total control over the students the only possible outcome is total chaos. This control is not limited to controlling what they see as improper behavior. It extends to every aspect of students existence in school. Students are told when, where, and how to sit, when to talk (almost never unless answering a question from the teacher), when and where to work, when to eat, when to drink, and even when to go to the bathroom. Every second a student is in school there is a teacher telling them what to do, feel, and think. Looking from the outside, one would believe our culture values complete conformity, blind obedience to authority, as well as never questioning the status quo. This could not be farther from the true ideals and values we hold in America and yet our schools are supposed to prepare our children to be productive members of our society. In order to take their place as adults in the US, children need to be able to do the opposite from what we expect and teach them in school.

One wonders what teachers believe will happen if students suddenly where allowed to think for themselves. Look at some of the practices we traditionally see in schools and see what they are teaching, how they could be done differently to teach children to think for themselves and control their own behavior, and what would happen to the classroom if changes were made. Remember the goal of school is learning and management is creating an environment that promotes learning. If our routines and practices add to learning they are good if not they should be replaced.

The first example that comes to mind directly relates to learning. In most classrooms in America students are expected to work alone, silently, at their desk, when it is time to do what is called seatwork. If we look outside of school to the "real world" we rarely see anyone working alone at a desk silently. There are few (I can't think of any) occupations that call for this type of work setting. In most, if not all, situations we find ourselves in and out of the work place we as adults tend to work with others at a wide variety of places. It is highly unusual to find anything close to the environment most students find themselves in for hours a day.

This type of total control creates several negative results. First and foremost, working silently, alone, and at a desk detracts from learning. How many of you study under these conditions? None of you do. You probably study lying on the bed with the TV on, a Coke on the night stand and a bag of chips beside you. Or you study with a group of classmates talking about a variety of subjects in addition to the classwork. Under which set of conditions do you learn better? Each student is an individual with individual needs when it comes to learning. Why do we think that everyone should study in the same way in order to learn?

This approach to seatwork also has other negative effects on students and their learning. It makes learning boring. Working by yourself is not as much fun as working with your friend. It turns the teacher into the talk and movement police. Instead of using her time to work with student to help increase learning the teacher is forced to look for those breaking the rules. Instead of helpful guide we turn into the wicked witch of the west. All of these detract from learning.

So if the way we traditionally handle seatwork does not seem to be the best approach, how could we make it better? We have reflected on our practice, looked at the results of our procedures, and refined our management to improve learning. If you expect that we could learn more through better management of the seatwork time, then we must change our practice. Let's look at each part to see what might be the result if we made changes. What would be the results if we let students work in places other than their desk? Most teachers' reliance on total control would lend you to think that the result would be total chaos. However, there is a middle ground and there is where you will find management for learning.

Imagine if you will a classroom where not all students are at their desks. Some may be sitting or even, God forbid, lying on the floor. Some students might be working under a table or in a beanbag chair in the corner. Students might be working at a table or leaning against the wall. What would be the results of letting students work where they wanted instead of where they were told to sit? Would chaos reign? No. Students would feel more comfortable, better able to focus on the task at hand, and more willing to work hard. In effect more learning would occur.

A Climate for Learning

All of a teacher's procedure, practices, communication and actions set a tone for the class. That tone can promote or detract from learning. The Office of Educational Research and Improvement (OERI) defines classroom climate as an ethic of caring that guides interpersonal relationships in the school. There are many aspects to effective classroom climate. Farley (2002) states that the major difference between students who succeed in school and those who don't is the difference between students who have be taught by positive teachers and those students taught by negative teachers. Nelsen, Lots, and Glenn (2000) contend that there must be a climate of acceptance, dignity, respect, and encouragement. Teachers must show they truly care about their students. The attitude must be that all students are worth all the effort teachers can expend on them (Coloroso, 2002).

Teachers and students must work together to maintain a positive and productive classroom climate. Teachers who approach classroom management as a process of establishing and maintaining effective learning environments are more successful than teachers who emphasize their roles as authority figures or disciplinarians (Brophy, 1988).

Both students' future success and the quality of learning will be enhanced in classroom and school environments that emphasize collaboration and caring (Kohn, 1996). Establishing a positive climate for learning has many positive effects including higher academic performance, stronger motivation to learn, greater liking for school, less absenteeism, greater social competence and fewer conduct problems (Lewis, Schaps, & Watson, 1996). As Jones (1987) state we can be proactive and spend time building a positive classroom environment in which behavioral norms are developed by, agreed upon and practiced by students. Or we can be reactive and spend countless minutes responding to the disruptions caused by our decision not to spent time building a community of support.

Physical environment

There are many aspects to designing a classroom for learning. Every part of the room and atmosphere are important. Teachers need to consider how the desks are arranged, the lighting and temperature in the room, the wall decorations, the amount of student input, even the flooring can add to or detract from learning. Everything from floor to ceiling can add to or detract from learning.

When students walk into the classroom, be it for the first time or the hundredth time, what do they see, think, and feel? Do students feel comfortable, welcome, and safe? Is the room what Dr. William Perky would call "inviting?" When the students (and the teacher) enter the room is it a place they want to be? As you look at the room ask yourself would I want to be in this room learning for the next seven hours? Teachers need to take the time to reflect on each part of the classroom and determine the impact on learning.

There are many parts to the inviting classroom. Many of the choices to make have to do with what type of activities will be performed during learning. If students are going to work in groups, there needs to be grouped desk, tables, and/or open floor spaces. If teachers are going to allow students to move around the room for various activities, the room needs to be arranged for traffic flow.

Take a few minutes to design the ideal classroom. If you had the ability to create a classroom that would maximize learning, what would it look like? Take a blank piece of paper and start drawing. Don't let what has always been done in schools be a stumbling block for your imagination. Let your mind go wild. Look at each aspect of the classroom design and ask yourself what would increase the learning? Go ahead I will wait............................... Done yet? I know it takes a lot of thought. I hope you didn't injure yourself. What did you come up with? There is no right or wrong answer (the same with most problems in school). Trade papers with a peer and describe your classroom setup. Give your reasoning for each decision you made. If you can't identify a reason you chose to include some aspect of your design, you need to go back and work on it some more. Go ahead and discuss each others designs, I will wait............................. How different were the two rooms? Is there some aspect of your peer's room you have decided to incorporate into your room? Good. You should go out and see as many different classrooms as you can. The more you see the more ideas you will have for your classroom design. Hint: Take a notebook along or better yet a camera, and write down everything you see. If you don't write it down you will forget. What do you see that you think will add to learning and what do you see that might detract from learning?

Student/teacher relationship

An even more powerful component of the classroom climate is the teacher/student relationship. A significant body of research indicates that academic achievement and students' behavior are influenced by the teacher/student relationship (Jones, 1987). In order for the teachers to create a positive relationship with students there must be a learning environment that is warm, caring, and noncoercive (Glasser, 1986). Teachers must approach teaching as a relationship with individual children not controlling a class. Even management theory that began in the Behaviorist models of the 1970 have come to see the value of positive student/teacher relationships. Canter (1996) stated that, to be effective, any discipline system must be grounded in respectful, supportive, teacher-student relationships. Students come to behave more respectfully when important adults in their lives behave respectfully toward them, they are more likely to care about other if they know they are cared about. If their emotional needs are met, they show a tendency to help meet other people's needs (Kohn, 1996).

Ideas to Improve Teacher/Student Relationship

- **Students as individuals** – Teach and treat each student as an individual. It is easier to go out of your way as a teacher for a student if you see then as an individual. When deciding how best to handle a situation or what the best teaching strategy would be consider each student's individual needs, strengths, and weakness. What would help this student learn?
- **Teacher As a Model** – Model for your class the type of personal interactions you expect. If you want students to treat each other with respect, the teacher must treat each student with respect. If you want the class to use good anger management, the teacher must model good anger techniques. What are the students learning from my actions?
- **High Expectations** – Having high expectation for student learning and behavior and expressing those expectation in positive ways leads to positive relationships.
- **Meeting Student Needs** – Students' actions in the class are a struggle to meet five basic needs: survival, belonging, power, fun, and freedom (Glasser, 1986). Teachers who provide a stimulating learning environment, encourage students, and help them as much as possible be a part of the classroom community are most effective with today's learners. Almost all students have a primary compelling desire to feel they are a valued member of the class, that they belong (Dreikurs & Cassel, 1995).
- **Allowing Student Input** – The more of a voice students have in the classroom the more likely they are to behave and learn. When a student has a say in the rules, procedures, and even the academic choices, they see the reason and need for

order in learning. It is the experience with decisions that helps children become capable of handling them (Kohn, 1996). The process of making decisions produces many benefits for students, such as helping them become more self-reliant, causing them to think issues through, and encouraging them to buy-in to the classroom.

- **Positive Communications** – How teachers communicate with their students sets the tone for the classroom climate. It can be a positive tone or a negative tone. Teachers should show a sense of humor, a positive attitude, a supportive tone of voice, be optimistic, compassionate, enthusiastic and excited about the students and the learning in the classroom (Dreikurs & Cassel, 1995, Nelson, Lots, & Glenn, 2000, Marshall, 2001, Kohn, 1996)
- **Listening To Students** – In order to have positive communications and positive relationships with students, a teacher must listen to students. Teachers must listen to students, taking their thoughts and feelings seriously (Nelson, Lots, & Glenn, 2000). Students must feel that the teacher wants to hear their ideas, feelings, and even their stories in order for positive relationships to occur.
- **Showing Interest in Students' Lives** – Teachers need to take a personal interest in students' lives. Showing an interest in and respect for students outside interest leads to more positive relationships within the classroom.

- **Other Ideas for Improving Relationships:**
    - **Eating lunch with students**
    - **Encourage students to strive for improvement, not perfection**
    - **Emphasize students' strengths**
    - **Help students learn from mistakes**
    - **Encourage students to help each other**
    - **Show pride in the students' work**

- **Impediments to Positive Teacher/Student Relationships:**
    - **Teacher control**
    - **Group punishments**
    - **A demand for silence**
    - **Negative communication**
    - **Criticizing, blaming**
    - **Complaining**
    - **Threatening**
    - **Punishing and rewarding students to control them**

- **Golden Rule of Teacher/Student Relationships** - Teachers should never treat students in ways they, the teachers, would not want to be treated (Coloroso, 2002).

Parent Involvement for Improved Classroom Climate

There is widespread consensus among parents, educators, practitioners, policy makers, and researchers that parent involvement is critical to children's success in school. School-family partnerships can significantly impact student achievement. Schools are a social organization and the triangular relationships between parents, students, and teachers are essential for school effectiveness. We cannot look at the school and the home in isolation from one another. They are inextricably interconnected with each other. Unfortunately, many teacher preservice education programs do not provide extensive opportunities to develop the necessary skills needed to communicate effectively with parents (Kessler-Sklar & Baker, 2000).

A significant body of research (Henderson & Berla, 1996; Olmstead & Rubin, 1983) indicates that when parents participate in their children's education, the result is an increase in student achievement and an improvement of students' attitudes. Studies that compared levels of parent involvement found that student achievement increased directly with the extent to which parents were engaged in the school (Henderson & Mapp, 2002). In addition, increased attendance, higher student motivation, and fewer discipline problems have been correlated with an increase in parent involvement.

There are many benefits of parent involvement for schools. Higher levels of parent involvement can serve to increase student achievement, improve teacher morale, and leads to stronger reputations in the community. Teachers report that their professional lives are more fulfilling when they receive help and support from parents (Epstein, 1992). Hara and Burke (1998) point out that increased parent involvement also leads to a significant increase in parents' interest in and appreciation for education, teachers, and learning.

In 2000, a study was completed which surveyed 200 superintendents in 15 American states regarding their districts' parent involvement policies and programs (Kessler-Sklar & Baker). Over 90% of the participants indicated having at least one district-level policy that addresses parent involvement. The two most commonly reported policies were to communicate with parents regarding students' progress and school programs and to provide parents with opportunities to serve as decision makers. The survey also found that districts were least likely to indicate they had policies or procedures in place to train teachers to work with families. The authors recommended that schools should evaluate the need to train teachers to work with families. The Parents As School Parents: Research Report (1996) had four major conclusions:

- There are few parent involvement programs for parents of children older than elementary school-age;
- Few parent involvement programs have been rigorously evaluated;
- Most parent involvement programs aim to change parents' behavior; and
- There are few parent involvement programs for training teachers or changing the way that schools and parents interact.

The authors of this report indicate that professional and in-service training for teachers on how to effectively work with parents is not yet widely available. Their research also suggests there are few opportunities for personal and individualized contact between parents and teachers. They also acknowledge that more open dialogue is needed between homes and schools, especially interactions that are positive and not problem-focused.

Schools' efforts to involve families are most effective when they are comprehensive, well-planned, and long-lasting. Parents are most likely to become involved if they understand they **should** be involved, if they believe they are **capable** of making a useful contribution, and if parents are convinced the school and their children **want** them to be involved (Henderson and Berla, 1996).

Teachers' expectations have a positive or negative affect on how well students perform. Research indicates that when teachers get to know families, they have higher expectations of the students. Teachers also develop higher expectations of the parents as they get to know the families of their students.

Good education requires support and collaboration between school officials and parents. Initiating and strengthening the working relationship between home and school are major responsibilities of teachers. We must help parents understand they are important contributors to their child's success in school. A relationship build on mutual trust facilitates effective instruction.

Ideas to Increase Communication Between Home and School

Ames' (1995) research indicates that parents' evaluation of the teacher, their sense of comfort with the school, and their involvement with school activities was higher when parents received frequent and effective communications from teachers. Effective teachers demonstrate professionalism and confidence in every interaction with parents. The following are ideas focused on improving parent/school communication. They are generic K-12 suggestions and may not be appropriate for every grade level.

- **Send a personal welcome card or note to each student before school begins (if possible).**
- **Invite parents to special events throughout the year.**
- **Send home weekly or monthly newsletters.**
- **Don't let your first contact with parents be in connection with a negative incident.**
- **Schedule "good news" phone calls to parents throughout the year.** Most phone calls to parents are of a negative nature. Try to balance this with periodic positive calls as well. Consider keeping a parent communication form documenting the dates of phone calls along with a brief description of the purpose of the call (positive or negative).

- **Provide interactive homework or projects that involve the entire family** (time capsules, family trees, my life history).
- **Celebrity of the Week.** Choose one student each week to highlight on a class bulletin board. Send home a zip lock bag and a personal inventory form for students to complete. The family will send the completed inventory and pictures of the child in the bag. The teacher should consider being the first Celebrity of the Week.
- **Parents and Students As Teachers.** Invite parents and their students to share a talent, skill, or their occupation with the class.

There are two major occurrences when teachers will be required to interact with parents. Every school has some type of open house and parent/teacher conferences. Teachers must be prepared to interact effectively with parents and must make the effort to make a good impression. The following are ideas that can be implemented to increase the likelihood of having a smooth open house.

Ideas for an Effective Open House

Prior to Open House

- **Meet with other teachers in your grade level and your mentor** to identify what needs to be covered during this Open House meeting. Ask them for advice! Use their suggestions to **create a written agenda** for you to follow and to share with parents.
- **Create a welcoming environment for parents! (See ideas below.)**
- **Have a "Welcome To Open House" poster on your classroom door** signed by all of you. You could also do "Welcome Parents and Friends of (then list each student in your class).
- **Provide nametags for parents.** _____Parent of_______. The children can make the nametags for their parents and have them on their desk. This enables parents to network and make connections with each other.
- **Encourage parent involvement in your classroom.** Provide a volunteer sign up sheet. Create a list of possible activities: reading to students, tutoring, developing academic games and activities, assisting with special activities, chaperoning field trips).
- **Send home personal invitations designed by your students.** This can be an in-class writing assignment.
- **Display student work everywhere!** Use hallways too! Be sure there is something from every student!
- **If appropriate, prepare something special for the parents on his/her child's desk.**

Open House Night

- **You need to appear caring and competent!**
- **Dress professionally!** Always dress professionally when you are meeting with parents!

- **Welcome parents warmly and try to greet them by name.** Prepare yourself beforehand with some positive things to say to parents about their children as you greet them.
- **Provide a written agenda for parents along with a pen at each desk for them to take notes.**
- **Introduce yourself and your paraprofessional (if you have one).**
- **Express your excitement about the year!** Parents want to see that you are enthusiastic about teaching their child.
- **Clearly and carefully explain your policies and procedures (especially your grading system, discipline and homework policies).** Send home your discipline and homework policy and ask parents to read and sign both documents. Keep these in your files.
- **Emphasize that you are firm but fair and explain your discipline policy thoroughly.**
- **Discuss your "clean slate" philosophy** that students are beginning with a brand new slate this year and you have high expectations for them.
- **Emphasize your willingness to work with parents and encourage them to contact you immediately with any concerns!** If you aren't aware of a problem, you certainly will be unable to solve it.
- **Provide a list of strategies parents can use to help their children at home during the year.** Many parents want to help their child in school, but they do not know how to assist them.
- **Encourage them to set up a conference with you if they want to discuss an individual student's problems. Make it a policy to NEVER ADDRESS THE PROBLEMS OF AN INDIVIDUAL STUDENT during a school event.** Politely tell the parent that you appreciate his/her concern and you would be happy to meet at a later time to discuss the matter. Kindly but firmly, ask him/her to call you to set up a time to meet privately.
- **Provide a time for questions and answers at the end.** Respond to parents' questions quickly and honestly. If you are unable to answer the question, tell the parent you will research the question and communicate the answer with them as soon as possible.
- **Thank parents for allowing you the opportunity to work with their child this year.**

Effective Parent Conferences

The second time all teachers will meet with parents occurs during parent/teacher conferences. These conferences can be formal (an event planned beforehand) or informal (in the hallway, on the phone, or in the car rider line). In most schools, formal school-wide conferences occur twice a year. Conferences can be stressful or stress-free. It depends on the teacher and how well prepared he/she is. It is essential that teachers are organized and well prepared for conferences. Effective parent conferences rate as one of the best approaches to encourage parental involvement in a child's educational program. Most often the teacher understands the curriculum, the educational process, and how well the child is performing academically. The parent knows the child, his/her interests, needs, and fears. Together, parents and teachers can do more to assist students in achieving success in school than either can while working alone. The following are some suggestions on how to effectively prepare for formal parent/teacher conferences.

Pre-conference Suggestions

- **Send conference request forms home early enough to allow for parent planning.**
- **Always encourage both parents to attend.**
- **Work with the other teachers in your school to schedule consecutive conferences for parents of several children.**
- **Schedule parent conferences carefully.** Do not schedule too many conferences on one day, especially with parents of students who are struggling.
- **Consider scheduling a few conferences a week before the official parent-conference week.** This will make your conference week a little less hectic. Obtain administrative approval first if necessary.
- **Make sure your parent-conference schedule is convenient for working parents.**
- **Send a colorful conference reminder home a few days before the scheduled meeting.** With little ones, you may want to safety pin them on the child's outfit or coat.
- **Be sure you know as much about the home situation and parents as possible beforehand.**
- **Be aware of school policy regarding promotion and retention before the conferences begin.**
- **Learn parents' names and use them correctly.**

Conference Day Suggestions

- **Place a few adult-size chairs in the hallway so parents will be comfortable while they wait for their conference.** Also, try to have student work displayed outside the classroom for them to look at as they wait. Leave a few magazines or professional journals for them.
- **Identify your classroom and name clearly on the door to assure parents they are in the right place.**
- **Post an updated daily conference schedule on the door (with names and times). Stay on schedule!** If a parent arrives late and it is going to upset your schedule, reschedule their conference. If a conference is lengthy (and goes beyond the scheduled time), reschedule a time when you can meet again to discuss the concerns. If you want to schedule a bathroom/snack break for yourself, write it on the schedule as a "meeting."
- **Put parents at ease immediately.** Always welcome parents at the door with a smile and thank them for attending. This will help set the tone for a positive meeting.
- **Always conduct conferences at a table.** Never conduct conferences from behind your desk. This will be a more informal atmosphere and less threatening for parents. Provide paper and pens so parents can take notes or sign papers. Make

sure you have adult-size chairs available for everyone (in case they bring grandma, too).

- **Be organized and prepared!** Prepare a written agenda beforehand. Write down specific items you want to discuss during the conference (this ensures you won't forget important items).
  Ex. Conference Goals for ____
  1. Daily work (attach copy of grades and examples of work)
  2. Recent changes in behavior (list specific examples)
  3. Interaction with peers (site specific examples)
- **Encourage parents to express their ideas and to react to the issues that are being discussed.** If there are problems, you need to be "armed" with several specific suggestions on possible solutions. Mentors can help with developing concrete suggestions beforehand!
- **Emphasize the child's individual progress rather than compare with other children in the class or the home. Keep all conferences confidential!**
- **Begin and end the conference on time and keep them focused.** If a parent digresses, it is your job to get the conference back on track. If more time is needed, schedule another appointment.
- **Set up a folder for each child and place the conference agenda, student work, grades, and copies of tests in the appropriate folder.** Put them in order by conferences so that all you have to do is grab the appropriate child's folder and you are ready to go! Add the names of the parents on the agenda (in case you forget!)
- **Begin each conference with something positive about the child.** Plan this ahead of time for difficult students!
- **If you don't understand what a parent is saying, paraphrase it and then ask if you are correct.** If you are unsure what a parent is saying, use phrases such as: "Can you tell me more about that concern?" or "I'm having a problem understanding exactly what you mean." or "Can you give me an example?"
- **Listen! Listen! Listen!** The ability to listen is basic to good rapport. When dealing with an angry parent, silence is golden!!! Let parents talk! A defensive attitude will only alienate a parent. Avoid arguments completely. Quarreling doesn't solve problems. Keep your cool. If there is a difference of opinion, be diplomatic. Make an effort to understand the parents' point of view. Let the parent vent if necessary!
- **Place yourself in the parent's shoes.** How would you feel if your child's behavior was being discussed? Even the most difficult child has positive attributes. Be honest but be tactful.
- **Avoid long words or educational jargon!** Many parents will miss the point because they are too embarrassed to admit they do not understand. Keep vocabulary simple and use a lot of specific examples.
- **End with a summary of the conference.** Summarize what has been established and what is to be accomplished as a result of this conference. Determine what is expected of the student, the parents, and the teacher.
- **End the conference optimistically and positively.** Consider saying "You've helped me a lot by sharing _______ about your child," or "I appreciate your

concern for your child and your willingness to help us get him/her back on track academically. Thank you for your support as we work together to help ____ learn to interact more positively with his peers." Stand at the end of the conference and shake the parent's hand.

- **Set up a follow-up time to meet if necessary.**

Suggested Follow-up

- After the meeting ends, take a moment to make a note about major points discussed or to remind you of follow-up action that is needed.
- Follow through with any suggestions made during the conference.
- Communicate with parents and keep them informed of progress.
- Following school policy, report to your administrator that you have held the conference and notify them in writing of any potential negative reactions or responses. This will enable them to know your side of the story beforehand (should the matter come to their attention).

The Importance of the Home

Another focus of parental involvement efforts is the home. Even after children are of school age, they still invest 70% of their waking time outside the school setting. This time represents a tremendous learning opportunity that families and schools need to recognize (Clark, 1990). Kessler-Sklar and Baker (2000) suggest that schools need to assist parents in increasing opportunities for learning at home. Hopefully, this will lead to students arriving at school better prepared and performing better in school. Some programs assist parents by helping them improve their parenting skills (Yap and Enoki, 1994). Other programs (Scott-Jones, 1987) offer parents instruction on at-home activities to support learning. When parents' time for school involvement is limited because of personal or professional obligations, implementing learning activities at home is an efficient way for parents to spend their time (Toomey, 1986). Teachers, through their interactions with parents, play a major role in encouraging parents to support their children's learning at home.

Joyce Epstein, a well-known parent involvement researcher has researched the effects of numerous Teachers Involve Parents in Schoolwork (TIPS) programs. This is a highly successful interactive homework program that involves parents and students in learning activities at home (2001). Van Voorhis's (2001) study also indicated that well-developed, teacher-generated homework assignments in science help students academically as well as promote parent-child relationships and develop stronger parent-teacher communication.

Ideas for Extending Parent Involvement

There are many different ways for extending parent involvement in the schools.

- **Develop a Parent Packet.** Provide information about your philosophy, program, daily schedule, supplies, birthdays, curriculum, contact information, etc. to distribute at Open House.

- **Keep a checklist outlining contact with parents.** This is an excellent incentive to continue ongoing parent contact throughout the year with ALL parents (not just those who demand more time).
- **Create a Home/School Dialogue Journal.** A dialogue journal is a notebook that parents and teachers can use for communication purposes. It could also be a homework assignment notebook that is checked each day by both parents and teacher. This establishes an ongoing method of two-way communication throughout the school year.
- **Develop Parent Education Seminars.** This will enable you to expose parents to a variety of ways to assist their child at home. Many schools have created Math Night, Science Night, or Reading Night where parents and students learn together through interactive and creative instructional games and activities.

The importance of parent involvement has been acknowledged and well documented by numerous researchers, practitioners, and policymakers.

References

Ames, C. (1995). *Teachers' school-to-home communications and parent involvement: The role of parent perceptions and beliefs* (Report No. 28). East Lansing, MI: Michigan State University, College of Education, Center on Families, Communities, Schools, and Children's Learning.

Brophy, J. (1988). Educating teachers about managing classrooms and students. *Teaching and Teacher Education, 4*(1), 1-18.

Canter, L. (1996). Fist, the rapport – then, the rules. *Learning.* 12-14.

Charles, C. M. (2005). Building Classroom Discipline (8th ed.). Pearson Education Inc. Boston, MA.

Clark, R.M. (1990). Why disadvantaged students succeed: What happens outside of school is critical. Public Welfare.

Coloroso, B. (1990). Kids are Worth It! Giving Your Child the Gift of Inner Discipline. New York: Harper Collins.

Dreikurs, R., & Cassel, P. (1995). Discipline Without Tears. New York: Penguin.

Epstein, J.L. (1992). School and Family Partnerships. In M. Alkin (ed.) Encyclopedia of Educational Research. New York: MacMillan.

J.L. Epstein (Ed.). (2001). *School, family, and community partnerships: Preparing educators and improving schools.* Boulder, CO: Westview Press.

Farly, J. K. (2002). All Eagles are Supposed to Fly. New York: Writers Club Press.

Ginott, H. (1971). Teacher and Child. New York: Macmillan.

Glasser, W. (1986). Control Theory in the Classroom. New York: HarperCollins.

Hara, S.R., & Burke, D.J. (1998). Parent involvement: The key to improved student achievement. *School Community Journal, 8(2),* 9-19.

Henderson, A. T., & Berla, N. (1996). A new generation of evidence: The family is critical to student achievement. St. Louis, MO: Danforth Foundation and Flint, MI: Mott (C.S.) Foundation.

Henderson, A. & Mapp, K. (2002). *A New Wave of Evidence: The Impact of School and Community Connections on Student Achievement,* Austin, Texas, Southwest Educational Development Laboratory.

Jones, F. (1987). Positive Classroom Discipline. New York: McGraw Hill.

Kessler-Sklar, S.L., & Baker, A.J.L. (2000). School district parent involvement policies and programs. *Elementary School Journal,* 101(1), 101-18.

Kohn, A. (1996). Beyond Discipline: From Compliance to Community. Alexandria, VA: Association for Supervision and Curriculum Development.

Lewis, C., Schaps, E., & Watson, M. (1996). The caring classroom's academic edge. *Educational Leadership, 54,* 16-21.

Lipsitz, J. (1984). Successful Schools for Young Adolescents. New Brunswick, NJ: Transaction Books.

Marshall, M. (2001). Discipline Without Stress, Punishments, or Rewards: How Teachers and Parents Promote Responsibility & Learning. Los Alamitos, CA: Piper Press.

Nelson, J., Lott, L., & Glenn, H. (2000). Positive Discipline in the Classroom. Rockin, CA: Prima.

Olmstead, P.P., & Rubin, R.I. (1983). Linking parent behaviors to child achievement. Four evaluation studies from the parent education follow-through programs. *Studies in Educational Evaluation, 8*, 317-235.

Phelan, P., Davidson, A., & Cao, H. (1992). Speaking up: Students' perspectives on school. *Phi Delta Kappan, 73*, 695-704.

Scott-Jones, D. (1987). Mother-as-teacher in the families of high-and-low-achieving low income black first graders. *Journal of Negro Education, 56*(1), 21-34.

Toomey, D. (1988, April). Home-school relations and inequality in education. Melbourne, Australia: La Trobe University, School of Education (Eric Document Reproduction Service No. ED 269 495)

National Council of Jewish Women. (1996). *Parents as school partners: Research report.* New York: ERIC Clearinghouse on Urban Education/Columbia Teachers College. http://eric-web.tc.Columbia.edu/families/NCJW_child/index.html

Van Voorhis, F.L. (2001). Interactive science homework: An experiment in home and school connections. *NASSP Bulletin, 85*(627), 20-32.

Wehlage, G., Rutter, R., Smith, G., Lesko, N., & Fernandez, R. (1989).Reducing the Risk: Schools as Communities of Support. Philadelphia: Falmer Press.

Yapp, K.O. & Enoki, D.Y. (1994, April). Search for the elusive magic bullet: Parent involvement and student outcomes. Paper presented at the Annual Meeting of the American Educational Research Association, New Orleans, LA.

Technology in Education

David Martin, Mark Warner, Thomas Brown, and Debra Coffey

Guiding Questions

1. How can technology be used to bring the world into the classroom and transform the learning environment into a place where students are more actively engaged in learning?

2. How can you design and develop student learning activities that integrate technology for a variety of student grouping strategies for diverse student populations?

3. Describe technological opportunities that can make learning more accessible and fun for students.

4. What are sources for technology activities that can benefit you and your students?

Technology in Education

David Martin, Mark Warner, Thomas Brown, and Debra Coffey

Introduction

We live in an age of technology where children in our schools often know more about technology than their teachers. Most teachers did not grow up with the technology that has become part of the everyday lives of today's children. Only in the last few years have talking on cellular phones, playing video games, and surfing the Internet and television channels become commonplace activities. Internet capability in schools is widespread. So if most school systems in the United States are already wired for the Internet, how then shall today's teachers be prepared to deliver education in tomorrow morning's classrooms (Warner and Aiken, 1999)? Any response to this question is hazardous in view of the fact that technological change has increased at such an accelerated rate that proposals for pre-service and in-service teacher preparation in technology have a brief shelf life. Daunting though the task may be, one must take aim at such a dynamic, moving target and fire away. National standards for technology use in today's classrooms include a demonstration of a student's ability to: 1) explore, evaluate and use computer technology-based materials; 2) use computers for problem solving data collection, information management, communications, presentations and decision making; 3) design and develop student learning activities that integrate computing and technology for a variety of student grouping strategies and for diverse student populations; and 4) demonstrate skill in using such productivity tools as word processors, databases, spreadsheets and print/graphic utilities.

In addition to providing the experiences mentioned above, teachers are strongly encouraged by local school systems to develop exemplary web sites that contain opportunities for students, other teachers, parents and members of the community to: 1) view teacher-made slide show presentations including such data displays as graphic organizers, educational images, charts, tables, and spreadsheets; 2) engage in inquiry-based learning activities with external links to web sites containing primary source documents; 3) view student-made projects or field trips using scanned images or digital photography; 4) read student-made publications of their own writing using a desktop publishing format; 5) receive information regarding assignments, classroom and school wide events, field trips, classroom and school policies; and 6) engage in a wide variety of distance learning opportunities especially designed for students with extended absences. Online classroom delivery systems also encourage a variety of discourse opportunities through interactive asynchronous bulletin boards and email. Students can send projects to their teachers as attachments and teachers can provide electronic feedback to students through a wide array of word processing tools.

Integrating technology into curriculum, instruction, and assessment has obliged teachers to think about organizational and time management strategies that provide all of their students the opportunity to have access to enhanced learning tools. Access to technology enables teachers from the same school to collaborate on technology rich projects that provide their students opportunities to experience interdisciplinary curricula. Thoughtfully designed multi-media projects permit students with various kinds of intelligence to experience success in academic enterprises that have value beyond school. In this kind of learning experience, students who are less likely to exhibit verbal skills can have a visible voice in the classroom. For example, a teacher can establish links from her web site to student created web pages that contain a variety of projects. Students can provide an email link at the bottom of their web pages so that other students can ask questions and engage in constructive dialogue. Teacher mediation of this interactive dialogue is a powerful alternative instructional strategy.

It is evident that technology is promising for those who desire students to take more responsibility for their own learning. Teachers who facilitate student leaning need more structured time to develop skills working with new technology-based educational tools. These tools need to be presented in a context of learning in which the overall objective requires an authentic demonstration in a performance context. Teachers must be convinced by their own successes that new technological tools have an every day practical application and that parents and local infrastructures support the use of these new tools.

A Brief History of Technology in Education

Education has utilized technology for many years. Films, videos, and filmstrips have become staple supplements to the curriculum. Models, charts, and displays continue to provide enrichment and depth to programs. Audiotapes continue to have uses in song and dance. We use overhead projectors to show transparencies, manipulatives, money, clocks, color tiles, pattern blocks, the spectrum of visible light, and even magnetic fields (by sprinkling iron filings onto a sheet of acetate that has been placed over a magnet on the projector glass). Calculators continue to be used to help children in both mathematics and science.

Computers have been used in education since the late 1950s; the early focus was on computer-assisted instruction (CAI) involving tutorials, drill-and-practice formats, and the mechanics of computer hardware and programming techniques. The 1960s brought computers solidly into the field of education through computerized applications of programmed instruction. However, it is the emergence of the personal computer in the mid-1970s and the Internet in the 1990s that has expanded the educational use of computers to include word processing, spreadsheets, databases, graphing programs, laboratory computer interfacing systems, presentation software, electronic mail, the Internet, and a multitude of increasingly sophisticated applications. Computers can provide practice, create realistic simulations, gather experimental data previously impossible to obtain, process experimental data rapidly and accurately so valid conclusions can be reached, provide instant access to huge amounts of information, and enable children and their teachers to communicate with peers and experts throughout the world.

Widespread Use of Computer Technology

Nearly every American business, from banks and brokerage firms to warehouses and fast-food restaurants, requires some knowledge of computers. Nearly every manufacturing facility utilizes computers and computer-based technology. More than half of American homes have computers. In 2000, 57% of U. S. households had personal computers, and 51% of these had access to the Internet (*World Almanac*, 2004, p. 717). According to the 2000 United States Census, sixty-four percent of children aged 6-11 had access to home computers, and 25% of these children used the Internet at home (Home Computers, 2001, p. 4). These statistics suggest one reason for employing computers and advanced technology in our schools: *They are used everywhere.*

Familiarity with Advanced Technology

A second reason for using advanced technology in the classroom is that many children are accustomed to using it at home in the form of videos, television programs, digital cameras and camcorders, cell phones, iPods, Palm pilots and other handheld computers, video games, computer games, CD ROMs, learning programs, e-mail, and the Internet. Just as educational videos seek to teach children through media familiar to children, today's educational technology seeks to provide a comfortable learning atmosphere for children used to technology.

Technological Access to Information

Third, technology can be used to gain access to amounts and types of information previously unavailable to children. For example, using CD ROMs and the Internet, children can witness experimental procedures too dangerous or too expensive for the classroom; they can see photographs and action scenes and hear explanations and information presentations on just about any topic of interest, from animal habitats to aviation, from plate tectonics and volcanoes to nuclear reactors. Entire encyclopedias are available on CD-ROMs, some of which are "talking" encyclopedias with videos, from which children can obtain desired information in a matter of seconds. The Internet enables children and teachers to access huge amounts of specialized information on any topic from anywhere in the world.

Computer Support in Inquiry Investigations

Fourth, technology provides speed, accuracy, and convenience in inquiry investigations. Technology enables children to spend less time on data collection tasks and mathematical manipulation and more time processing and interpreting experimental data, thus achieving greater accuracy in data collection, mathematical operations, and experimental results. Probes and sensors that accompany laboratory computer interfacing systems enable children to measure force, temperature, light intensity, barometric pressure, and even heart rate with a degree of accuracy, sensitivity, and speed not otherwise available. For example, temperature probes can be used to compare the small difference between air temperatures at the floor and the ceiling of the classroom. Motion sensors can be used to record the continuously increasing speed of a cart rolling down an inclined plane.

Spreadsheets

Spreadsheets can be programmed to do mathematical calculations on raw data entered by children to provide desired information. For example, children can enter the number of swings a pendulum makes in 15 seconds into a spreadsheet; by means of the equations programmed into the spreadsheet by the teacher, they can calculate the average period.

Database Programs

Database programs can be used to store a variety of information that children (or the teacher) have researched on a topic; this information then can be sorted in different ways to help children answer their questions. For example, children who are investigating dinosaurs can research facts about a number of different dinosaurs. These facts are entered into a "dinosaur database," and commonalities among dinosaurs are searched, such as which dinosaurs were plant eaters, how many dinosaurs were less than 10 feet long, and where the most dinosaur bones have been found.

Graphics programs can be used to generate instant graphic portrayal of data collected by children (such as daily outdoor temperature or rate of plant growth), providing visual assistance in interpreting data.

Support of Learning Differences through Technology

Fifth, advanced technology can be used to provide learning experiences suitable for individual needs of children. For the visual learner, the array of video material available is virtually unlimited, ranging from programs that air on commercial and public television channels to videos, DVDs and CD ROMs prepared specifically for educational use on specialized topics and videos and photographs available on the Internet. With the appropriate technology, it is possible for children to access information about chosen topics from a variety of sources and then to manufacture their own video on that topic. Presentation software such as PowerPoint® makes it possible for children (and teachers) to develop multimedia presentations. These presentations might include material extracted from the Internet, video and audio clips that the children themselves produced, photographs that children took with digital cameras, and text—all in the same presentation. In addition, children can develop their own classroom publications and can publish their investigations and accomplishments in Internet sites.

Use of Computer Technology by Professionals

Finally, perhaps the most compelling reason for using advanced technology in education is that *real world professionals use it*. For example, one of the premises underlying elementary science education is that children should *do* science, not just read about science, and that children should do science the way scientists do science. This means using technology. The National Science Teachers Association (1999) adopted this posture in their position statement, "The Use of Computers in Science Education":

> Just as computers play a central role in developing and applying scientific knowledge, they can also facilitate the learning of science. It is, therefore, the position of the National Science Teachers Association that computers should have a major role in the teaching and learning of science.

Computers in the Elementary Classroom

The development of the personal computer and the rich array of educational software and related technologies now available have virtually transformed the use of technology in the classroom. In 2003, 91% of elementary schools in the United States had computers (*World Almanac*, 2004, p. 289). This is contrasted with 11.1% of elementary schools in the United States that reported using computers just 20 years ago (*World Almanac*, 1994, p. 196). In 2002, 92% of American elementary school classrooms had access to the Internet as opposed to 30% of American elementary schools that had access to the Internet in 1994 (National Center for Education Statistics, 2003).

A Technology Inquiry Continuum

A continuum can be constructed for the wide array of computer technology applications available.

TUTORING ◄——— INTERACTIVE ———► EXPERIMENTING

Tutoring applications are expository in nature. They dispense information. They teach something to the child. Tutoring applications include such programs as drill-and-practice, tutorials, course reviews, remediation, and testing.

Interactive applications are those that allow children to interact with the computer in some fashion, and include applications such as games, word processing programs, spreadsheet programs, database programs, graphic programs, simulation programs, graphic organizer programs, CD ROMs, presentation software, e-mail, and the Internet.

Experimenting applications are those that allow children to use technology as an adjunct to their own experimental procedures. Laboratory computer interface systems permit data gathering that would not otherwise be possible, especially long-term data (such as overnight effects), short-term data (such as increase in speed of a cart rolling down an inclined plane), and hard-to-obtain data (such as air temperature differences between the floor and the ceiling). In laboratory computer interface systems, a probe or a sensor is used to collect data, and the computer to which it is connected (interfaced) displays and processes the data. In addition, there are many Internet applications that encourage children to pursue their own inquires with the aid of Web-based resources such as communicating with scientists and interfacing with specific inquiries through using WebQuests, the Apple Learning Interchange, and other online facilities.

Tutoring Uses of Computers

Tutoring programs are used as dispensers of information and testers of children's mastery of the information. Typically a piece of information is presented on the screen, and the child is asked to key a response to a question about this information. The computer gives a "yes" or a "no" response. The "yes" response may be in the form of points awarded, or distances along an animated path, or height up a mountain, or some other system of portraying success. The "no" response typically refers the child to additional screens that "teach" the material, after which the child tries a similar question. The tutoring programs provide immediate positive reinforcement of children's responses and are similar to the programmed texts of the 1960s and 1970s; in a sense, they are a newer generation of programmed texts.

A tremendous array of electronic tutorial curricula exists, in the form of computer programs and on the Internet. Programs range from simple to relatively complex and should be selected on the basis of their intended uses and the age, grade, and sophistication of the children. Computer tutorials often include the basic elements of quality expository teaching: gaining attention, overviewing the lesson, providing objectives, reviewing prerequisite information, delivering new information, providing guidance, giving items for response, and providing feedback. A good example of such programs is the tutorials that accompany many computer programs you might purchase. You may have used one yourself to help you master a word processing program. Tutoring programs can be purchased; many are available for use directly from the Internet.

Tutoring programs can be used as part of an advance organizer or introduction to a lesson or unit of study. Those available on the Internet are particularly useful for this purpose. They can be used as part of an advance organizer or initial introduction, for follow-up on a topic the teacher has introduced, or for review of material. They can be used to reinforce concepts explored in class from different perspectives. They can be used to enable children to learn about something that has captured their interest or to cover material they missed due to absence. Tutorials are also extremely useful in helping teachers study scientific material where they may feel the need.

Computerized tutoring has been shown to exert a small but positive effect on learning (Hancock & Betts, 1994). However, these programs are designed to lead the child to correct responses and, as such, are clearly expository in nature. There is no room in these programs for children to interact or to apply their own thinking. The computer "owns" the knowledge, and it is the job of the child to discover what this knowledge is.

Interactive Uses of Computers

Interactive uses of computers permit children to use computers as tools to aid them in their inquiries. Although limited in scope by the material written into the programs, these applications allow some degree of mental manipulations directed by children.

Word Processing and Desktop Publishing Applications

Word processing programs are used for written reports, essays, descriptions, and the like. Features such as spell-check and grammar analysis permit attention to the substance of the material without having to worry unduly about mechanics. It has been shown that children who regularly use word processors for their writing exhibit higher quality and greater quantity of writing (Hancock & Betts, 1994). Children can use word processing programs to record experimental data; however, they cannot manipulate data using word processing programs.

Desktop publishing programs are word processing applications that allow children to put together such products as newsletters and information pamphlets with a professional look. How better to show the community what is happening in your class than to distribute a professional looking periodic newsletter? Programs are available for producing signs and banners, flash cards, calendars, and even your own big books. Children can make banners to advertise special classroom events such as "Science Day" or to welcome guest speakers. They can make signs to label where various kinds of equipment are stored.

Spreadsheet, Database, and Graphing Applications

Spreadsheet programs are used to record quantitative data and to provide rapid and accurate calculations by using mathematical formulas to process the data. For example, a spreadsheet can be used to calculate average period of a pendulum from raw data. Children first input the number of washers they used, the length of the string, and the distance of the pull. They then count the number of swings in 15 seconds for each of three trials, and enter the result in the appropriate blank after each trial. Each time a variable is changed, they enter the new values and the results of each of the three trials of swing counting. Formulas entered into the spreadsheet calculate the average of the three trials, the average number of swings *per minute*, and the average *period* of the pendulum (length of time for one swing). By using the spreadsheet, children can interpret the results of their explorations from accurately calculated averages.

Spreadsheets can be used to calculate the rate of growth of each of several plants; children input periodic height measurements, and the spreadsheet is programmed to calculate averages. Spreadsheets have many other uses where calculations from raw data are needed to interpret experimental results. Spreadsheets aid children in their development of the processes of prediction, inference, and interpreting data.

Database programs enable users to search large amounts of information about particular topics in any of a number of categories. For example, commercial searchable online catalogs and fast food nutrition facts are stored in databases that the user can access to retrieve specific information such as a listing of umbrellas available from a catalog or the nutritional value of a Big Mac. Database programs are used to help children sort and analyze large amounts of data about related phenomena. After entry of many items of information about each of many examples of a set, children can sort the information in different ways to answer questions. For instance, one could develop a database of characteristics of birds. Such characteristics as length, male–female resemblance, habitat, song, and nesting habits might be included. Each child might be assigned responsibility for researching the agreed-upon information about one or two birds. This information is recorded in the labeled sections of each database cell, one cell per bird. The information also can be presented in tabular form. Once the information has been entered, children use the sorting function to discover similarities among birds, such as which birds are located in certain areas, in which birds the male and female look alike, and the most common nesting habits.

Databases can be developed for just about any topic from dinosaurs to populations, animals to planets. Many databases are available commercially, and there are a huge number of databases on the Internet, many of which can be used to help children in their inquiries. However, as Braun (2004) points out, "Students' learning reaches its highest stages when students actively participate in the design of the database, collect the data themselves, and then develop questions and probes for other classmates or adults" (p. 71-72).

A good way to introduce children to the concept of databases is to have them write the data on cards and then sort the cards by common characteristics. For example, children record the information about each different kind of bird on a different card labeled with the name of the bird. They then flip through the cards to find similar characteristics, such as which birds live in cities. The electronic database is the next logical step, and has the advantage that it can manipulate large amounts of information quickly and can sort by numerical parameters, such as finding birds longer than 15 inches, between 15 and 20 inches long, or up to 18 inches long. Having done these tasks manually, children develop understanding of how database programs work and the power of electronic database programs. Database programs aid children in the processes of classification and interpretation of data.

Graphing programs use the computer to construct any of a variety of graphs from data entered by children. Options for graph construction normally include line graphs, bar graphs, and pie graphs, drawn either to predetermined specifications or to the child's specifications. Graphing programs are extremely useful in helping children visualize the impact of their data and interpret the meaning of the data. A graphing program was used to portray the depths and diameters of simulated moon craters formed by dropping marbles from different heights. Graphing programs can be used as early as kindergarten to chart plant growth, daily temperatures, times of sunrise and sunset, and the like. Teachers may need to provide the set-up, but children can input the data.

Graphing programs can show percentages and frequencies (quantities) of non-numeric variables in the form of pie graphs and bar charts. These programs are appropriate for charting data that are partially qualitative, such as percentages of basic food groups consumed during a day, numbers of children with certain hair color or eye color, numbers of days with given weather conditions, and the like.

Software such as Microsoft Excel combines database, spreadsheet, and graphing functions in a single powerful program that can be used for any of these functions independently and can combine utilities to produce rich arrays of information manipulation and presentation. For example, using Excel, the dinosaur database referred to earlier in this chapter cannot only sort and retrieve in a traditional database mode, but also can display the results in any of a number of graphic forms without having to reenter information.

Presentation Applications

Presentation software such as PowerPoint® is used for creating presentations that can include headline slides, pictures, photographs, videos, graphs, and sound. The presentations are used by elementary science students to show what they did in their investigations and illustrate summary results. Presentation software is very flexible, and its components can be manipulated to show topics succinctly and thoroughly.

Graphic Organizer Software

Graphic organizer software is used to depict pictorial or graphic organization of material. Graphic organizers, which include mind maps, concept maps, webs, and the like, are powerful tools to help people organize information. Electronic graphic organizers include concept mapping programs such as *Inspiration* (for upper grades) and *Kidspiration* (for lower grades); several other programs are available on the Internet. Graphic organizers help students develop plans for their inquiries, show visually how they are fitting information together, and show how they reach their conclusions.

Simulation and Animation Applications

Simulation programs enable the child to input a series of inquiries and actions for realistic or hypothetical problems and receive graphic information about the effect of the actions. For example, an upper elementary grades program called *SimCity*, by Brøderbund Software, invites children to inquire into urban ecosystems. A city plan is presented and children are asked to respond to hypothetical community changes, such as sudden population changes, natural disasters, and poor planning, by suggesting redesigns of the city. Effects of their newly input designs are shown so children can see the results of their planning suggestions. Simulation programs are used to train pilots and astronauts and to pose clinical problems for medical students. In elementary education, simulation software is often used to explore concepts that require (1) expensive or hazardous materials or procedures (such as nuclear reactions and experiments involving strong acids or highly reactive chemicals), (2) levels of skill not yet attained by children (such as activities involving micromeasurement, vacuum treatment, or supercooling), or (3) more time than is possible in a classroom situation (such as population growth simulations). Computer-based simulations enable students to "see" and manipulate abstract concepts such as density and to model complex ideas like predator-prey relationships.

Many simulation applications enable children to explore science topics through the virtual reality actions of scientists. For example, in *Dinosaur Hunter* (DK Interactive Learning), children travel in the footsteps of paleontologists in search of dinosaur fossils and learn about each dinosaur through videos, animations, and 3-D manipulations. Simulation programs for virtual dissections are available for helping children learn dissection techniques while concurrently demonstrating the sanctity of life.

Animation programs simulate processes such as acceleration, cell division, and mountain formation. Programs range in content sophistication from very simple (such as blood coursing through the body) to very complex (such as forces acting on space vehicles). They enable children to see models of phenomena that otherwise cannot be seen and allow children to manipulate given variables to see what happens, thus encouraging children in their development of the process skill of model making.

CD-ROM information bases enable children to isolate desired facts and other information through search-and-sort mechanisms. A CD-ROM is a compact disc that has the capability of storing huge amounts of information. The *ROM* in the term means "read-only memory," because you cannot add anything to the disc. A single CD has the capacity to store some 550,000 pages of print information; many are multimedia in nature and provide videos, sound, and pictures in addition to textual material. For example, illustrated encyclopedias, talking dictionaries, and maps with databases showing facts about major cities and geographic features are available on CD-ROM. The National Geographic Society has produced a number of CDs that contain facts, essays, color photos, maps, sounds, video clips, and games. A number of *Magic School Bus* titles are available in interactive CD-ROMs. The CD-ROM normally has a menu built into the program, enabling children to quickly access the desired information by category. Library catalogs and the ERIC, PSYCHLIT, and other reference databases in your college or university library are probably provided on CD-ROM.

CD-ROMs are available for multitudes of scientific topics and can take the form of databases, providers of multimedia information, simulation programs, or combinations. Although CD-ROMs cannot save children's work, they can provide exciting information presentations and interactive simulations.

Experimenting Uses of Computers

Microcomputer-Based Laboratories (MBLs) consist of computer-operated software with probes designed to collect data beyond the range normally available in the classroom. The probes extend observation capabilities by detecting very small differences in data (such as hundredths of a degree in temperature readings) and recognizing sensory input to which humans are not sensitive (such as ultraviolet and infrared radiation and inaudible sounds). They can provide data points at very small intervals (such as the speed of a falling object at 1/100-second intervals), and they can record observations over very long periods of time (such as the temperature of the classroom every 10 minutes for 24 hours).

Accompanying the probes and sensors are programs that provide readouts of the data, graph the data according to the experimenter's specifications, and perform mathematical manipulations of the data to meet the experimenter's needs (such as averaging trials and calculating acceleration from change in velocity). Although children are limited in their investigations by the capacity of the program and sensitivity of the probe or sensor, MBLs greatly expand the range of inquiry available. The use of MBLs supports the constructivist approach to elementary science teaching and learning.

MBLs are available for a wide variety of experimental purposes. The temperature probe is an electronic thermometer that detects and records temperatures from below freezing to above 100° Celsius. Temperatures can be read to the nearest tenth of a degree (or finer), and readings can be taken at any interval (long or short) over any period of time (long or short). For example, a child may wonder how fast warm water cools. Using the temperature probe provides data to answer the question. The temperature probe also can be used to record outdoor temperatures, monitor aquarium temperatures, and record the conversion of light energy to heat energy.

The light sensor is a photoelectric cell used to detect and record light intensity. Children experimenting with the effect of distance on intensity of illumination can use the light sensor to obtain measurements of actual amount of light received from a light source as the distance is changed. The light sensor can be used to provide visual portrayal of the effects of the tilt of the earth's axis on amount of radiant energy received at various latitudes on a globe. Using a flashlight to simulate the sun, children focus the light beam onto various latitudes of a globe or balloon that simulates the earth to investigate the tilt of the earth in its revolution about the sun and the effect of that tilt on concentration of radiant energy.

Motion detectors allow children to gather data on the motion of objects. Similar to the automatic range finders on Polaroid® cameras, they send ultrasonic pulses at high frequency and record the time each pulse takes to make one round trip from the device to the moving object and back to the device. From the time for each round trip, the accompanying computer program can calculate distance, velocity, and acceleration of a moving object. The motion detector is ideal for measuring the rate of acceleration of a cart rolling down an inclined plane, rate of deceleration of an object rolled down a hall floor, or rate of acceleration of freely falling objects. The results can be displayed graphically, in terms of actual data and as reductions in velocity, acceleration, or distance.

Heart rate monitors are similar to those found on exercise equipment. The sensor clips to the ear or slips onto a finger and measures pulse rate, which is recorded over time. This sensor is ideal to help children explore the effects of exercise and rest on heart rate. These and other kinds of probes and sensors are available from science supply companies and can be installed in a matter of minutes by anyone familiar with computers.

Sources of Computer Software

Many journals and magazines, such as *Educational Technology* and *Journal of Computers in Mathematics and Science Teaching*, contain software review columns; these will keep you apprised of new software and will aid in the evaluation process. *Technology and Children*, published by the International Technology Education Association (ITEA) is a journal devoted to technology education in elementary schools. *NSTA Reports*, published by the National Science Teachers Association, contains periodic listings of computer software that has been reviewed and assessed. Specialized journals such as *Science and Children* and *Childhood Education* also contain reviews of software.

Keep a running list of excellent software titles you come across, and add to it as you find new software that will help you meet the science inquiry needs of the children in your class. In all cases, you should give special consideration to the degree to which a particular technology or technological application supports the process-oriented inquiry method of instruction and the degree to which it enables children to explore on their own.

The Internet

The development and growth of the Internet probably is the largest factor contributing to the explosive growth in accessibility to information that we are experiencing today. It has been estimated that there are hundreds of billions of pages on the Internet, of which over 2 billion are readily accessible using common search engines (World Almanac, 2002, p. 628).

The Internet is a complex network of electronic communications that loosely connects millions of information sites worldwide. It was developed in 1969 as a military application to ensure that communications would continue uninterrupted even if global conditions were to become catastrophic. The World Wide Web was developed in 1991 to permit the inclusion of links in local sites that can take the viewer to other related local and distant sites.

Each and every site has its own unique address that normally starts with http:// (which stands for *H*yper*T*ext *T*ransfer *P*rotocol). The address is called the URL (*U*niform *R*esource *L*ocator) and contains several elements separated by dots or forward slashes. The letters at the end of the site designate its affiliation. Common designations include *edu* for an educational institution; *gov* for a government site; *com* for a commercial site; *mil* for a military site; and *org* for a site that is an organization. Web browsers such as

Netscape Navigator, Microsoft Internet Explorer, America Online (AOL), and others enable your computer to connect to the Web sites.

There are two ways to find a site on the Internet. (1) Enter the URL in the address box of the Web browser and click *enter*. The Web browser will find the site and will replace the browser screen with the site screen on your monitor. (2) Use a search engine such as Yahoo, Google, Excite, Infoseek, Alta Vista, Ask Jeeves, Lycos, or any of a number of other search engines. A search engine is a database of Internet resources organized by subject categories. In using a search engine, type key words in the "search for" window and click on the *submit* icon (sometimes called *button*). A list of Web sites matching your description will be displayed, usually many more than you can possibly examine, necessitating you to narrow your search. Click on promising Web sites until you find what you are looking for. Finding sites and exploring the links these sites provide is called "surfing the net."

Of particular interest to teachers is *The Gateway to Educational Materials* (GEM) Web site. GEM is an initiative of the United States Department of Education designed to expand teachers' capability to access many educational materials. When teachers connect to GEM, they are able to use the GEM database search facility instead of other Internet search engines to locate quality educational resources quickly and efficiently. GEM provides access to many thousands of educational resources including lesson plans, curriculum units, research, professional guides, activities, tips for teachers, background information, and other education-related materials available on the Internet.

The Internet provides limitless opportunities for searching and retrieving information on virtually any topic: art and museums, sports, news, weather, finance and stock quotes, travel and entertainment, government activities, educational sites for children and teachers, telephone and e-mail directories, reference material, health and medical topics, and practically anything else you can think of.

There are hundreds of thousands of Internet sites useful for education. Of course, much of this material is unsubstantiated, and you should look at sites with some degree of skepticism. It is a good idea to look for the source of information on Internet sites and to judge their value accordingly. For example, Web pages dealing with Gardner's theory of multiple intelligences that are developed and maintained by Harvard University are more likely to be authoritative than Web pages prepared by commercial developers of teacher materials.

The National Science Teachers Association (1999) has launched a *sci*LINKS project in which science textbook publishers can elect to include Internet icons and codes in the margins at key subject areas. SciLINKS also are included in the books NSTA publishes and in many of the articles that appear in their journals. To search for Internet information, students and teachers access the *sci*LINKS Web site and enter the code that guides them to several of the best Web sites on the Internet dealing with that topic. The Web site links are selected and maintained by teachers to ensure appropriateness and currency.

Constructing your Ideas

As you can tell, the Internet offers the full range of technological applications depicted in the continuum shown earlier in the chapter, from tutoring to interactive and experimenting uses. The Internet is the ideal classroom tool to support constructivist teaching and learning, and teachers must augment their curricula and instruction to incorporate this very important resource. In 1998, Congress established the national "Web-Based Education Commission," calling for educators to use the Internet "to improve achievement and to transform learning for all Americans" (Web-Based Education, 2001).

Using the Internet in the Classroom

The question arises of how you can incorporate the Internet into your curriculum. Craig (1999) suggests asking children to create a list of topics, perhaps relating to the subject matter being studied, that they would like to learn about, with the top choices becoming the focus of class investigations. Those topics for which information is unavailable in libraries or through community resources then become the subjects for Internet browsing. Students explore the Internet either individually or in groups. Of course, children must first learn how to explore the Internet; the technology or media specialist in the school often meets that need, frequently in technology lab settings.
The Internet also provides an opportunity for students to explore issues and ideas from a more global perspective. The development of such a point of view involves taking a more reflective view of our learning in a way that seeks to understand the links between our own lives and those of people throughout the world. Regarding science education, the Internet provides students with an opportunity to explore environmental problems at both the local and global levels. Globally, they can observe a human population counter as it increases by an amazing 2.7 people per second. They can also plot human population changes over time and relate these changes to the wide range of environmental problems that threaten the health of our planet. They can even calculate their own Ecological Footprint to see the impact of their own choices on the health of our environment. Such explorations can help students to develop the skills, attitudes, and values that will allow us to work together across countries and cultures to solve the complex challenges that await our fragile planet.

WebQuests

One of the more sophisticated uses of the Internet in classrooms is the WebQuest. A WebQuest is a student-centered inquiry-oriented activity designed by teachers in which some or all of the information students interact with comes from the Internet (Norton & Wiburg, 2003). It is a semi-directed plan for students to use in independent investigations of topics using the Internet. WebQuests combine discovery learning, integrated approaches, and technology in topic-centered learning units that are "among the most fascinating applications on the Web for K-12 educators" (Spartanburg County School District Three, n.d., p. 1). A WebQuest is a tried-and-true format for investigating a real-world problem using various available technologies. It includes the following six components (Dodge, 1995):

1. An introduction that sets the stage for the inquiry
2. A basic task
3. A set of information sources including links to Internet sites, email conferencing, searchable databases, computer programs, books, magazines, and other available resources
4. A description of the process the students should go through in accomplishing the task, broken into steps
5. Guidance on ways to organize the material
6. Conclusion that also includes ideas for further study

In addition, students' WebQuest projects are evaluated through a rubric that is part of the WebQuest.

The WebQuest employs the guided inquiry method of instruction where the teacher's role is to get students started on an investigation and facilitate their continued inquiry in the directions their efforts and interests take them. Using WebQuests, students can investigate virtually any subject they would like to pursue as thoroughly as they would like. For example, they can analyze the effects of the space program, take a virtual trip to bird or turtle nesting sanctuaries, prepare a virtual zoo exhibit, investigate the destructive forces of tornadoes and hurricanes, simulate animal survival in a disappearing forest, and build a better mousetrap.

Many WebQuests dealing with a wide variety of topics have been prepared and are available on the Internet. These can be adopted intact, or can be tailored to meet the needs of your class. Once you "get the hang" of WebQuests, you may want to develop your own and possibly post them on the Internet for others to use as well. Direct links to some of the highest rated WebQuests are provided on the companion Web site. We also have provided a direct link to the WebQuest site at San Diego State University, its birthplace. At this site, you can access teacher training materials and full information about WebQuests.

WebQuests center on real-world problems and require students to investigate the problem, come to workable solutions, and prepare some sort of presentation to show the results of their inquiries. Of necessity, they are interdisciplinary and are guided-inquiry in orientation. Because they are discovery in nature and use a multitude of exciting and virtually limitless technological resources, they truly "expose children to the scientific processes and the thrill of discovery" (Bollman, Rodgers, & Mauller, 2001, p. 68).

School and Class Web Sites

Many schools have their own Web sites, and teachers and children can download information to the Web sites through the "Web master" (person who controls the site). It is becoming increasingly commonplace for teachers to have their own Web sites that contain information about their classes, homework postings and helps, notices of class activities and examples of children's work. There are numerous Internet sites that provide step-by-step instructions for developing your own Web site. Some have templates you can use to simplify the process, and some allow you to post your self-prepared Web page free. Many teachers have the children in their classes develop their own Internet sites to which they publish their work as a means of demonstrating their achievement. These sites normally are linked to the main class Web site.

Scientific Research

In addition to using the Internet to find information, you and the children in your classes can use it to participate in scientific research efforts. For example, bird migrations are tracked through several Internet sites, such as *Journey North*, and children can forward their sightings through the Internet to be included with the data. Periodic results are forwarded to all contributors to enable them to chart the migration habits of given species of birds. A direct link to the Web site is provided on the companion Web site.

In a project that was conducted by successive classes over many years, 1st and 2nd graders investigated several factors about a local water habitat that appeared to be deteriorating. The teachers and students used word processors, spreadsheets, and presentation software to develop a Web site where they presented the results of their inquiries. They also prepared presentations for their City Parks commission which approved funding to restore the habitat based on the work the classes did (Wiske, 2004).

The Jason Project is a science-based interdisciplinary curriculum in which children participate in multimedia virtual research expeditions. A different focus is provided each year. Although the project is designed for older children, children as young as fourth or third grade age have participated successfully with modifications in reading level requirements (Jason Project, 2001).

Bringing the World In to the Classroom

Internet technology also permits teachers to bring the world into the classroom, such as in the following examples:

- *Operation Ruby Throat* is an international cross-disciplinary research initiative designed for K-12 teachers and their students in North and Central America. Students make observations of the Ruby-throated Hummingbird and input their observations into the Internet site. Data are exchanged among all participants via the Internet, and are made available to practicing scientists who are studying the habitats of the birds and the effects of habitat disruption. The scientists provide input and guidance to the participating teachers and students during all phases of the project. The companion Web site has a direct link to the *Operation Ruby Throat* site.

- K–12 science teachers can access a 24-inch research-grade telescope located in the California mountains for astronomy projects. After reserving a block of time, the telescope can be controlled by the computer in the teacher's classroom and directed to move across the sky to a certain object. The object is photographed and the image is sent back to the computer where it is downloaded. Children can repeat the process to obtain additional images and thus study change ("Classes View Telescope," 1995).

- Children who are working on projects in their schools in the United States and desire information, experiment replication, or feedback from children elsewhere can make the request through e-mail or the Internet. For example, if children wanted to find out why underwear turns inside out in the drier. One child wondered if the same thing would happen in Australia, because it is in the Southern Hemisphere. E-mail would enable the child to ask the question and enlist Australian children in pursuing the same project.

- Using closed-circuit video, children in American schools have communicated with astronauts in space, deep-sea divers, and archaeologists, asking questions, receiving answers, and being shown first-hand demonstrations of operations and responses to their questions.

- Children can communicate with astronauts in orbit via e-mail and closed circuit television transmitted by satellite to ascertain the current status of experiments they themselves designed to be carried out in space. Indeed, children and their teachers are invited to prepare experiments to be carried out in space aboard NASA spacecraft. If accepted, the astronauts perform the experiment in space while communicating with the classes of children through closed-circuit television.

Incorporating Internet technology into the curriculum transforms classrooms. Owston (1997) reports that when computers are introduced into classrooms, teachers change their teaching style to allow students greater autonomy in their learning--teachers tend to shift their style of teaching from a didactic to a more project-based approach. The overriding questions about how to incorporate Internet technology into the curriculum are "Does this application help children *do* science?" and "Does this application help children assume ownership of their inquiries?"

Video in the Classroom

Many advances have been made in the field of video. Commercial and public television stations offer carefully designed instructional videos that are telecast during typical school hours so schools can receive them and pipe them into appropriate classrooms. For example, the Public Broadcasting System (PBS) regularly airs programs on science and nature. The Learning Channel airs programs on topics suitable for children. The Weather Channel broadcasts daily 10-minute explanations of weather phenomena and offers documentary videos for use in schools. Most educational television material is copyright-cleared and free of commercials. *Cable in the Classroom* monitors and publicizes educational telecasts and also provides schedules of upcoming educational programs. One of the recent advances in educational technology is video production by children. All it takes to help children make their own videos is a little know-how (or the assistance of the media specialist) and a desire to let children expand their horizons. To aid teachers and students in making their own videos, the Apple Computer Company has developed the Apple Learning Interchange (ALI), and Internet site whose purpose is to provide materials to help teachers in their teaching and their professional growth. A major section of the site is devoted to lesson ideas and teacher helps for developing videos on a variety of topics.

Conclusion

The array of technology available to support process-oriented inquiry programs of instruction is dazzling. Terminology often seems indecipherable, choices are seemingly infinite, and hardware can be expensive. How do you get started? If you already are familiar with computers and other technology, you may feel ready to jump right in and enrich your classes with a wide array of computer applications. However, if you are uncomfortable with technology, it is a good idea to start slowly.

Every teacher should know how to use at least a word processing program, a spreadsheet program, a database program, a graphing program, e-mail, and the Internet. As you begin to incorporate technology in your classroom, try one or two applications that seem to have particular merit, such as using a word processing program to write letters and reports, using a spreadsheet to keep track of grades or attendance, using a program to create signs and banners, or searching the Internet to find ideas for a unit or lesson you are planning. Do not be dismayed by initial difficulties; we all experience them at first. Keep working with the programs you choose, and you will be amazed at how rapidly you achieve proficiency and you will be amazed at how much work and time you save.

Then try a scientific application, perhaps a tutoring program that presents a unit you are teaching. Children can run through this program as an additional activity or as a review activity. Many teachers allow children to include computer work in their free-time choices. Perhaps a game or two might be appropriate, or a program on some topic that is interesting to your children but that you will not be able to include in your curriculum.

When the time comes for you to provide input into the district's or the school's budget, be prepared to discuss the virtues of technology; your voice and your expertise may help put your school on the cybernetic information highway. You can serve on your local school committee for software evaluation and you can help develop the 5-year plan for technology in your school. You can request that your school subscribe to technology magazines.

As you progress in your quest to use modern technology in your classroom, your excitement will mount from day to day. Keep adding to your store of information, expertise, and software, and you will find you are helping your students to open doors to inquiry never before available. With technology, there is no limit to children's inquiries.

References

Braun, Jr., J. A. (2004). Technology in the classroom: Tools for building stronger communities and better citizens. *Kappa Delta Pi Record, 40*(2), 69-73.

______ (1995). Classes view telescope via computer. February/March *NSTA Reports*

Collings, J. N. (1985). Scientific thinking through the development of formal operations: Training in the cognitive restructuring aspect of field-independence. *Research in Science & Technology Education, 3*(2), 145–152.

Craig, D. V. (1999). Science and technology: A great combination. *Science and Children, 36*(4), 28–32.

Dodge, B. (1997). Some thoughts about WebQuests. Retrieved 12/05/04, from http://webquest.sdsu.edu/about_webquests.html.

Edelson, D. C. (2001). Learning-for-Use: A framework for the design of technology-supported inquiry activities. *Journal of Research in Science Teaching, 38*(3), 355–385.

Foshay, J. D. (1999). *Project-based multimedia instruction* (Fastback No. 445). Bloomington, IN: Phi Delta Kappa Educational Foundation.

Frisch, M. (1957). *Homo Faber.* Frankfurt: Suhrkamp Verlag.

Hamilton, A. (1949). Brains that click. *Popular Mechanics Magazine, 91*(3), 162-167, 256, 258.

Hancock, V., & Betts, F. (1994). From the lagging to the leading edge. *Educational Leadership, 51*(7), 24–29.

Hernandez, S. & Leung, B. P. (2004). Using the Internet to boost parent-teacher relationships. *Kappa Delta Pi record, 40*(3), 136-138.

______ (2001). Home computers and Internet use in the United States, August 2000. Washington, DC: U.S. Census Bureau. Retrieved 11/07/04 from http://www.census.gov/prod/2001pubs/p23-207.pdf.

International Society for Technology in Education. (2004). Curriculum and content area standards: NETS for students. Retrieved 12/07/05 from http://cnets.iste.org/currstands/cstands-netss.html

IsteNETS. (2004). National educational technology standards for teachers. Retrieved 12/12/04 from http://cnets.iste.org/teachers/t_book.html.

______ (2001). Jason Project. Retrieved 12/09/04 from http://www.jasonproject.org

Mohler, R. R. J. (2000). More space shuttle experiments take flight. *Science and Children, 38*(2), 39–43.

______ (2003). National Center for Education Statistics. *Issue brief: Internet access in public schools and classrooms: 1994–2002.* Retrieved 10/04/04 from http://nces.ed.gov/pubsearch/pubsinfo.asp?pubid=2004011

National Science Teachers Association (1999). NSTA position statement: The use of computers in science education. Retrieved 11/21/04 from http://www.nsta.org/positionststement&psid=4

______ (1999). National Science Teachers Association. NSTA launches *sci*LINKS. *NSTA Reports!, 10*(5), 1.

Norton, P. & Wiburg, K. M. (2003). *Teaching with technology.* Belmont, CA: Wadsworth/Thomson Learning.

Oppenheimer, T. (2003). *The flickering mind.* New York: Random House.

Owston, R. D. (1997). The world wide Web: A technology to enhance teaching and learning? *Educational Researcher, 26*(2), 27–33.

Pastor, E., & Kerns, E. (1997). A digital snapshot of an early childhood classroom. *Educational Leadership, 55*(3), 42–45.

Spartanburg County School District Three. (n.d.). WebQuests. Retrieved 08/26/04 from http://www.spa3.k12.sc.us/WebQuests.html

Steinberg, E. R. (1989). Cognition and learner control: A literature review, 1977–1988. *Journal of Computer-Based Instruction, 16*(4), 117–121.

______ (2000). Technology training. *Kappa Delta Pi Record, 36*(4), 189.

United States Department of Education (1999a). E-Learning. Retrieved 09/06/04from http://www.ed.gov/print/about/offices/list/os/technology/reports/e-learning.html

United States Department of Education. (1999b). *Preparing tomorrow's teachers to use technology.* Retrieved 09/22/04 from http://www.ed.gov/programs/teachtech/index.html

United States Department of Education. (2000). Revising the 1996 national educational technology plan. Retrieved month day, year, from http://www.air-dc.org/forum/

______ (2001). Web-based education commission calls for "National mobilization" around Internet. American Association of Colleges for Teacher Education. *Briefs, 22*(1), 1.

Warner, M. & Aiken, M. (1999). Training today's teachers for tomorrow's classrooms. *Technological Horizons in Education Journal,* 27(3) 118-122.

Wiske, S. (2004). Using technology to dig for meaning. *Educational Leadership, 62*(1), 46-50.

World Almanac. (2004). New York: World Almanac Books.

World Almanac. (2002). New York: World Almanac Books.

World Almanac. (1994). Mahwah, NJ: Funk and Wagnall's Corporation.

School Leadership and Teachers' Needs: A Case for a Moral Posture
Samuel B. Hardy, III

Guiding Questions

1. Does humankind seek the "good" outcome in each endeavor?

2. Is it in man's nature to habitually strive toward success?
   Should leaders guide others from a moral perspective (always doing the right thing), or direct subordinates in step-by-step task performance?

4. If teachers naturally desire the "right" outcome for their students, what is the role of the school leader, and how do we gauge his effectiveness?

5. Is there a "best practice" a principal can utilize to motive her faculty? How much effort is required?

School Leadership and Teachers' Needs: A Case for a Moral Posture

Samuel B. Hardy, III

An Ethical Basis

Tracing back to the early Greeks as an historical preview, Beckner (2004, as cited from MacIntyre, 1966, p.57) uses the first sentence from Aristotle's *Nicomachean Ethics* to serve as a partial explanation for why we act as we do: "Every craft and every inquiry, and similarly every action and project, is thought to aim at some good; and for this reason the good has rightly been declared to be that which all things aim" (p.10). The word in Greek used by Aristotle to define "good" translates into *happiness*. The reader can assume therefore, that people, per Aristotle, will endeavor to do those things that bring them happiness - happiness derived from performing deeds that are good and virtuous. Immanuel Kant (Beckner, 2004) felt that an act to be moral must be done from a sense of good will. Kant developed his "categorical imperative" wherein he felt a rule of living must be universal, for all people, at all times. Kant's basic principle of morality "...completely transcends the realm of sense experience and specific characteristics of human nature." Kant felt that "good" actions were not necessarily "wise" actions but actions stemming from an inner sense of duty and calling to a higher moral law and not individual happiness (p.15). Kant's "categorical imperative" is consistent with our feelings that at times some things are right, and some things are wrong. According to Kant, our actions should follow those precepts that seem to be part of a universal law of nature (Beckner, 2004). If we accept either philosophical view, in this writer's opinion, then our actions originate from our own desire for happiness, or our desire for universal happiness (happiness for others). Whichever the motive, people strive for the "good" and virtuous outcome.

The ideal of doing "good" is not totally unique to Western philosophy. Confucius centered his teachings on human activities. His primary emphasis was in the establishment of a moral social order (Wong, 2001). The Chinese philosophers were not interested in purely abstract thinking or spiritual beings. This bent differs from the Western reliance on logic to explain the universe. The Chinese tended to be more concrete when they envisaged objects and they adopted a more pragmatic attitude toward life itself (Wong, 1998). Confucianism regards human nature as intrinsically good with man possessing the 'innate ability' to do good. It (Confucianism) seeks to build a moral order in life: "The primary concern is not in understanding what is right or good, but how good or right could and should be done." (Wong, 2001, p. 311).

China has a history since Confucius' era of preparing leaders on moral grounds. When comparing the West to China with regard to moral preparation Wong (2004, cited from Lo, 1996) points out that the West has been chiefly concerned with abstract concepts to understand the character of morality and to define good, right, ought and obligation. He goes on to point out that Chinese philosophers spent time on the meaning of moral values; they were more interested in the practical aspects of morality and, therefore, spent more time on bringing about ways of doing good. This concern for practical forms of morality was expressed very early in the history of China as ethical humanism.

Ethical humanism reached its zenith via the teachings of Confucius. Wong (2001, cited from Chan, 1963, p. 17), in articulating the concept, develops four elements (p. 314-315).

- *Confucius focused on human activities, paying little attention to spiritual matters.*

Prior to Confucius, in China, education had been reserved for the nobility and had been controlled by state officials. Confucius opened education to all and challenged the class system. Confucius' pupils were of all types: merchants, nobles, and the common folk. He did not reject anyone who had a desire to learn.

- *Confucius emphasized learning.*

Confucius felt that men were, by nature, basically alike and that learning created any differentiation. His attitudes toward life and learning have greatly influenced the Chinese worldview. The Chinese have long been known for the value they place on education. The assumption being, espoused by Confucius and others, that everyone can succeed in learning.

- *According to Confucius, learning does not serve a primarily vocational purpose. Its function lies in character training: learning to be faithful (chung) and altruistic (shu).*

It is not sufficient that a person keeps knowledge to himself. "'Man of ethical humanity must also practice what he has learnt. When he wishes to establish himself, he must at the same time establish the others. When he wishes to be prominent, he must also help others to be prominent.'" (p. 315). This obligation to empower others is known as the Confucian Golden Rule. Learning brings with it two requirements: First, learn to be a moral and upright person and, second, after serving the first purpose of learning, apply what has been learned to serve the people.

- *Confucianism took life as a given.*

Confucianism does not attempt to analyze and challenge life, but to accept it as it comes. Fate is beyond man's control and there are no guarantees of success despite the extent of the effort. Yet, good deeds and living life as a morally upright person are regarded as certain because being good is within one's nature; it requires no outside intervention, just one's own will and education can foster this process. A decided aspect of Confucianism is a belief in doing good (Wong, 2001).

The two general philosophical views of East and West, at least those of the philosophers mentioned herein, appear to this writer to differ in degree. The Western view centers on either an impetus in people to do good because it satisfies an inner urge (happiness) in Aristotle's view, or an impulse driven by a need to satisfy an extra urge (good will) or, duty to do right, put forth by Kant. Confucius' view is not far from both Westerners because he contends that it is in man's nature to do "good" and be morally upright. But being morally upright also requires that men learn, and through learning enable others with the knowledge. Aristotle's and Kant's Western philosophies are apart in terms of motivation, in this writer's view. A person cannot be driven to do good for himself (self-interest) at the same time he strives to help others through a moral sense of duty.

Whatever philosophical concept we accept, culturally it seems the societal perspective upon which moral behavior has developed is based in the notion that human actions, regardless of the motivation, are based upon tenets emanating from a distinctive human need to do "good". If one accepts the concept that "good" for one person is genuine, "good" meaning ethical and moral, it can only mean the results of that person's actions are "good" for all. Then it would stand that moral actions on the part of all people would promote society to a greater extent beyond the sum of its individual members' needs. What are the implications of "good" deeds for leadership? What are the implications for school leaders? We will return to these points later.

Leadership

There appears to be no set definition for *leadership*; at least not one serving as a guide for all settings and circumstances. Hughs, Ginnett and Curphy (2002) stress this and point to the multitude of factors that impact each situation as the reason. These authors do accept a definition they cite from Roach and Behling (1984): "the process of influencing an organized group toward accomplishing its goals" (p.8). Snowden and Gorton (2002) use a definition by W.H. Cowley dating from the 1920's: "The leader is the one who succeeds in getting others to follow him [her]" (p.69). Still another definition is by Hoy and Miskel (2005) which they credit to Martin M. Chemers (1997): "Leadership is a process of social influence in which one person is able to enlist the aid and support of others in the accomplishment of a common task" (p.375). These same authors do offer the following statement: "The only assumption shared by this [Chemers' definition] and most definitions is that leadership involves a social influence process in which one individual exerts intentional influence over others to structure activities and relationships in a group or organization" (p.375). If we accept that the above definitions are representative of the literature in general regarding the work done on the subject of leadership, it appears to this writer that leadership, or getting things accomplished by directing a group endeavor, is, as Hugh, et al (2002) put forth, a function of the leader, the follower, and the situation.

Leaders

Leaders are all different but it is fair to say that they all share some common attributes. Hughes, et al (2002) with reference to the work of many others point out that leaders who are effective differ from those who are not. The differences start with personality. A leader's personality will affect his personal style. Whether he views followers as needing his strict direction or whether he is willing to delegate actions and responsibilities are innate personality qualities the leader carries with him through life. Often personality traits are so ingrained in us that we seldom adapt alternative styles for very long. A second way personality affects a person's style is through temperament. If a leader has an even temper and is not susceptible to loud outbursts when brought bad news, he/she is likely to be brought information by followers in a timely manner. Subordinates who expect to be "shot" when approaching the boss with disquieting information will not do so. This is often just the information the boss needs to hear.

Hughes, et al, (2002) continue by noting another important aspect of being a leader is how the leader arrived at the position. Subordinates who rose through the ranks or were elected have more influence over followers than leaders appointed by higher-ups. If followers have direct input with the selection process they have a higher sense of identification with the leader. A greater sense of identification may, however, lead subordinates to expect more from the leader and place greater demands upon him/her. Regardless of how they achieved their current position, leaders must remain sensitive to those over whom they have authority.

Effectiveness can be determined by a person's level of experience in general and tenure with a particular organization. Those new leaders who "walked the walk" already are given a certain level of latitude by followers, and those leaders promoted from within an organization are treated in a like manner because they are better known than outsiders (Hughes, et al, 2002). A principal "rising from the ranks" because of his experience as a classroom teacher, in essence, will be accorded a certain level of respect by virtue of having "been there" already.

Followers

The leadership process is influenced by the leader/follower relationship. Hughes et al (2002), again citing previous research, tell us that followers' personalities along with their expectations, levels of maturity, overall competence, and motivation impact upon the leader. Of these traits, motivation to do the work is also important, "Workers who share a leader's goals and values, and who feel intrinsically rewarded for performing a job well, might be more likely to work extra hours on a time-critical project than those whose motivation is solely monetary" (p.31). The implications for understanding this about his teachers by the school principal are many and profound. Hughes, et al, go on to stress the importance of understanding the influence followers have on leadership due to the changing nature of the times in which we live.

The relationship is changing because pressure is mounting on organizations, and the people who work for them, to perform with reduced resources. Direct funding reductions, or reduced funding increases, have strained the relationship between followers and leaders. The second reason cited is the trend toward more openness between the leader and the led through an increased emphasis on power-sharing. Frequent and rapid change begets problems whose solutions require input from more than one perspective.

Followers can aide in problem solving by assuming a leadership role themselves. In the case of a school, the teachers are at times nearer the problem than the principal. They should, as Hughes and his colleagues suggest, "own" the change, a change for the betterment of the school by working together with the principal in a collaborative effort at problem solving. Next, followers (teachers) because they often see problems before the principal, can exert an influence on the leadership process by promptly and accurately relaying relevant information to the principal so that he can make a better decision. And, lastly, Hughes et al, citing from Senge, (1990) warn that the future will bring more change and followers should be open to the opportunities future change will bring. Facing change with a positive attitude and openness to self-development will result in greater employment value for the teacher.

The Situation

Just as there appears to be no set definition for leadership that applies across all settings, there is no set of leadership standards or rules that apply to all situations. The leader and each follower being their personal traits, backgrounds, perspectives, values, etc. to the situation. One leadership size does not fit all. The dynamic that results between the participants will dictate the level of involvement on the part of the leader. External factors such as availability of resources, space, policies and laws, also have an impact, and, therefore, each situation is unique.

Hoy and Miskel (2005) list the situational factors for educational leadership under four topic headings: **Subordinate** – personality, motivation and abilities; **Organizational** – size, hierarchy, formalization, leader role; **Internal** – climate, culture, and, **External Environment** – social, economic (p. 385). It is evident from this listing that there are many combinations of variables that can interplay in a school setting creating very complex situations. How can a principal unravel these combinations and effectively lead his school? One suggestion is to remain flexible.

In writing about situation leadership, Snowden and Gorton (2002) propose that less emphasis should be directed toward the *person* as an approach to effective leadership and more attention should be placed on the *situation* within which the person finds himself. They mention that the school of thought surrounding this leadership alternative is underpinned by two propositions: (1) that the leadership approach employed by an individual should be relative to the situation and (2) that different situations demand different kinds of behavior from the leader (p.73). They continue by noting observational evidence whereby persons who attain a leadership position, either elected or appointed, succeed until the situation changes and their constituents vote them out. The point being that certain leaders' styles "fit" certain situations well, and not others.

These authors continue by saying that this theory places a high price on a leader's ability to adapt and remain flexible. Critics of this theory per Snowden and Gorton say that many leaders are influenced by their own personality and needs and that they find it too difficult to adapt to new settings. Situations may change easily, but personalities do not - all the more reason for principals to know this about themselves.

Leadership, continued

A comparison between *leading* and *managing* is summed up by the statement that managers do things right, and leaders do the right thing. Kowalski (2003) elaborating on this difference points to the activities of managers to include: personnel supervision, materials' supervision, and conflict resolution. All actions required to maintain efficiency. Leadership, however, is centered on *what* should be done to better the organization (e.g., planning, visioning, and consensus building); not just the *how* of running the company, or managerial functions. Managers are trained to apply standard procedures to ensure uniformity whereas leaders are trained to think independently. He (Kowalski) continues the differentiation between the two by pointing out that managers are oriented toward *failure-avoidance*, but leaders are oriented toward *success-seeking* strategies – "a problem solving and risk–taking orientation to administration" (p.3). Managers focus on maintaining order and stability and tend to be inflexible in making decisions – they do only what the policy states. Leaders have a different disposition being open to new ideas and innovations. Leaders, therefore, will adapt their work methods more easily to change (Kowalski, 2003).

Continuing along with the same comparison of managing and leading, Cunningham and Cordeiro (2003) differentiate the two with leadership being concerned with organizational vision and the organization's direction, and that it (leadership) draws others into actively pursuing strategic goals. Managing, by contract, centers on the "nuts-and-bolts" of making the organization work. They go on to mention how important leadership is to schools because we have entered a time of transition. Educational reform is a process of continuous improvement and that leaders should be entrepreneurs in that they should empower employees to meet new societal challenges.

Sergiovanni (1992) goes a bit further in comparing a manager to a leader when he elaborates on Zalenick's (1989) term *managerial mystique.* In brief, the managerial mystique alludes to the tendency for managers (those in charge) to become engrossed in methods and not results; to so strongly become adhered to the methods, that form replaces substance and that results are gauged against how things are done, and not what good became of the end result. He uses school improvement plans as an example. Too many times, according to Sergiovanni, the *plans* themselves are viewed as good or bad, and not the *outcomes*: the outcomes being a better school and improved student performance. To overcome the mystique and truly return to the purpose of leadership, Sergiovanni proposes what he calls the head, heart, and hand of leadership.

The *heart* is referred to as what a person believes: his vision and dreams and what he is committed to. Each person's beliefs shape their own personal vision. The *head* is the person's mindscape – or, the set of principles and practices that a person fosters over time. A person's *head* (personal values) will guide his thinking depending upon the situations he faces. The *head,* or how a person reflects upon his circumstances, together with the *heart,* his personal vision, become the basis for directing his *hand,* or the decisions he makes. "The head of leadership is shaped by the heart and drives the hand;

in turn, reflections and decisions and actions affirm or reshape the heart and the head" (Sergiovanni, 1992, p. 7). So, per Sergiovanni, an administrator's practices are ultimately shaped by his head, or values.

James MacGregor Burns (1978) defines leadership "... as leaders inducing followers to act for certain goals that represent the values and motivations – the wants and needs, the aspirations and expectations – *of both leaders and followers"*. And, he continues, "... the genius of leadership lies in the manner in which leaders see and act on their own and their followers' values and motivations." (p.19). Burns goes on to delineate two types of leadership: transactional and transformational. Transactional leadership is brought about when one person contacts another to exchange something of value: physical or psychological. They "do the deal" and the parties part because there is no compelling reason for either to remain bound to the other once the transaction is finished. He contrasts this to transformational leadership whereby "... leadership occurs when one or more persons *engage* with others in such a way that leaders and followers raise one another to higher levels of motivation and morality" (p.20). Leaders' and followers' power bases become connected in shared support for a common purpose. And, transforming leadership inevitably becomes *moral,* per Burns, because it has a transforming effect by raising the level of "human conduct and aspirations" of both leaders and followers (p.20). Transformational leaders appear to leave followers better off after the experience of being led. In fact, these leaders become teachers in that they encourage followers to become leaders themselves. Given these two models, this writer would implore school principals to act as change agents to transform their faculty to reach beyond their limits as teachers.

Principals' Style

Being that transformational leadership has as its foundation a higher sense of moral purpose, what traits then should the leader aspire to acquire? What mode of interaction should become his norm when interacting with followers? Wong (2001) offers that to argue for a moral dimension of leadership suggests high moral standing in the person of the leader. Moral leadership carries two sets of implications. "The first suggests that the leader must appeal to the followers' sense of righteousness, obligation, and goodness, as motivations for action and work. The second is that leaders themselves must also possess a sense of righteousness, obligation, and goodness" (p.313-314). He contends that without this congruence between leaders and the led, it is hard to imagine how followers could be motivated. If principal's wish to *lead* their faculties in a changing world to improve student leaning and all the good that comes from it, they should strive to become, in this writer's view, transformational leaders. Safty (2003) in speaking about managing and leading states it best, in this writer's view:

> "Leadership, on the other hand, is – or at least ought to be – normatively apprehended as a set of values with connotations evocative of the higher achievement of the human spirit. Leadership, therefore, is irrevocably tied to morality. Measured by

> its results, leadership in whatever field should be the vision-driven achievement of those people who are able to transform their environment, morally elevate their followers, and chart new paths of progress and human development (p.84)."

The principal would work toward elevating his faculty to higher achievement if he/she would at all times remember the higher moral purpose of school leadership.

School leaders should become psychologically active in leading the school and the district. This suggests that the principal has a genuine enthusiasm for his leadership role. Principals must know themselves first: who they are as a person; what they believe, and how they feel. Only then will teachers and staff become committed to being members of the school and district, because followers will sense an apathetic or uncommitted leader (Rebore, 2003).

Self-understanding is an important beginning in relationship building and principals should endeavor to build relationships based on trust. Once trust is established, the principal can become the facilitator who promotes self-actualization on the part of all staff members. As he begins to see himself as a facilitator and not a direction giver, he can move away from the role of manager and into the role of leader. He will become more tolerant of uncertainty, more aware of his staff as a resource for problem solving, and more open with his teachers.

Following through on the above, the principal becomes, as Rebore states, a congruent person. "The more he becomes involved with others in a genuine way, putting up no professional front, the more likely that teachers, staff members, and others will take ownership of their responsibilities because they will be able to form a more trusting relationship with that educational leader" (p. 40). Rebore continues by noting that the genuine principal is a respectful person. Respect is a two-way dynamic (giving and receiving) between the principal and his staff. Once respect is established, it is the first step in creating genuine relationships; the others are: congruency, positive regard, warmth and trust, and the administrators approach to empowerment.

Rebore's articulation on congruency as an attribute of a school leader refers to a state of harmony between the leader's internal dispositions and external expressions. He cites Corey (1995), "Principals and superintendents who are congruent do not pretend to be interested when they are not, do not pretend to understand when they do not, do not say something they do not mean, and do not adopt a certain form of behavior just to win approval" (P.41). Congruency is often overlooked by principals because it is illusive. However, without congruency, Rebore warns, leadership becomes merely technique and ultimately meaningless; often devolving into simple control and manipulation.

Positive regard is the notion that a principal creates the atmosphere within a school whereby each person can freely express their ideas, feelings, etc. and all groups of persons can do so collectively. Rebore makes clear that it is built on the concept of unconditional acceptance. Establishing an environment that will allow for positive regard to flourish requires a nonjudgmental, caring attitude on the part of the building administrator.

The principal should accept each constituent's opinion and attitude and not screen them against his own thoughts and beliefs. The opinions of all have merit. This is difficult for any principal who views his job as including the regulation of speech and behavior of those he supervises. If he shows openness to a diversity of opinions, he is actually indicating that he values the rights or others to have their own views. His receptiveness to others' views and ideas will show to his staff, and others, that he is on their side. Showing positive regard does not mean that the principal will throttle his own opinions or ignore what he feels is improper behavior. Respecting teachers' rights to self-expression and respecting differences among people is key to showing positive regard (Rebore, 2003).

An essential to this notion of positive regard is an attitude of caring on the part of the principal – a genuine concern for his staff as human beings. Any false attempt or faint at caring will undermine the trust created between the principal and his staff. A caring attitude can be expressed by words, deeds, gestures, voice inflection and facial expressions, but only if the principal truly has positive regard for his staff. Rebore ends his discussion on the subject of positive regard by noting that a principal's attitude will be reflected in the attitude of all those he comes in contact with: faculty, staff, students, and parents. Positive regard is conducive to others' personal growth.

The element of trust continues to thread its way through a school's culture. People are not prone to respond to persons they feel are aloof, or cold. Persons with these characteristics are hard to get to know and become ineffective communicators because others will not engage them. Teachers will become suspicious and untrusting of a principal who seems aloof and too business-like and they will be reluctant to take risks. It is the principal's responsibility to establish a warm trusting atmosphere within his school, a culture wherein people can feel safe and know that the leader is concerned with their welfare (Rebore, 2003). Congruency, positive regard, warmth and trust are all noble ends and come under the penumbra of moral leadership. The last of Rebore's genuine administrator traits is the leaders' attitude on teacher empowerment.

Teachers because of their isolation within the classroom tend too often to see themselves as apart from the school administration. They (teachers) decide what's best for their students and they expect the administration to decide what's best for the district. In reality teachers' roles and school leaders' roles are intertwined and one cannot function effectively without the other. What teachers do while in their classrooms does affect the school. An understanding of this connectedness requires the administrator to adopt an attitude of inclusiveness with his faculty. An attitude of inclusiveness is built on mutual trust between the parties and the natural outgrowth is shared decision making. Empowerment or including teachers in decision making is essential to the idea of facilitative or inclusive leadership. Trusting the faculty is essential to a higher moral posture on the part of the principal. Rebore (2003) finishes his point on empowerment by noting that teachers and staff should be looked upon as stakeholders with a vested interest in the success of the school – their school. Including them in the decision making process adds value to the decision because they being different points of view from different backgrounds that enrich the discussion concerning school issues.

The points made so far through this writing have, for the most part, centered on the subject of the principal as school leader and what he should do. This is appropriate because he has the legitimate power within the school. But leadership implies followers, and now the focus will shift specifically to teachers.

Teachers' Perspective

The dynamic between the principal and teacher is not totally dissimilar to that of other work settings involving a supervisor and subordinate, but it is unique in that the followers (teachers) often do not accept fully the role of subordinate. Subordinate meaning the unquestioning "order taker". Teachers view themselves as professionals – instructional professionals, and they view the role of the principal as the administrative professional. This may lead to conflict. Potential conflict can be avoided, however, if the principal understands how teachers view his/her role in the school as that of setting the moral standard and the resulting culture. The principal should maintain a moral posture at all times, which is what the faculty expects.

In determining the teachers' perspective, the author obtained anonymous responses from individual public school teachers, enrolled in his graduate class, asking that they "design" a perfect school principal. If they could choose the characteristics they most preferred in a boss, what would those characteristics be? The intent was to "build" a perfect leader from their collective perspective.

The responses can be used to provide a leader characteristic makeup for which a principal can compare with his leadership style. Knowing if there are differences between what the leader feels are his/her strong traits and what his faculty perceives as desirable leadership traits, can only help to better the principal's role in the principal/faculty relationship and improve the chances for success. A representation of my students' responses is contained in the Appendix. A summation of the responses follows:

Desirable Characteristics
(Primary Reponses)

> Honesty (fair and trustworthy)
> Knowledgeable (subject matter, laws, policies, etc.)
> An effective communicator (both sending and receiving)
> Instructional leader (remembers when he was a teacher)

(Other Responses)

> Approachable
> Supportive of faculty and staff
> Is visible
> Consistent
> Will do the right thing
> Sense of humor
> Experienced

Citing work by Kouzes and Posner (1995) concerning their study involving 20,000 people, Snowden and Gorton (2002) list qualities subordinates expect in leaders; effective leaders were: honest, forward-looking, inspirational, and competent. Continuing, they point out that successful leaders, "keep their promises, align their actions to be consistent with the wishes of the people they lead, believe in the inherent self-worth of others, are capable of making a difference in the lives of others, admit their mistakes, arouse optimism about success, and create a climate of learning that is characterized by trust and openness" (p.73). Notice the marked similarity to my class and their expectations for principals' leadership qualities.

Lunenburg and Ornstein (2004, cited from Yukl, 1989, p.176) list traits and skills of successful leaders (p.143):

Traits
Adaptable to situations
Alert to social environment
Ambitious and achievement oriented

Traits Continued

Assertive
Cooperative
Decisive
Dependable
Dominant (desire to influence others)
Energetic (high activity level)
Persistent
Self-confident
Tolerant of stress, and willing to assume responsibility

Skills
Intelligent
Conceptually skilled
Creative
Diplomatic and tactful
Fluent in speaking

Skills Continued

Knowledgeable about group task
Organized
Persuasive
Socially skilled

These lists of traits and skills show behaviors not collectively inconsistent with characteristics delineated by Cunningham and Cordeiro (2003) for successful transformational leaders in their efforts toward goal achievement:

Vision – knowing your desired outcomes and methods of achievement through lots of idea development and the creation of vision.

Communication – expressing your ideas through various forms of presentation, including symbolic actions and shared meaning.

Trust – being predictable, accountable, persistent, and reliable and having integrity.

Deployment – knowing and nurturing of strengths, compensating for weaknesses, evaluating in relation to job requirements, and focusing on positive goals not problems (p. 167).

The result of these authors' work (each respectively draws from the work of many others) presents a consistent background of research on followers' perceptions of "good" leader qualities. My group of teacher/graduate students' responses – although not as elaborate is, nevertheless, aligned with the research. The results lead this writer to conclude that the *energy* necessary to transform a school; to improve the cultural milieu and better student achievement, lies with the teachers. The teachers themselves want to do "good" and they look for a principal (leader) who aspires to the same end. The principal rather than attempting to *lead,* or motivate, his faculty and thus separating himself from the *led* accordingly, would find his goals much more easily attainable if the faculty saw in him the same "good" intentions as they themselves possess. The principal would have to recognize that he and they are of like mind when it involves school improvement. Much less energy would have to be expended on the part of the principal in motivating his staff to take part in any intra-school project if he adapted himself to those traits emanating from a higher moral purpose – those same traits he wished for in a principal when *he* was a teacher. In fact, he ought to remember what motivated him to succeed.

Motivation

Gibson, Ivancevich and Donnelly (2000) define motivation as: "...the concept we use when we describe the forces acting on or within an individual to initiate and direct behavior" (p.127). Forces acting *within* an individual can drive that individual just as forces acting *on* that individual. Understanding motivation is important because it allows us to understand the intensity and direction of actions by others. It leads us to make deductions about outcomes resulting from individuals' behaviors. It is not measured directly, meaning we can not quantify motivation, but we can gauge it (the level of motivation) by observing the behavior of others. These authors caution, however, against making too quick an assumption about the actual causes for a person's actions. Seeing a person work hard by putting in overtime may suggest the person needs the extra money, or it may be because the person is very interested in the work and simply enjoys it! Gathering as much information as possible about the situation helps eliminate alternative explanations (Gibson, et al, 2000).

It is important that principals understand motivation because high levels of motivation can have a material impact on followers' performance. There is a direct relationship between high levels of motivation and high output, or desirable outcomes. Within the framework of public schools, for example, high test scores are a desirable outcome. Motivated teachers are more likely to produce higher student test scores than unmotivated teachers. Gibson, et al, (2000) list four reasons managers prefer motivated employees, and they suggest motivated employees are self-confident and decisive as well.

Motivated employees...

> are interested in producing high-quality products or services;
> are more likely to be productive than are nonmotivated or apathetic employees;
> want to come to work and become part of a team, and
> are interested in helping, supporting, and encouraging co-workers (p.127).

The starting point in developing an understanding of motivation begins with the individual. Motivational theory (Gibson, et al, 2000) suggests that behavioral patterns in persons are stimulated by needs. It is important to recognize that disparate groups of people have divergent needs and not all persons' needs cause the same level or reaction, but, however, needs or the lack of something become the stimulus for action in all people. Needs may be physical or emotional and the leader who can identify the relevant need deficiencies within his follower group can set goals and rewards, if necessary, for those followers. The ideal goal set by the leader is one that followers can achieve and at the same time satisfy personal needs. Goal setting is important also for goals represent a standard against which to measure the effectiveness of the groups' efforts. Teachers can gauge their efforts in improving test scores, for example, by weighing their students' scores against the state standard scores. Achieving the desired scores based upon the state requirements is the reward. The need is to know how effective their instructional efforts have been. Although test scores are not the end in themselves, learning is, high scores represent a "good" outcome. The scores also provide the teacher and principal with feedback - feedback that can be utilized for continued improvement.

Owens (2004) in writing about motivation differentiates between extrinsic motivation using the metaphor of the *carrot and stick* to show that people are motivated by external rewards and punishments, and intrinsic motivation which originates internally from a person's feelings and thoughts. Examples of extrinsic motivators used in educational settings are merit pay, performance reviews tied to positioning, teacher days, etc. All intended to reward the teacher for behaviors the administration deems acceptable. Intrinsic rewards, on the other hand, differ in that they originate from *within* the person (teacher) and are not - as are external rewards - intended to *control* the person. Owens continues by saying that a person's internal capacities are primarily cognitive and emotional and lead to feelings, aspiration, attitudes, and thoughts that themselves are motivating or demotivating.

If we accept that intrinsic rewards are more in-line with teachers' feelings and needs and serve as motivators, then principals' demonstrating the leadership traits teachers' place value on will satisfy this need. The principal by his everyday practice who exemplifies those characteristics most desired by his faculty (refer to the previous lists) will at the same time motive his staff to work for the betterment of the school, simply through his everyday actions. If his actions are always of a higher moral purpose, they will be consistent over time with his teachers' expectations of him. He will find that energy and resources needed to administer external reward systems will not be necessary. How should the principal expect to know his teachers' feelings and expectations? What should he do? This aspect of leadership – understanding fully the faculty's expectations – is of critical importance.

Communication

Probably the single most significant talent set utilized by an administrator involves communication skills. It is most often the case that problems among groups of people originate from poor communications. This is not surprising since the person sending the message has to verbalize his thoughts into the message; the message then has to be heard clearly and entirely by the receiver, and the receiver has to decode the message for understanding. Throughout this sequence of transmitting, receiving, decoding, and understanding a lot can go wrong. It is not hard to envision the damage that can be done to the morale of a faculty should the principal misunderstand his staffs' expectations. The teachers' lists of preferred characteristics previously mentioned include communication as one of a principal's desired traits. It would be wise then for the principal to hone this skill.

Snowden and Gorton (2002) citing work by Knoll list five communication behaviors that create a secure working environment and bolster staff performance. The reader will note the similarity in Knoll's list and the teacher's lists.

> Be honest by making open statements about your feelings, attitudes, and reactions to situations
> Be tactful and sensitive to staff needs, feelings, and problems, and treat people in a non-threatening manner.
> Accept people as they are by respecting individual staff differences, opinions, perceptions, and approaches.
> Have a positive approach when you greet people, smile at them, and inquire about their health, problems, and joys.
> Finally, be dependable, so that you will be trusted by the staff (p.36).

Snowden and Gorton continue by making the point that effective communication begins with the sender of the message – in this case the administrator. Each person has strengths and weaknesses and each should use the most effective medium to convey information, the medium that best suits their strengths. The principal has the choice of the medium and he should choose the method – either written or oral - that best fits the audience and situation. The message does not always have to be delivered in a staff meeting!

The success a principal will have as a communicator is ultimately measured by the degree of understanding on the part of the receivers of his message. If his message is understood and his directions complied with as he intended, he was successful. His success rate will be enhanced by the degree of trust that exists between him and the receivers of his communications (his teachers); his level of prestige within the school system as a whole (what do other principals think of him), and his perceived level of expertise on the subject. Continuing along this line, Snowden and Gorton elaborate on each of the above points.

There must be *mutual trust* between the parties. Trust has to be built and maintained by the principal for his messages to be believed. The authors stress that mutual trust is required for effective communications. The principal's *status* within the system's hierarchy is important as well. If he is not seen as influential or if he is not perceived as having the required level of experience or expertise, his message may not be listened to. Trust is important in *setting the tone* of the message; "Schools with high trust levels are more likely to be characterized by communication that is honest, and both communication and institutional effectiveness are better in a high-trust setting" (p. 35). The point is clear: Effective communication begins with trust, openness and honesty emanating from the principal. Teachers want to work with a principal who possesses these traits – traits of a higher moral purpose.

It is not the intent of this paper to give directions to the reader on communication skills. But the writer will suggest to the reader to always acknowledge that communication is a two-way exchange: sending and receiving the message. Effective communication requires effective listening. Lunenburg and Ornstein (2004) cite research indicating that as mush as 70 percent of a school administrators time is spent communicating; of this time, 85 percent is spent talking! This research would indicate that administrators do not spent a good deal of time listening. Listening completes the sender-message-receiver communication process. Listening – effective listening – is also a sign of respect for the sender of the message. Developing the ability to listen is not an easy thing to do, but it is an ability of persons who lead from a high moral posture.

The responses this writer received from his students together with the research cited herein should provide the reader with a basis for understanding the "message" being sent by teachers of their desires in a principal's abilities as a leader. Not all situations are the same, however, and opening channels of communications with his staff should be a priority for any principal. One-on-one meetings; group meetings, anonymous responses, are a few of the means a principal can use to understand his faculty's' perceptions on working in his school, and for him. The key to being an effective leader, a moral leader, lies in the way the principal responds to the information. The response should be honest, professional, and with the school' greater purpose and mission in the forefront. The faculty expects nothing less because the school's (your school's) success is always their goal.

The first implication for school leaders in realizing that the faculty is prepared to work toward the success of the school (i.e., they desire the "good" outcome) lies with the principal's approach to the faculty. To expect the faculty to respond to a direct (authoritarian) approach, in all cases, would not be effective. Hughes, et al (2002) in discussing research done at Ohio State University on leader behavior cite two distinct behavioral dimensions as the outcome, called: initiating structure and consideration. Initiating structure is a style whereby the leader concentrates on task-related outcomes; for example, meeting deadlines, achieving output standards, setting quotas, etc. Consideration, in comparison, is how a leader interacts and is supportive of subordinates. Principal's high in consideration would show support for subordinates (faculty) by showing an interest in their teaching and ideas, listening to their concerns, and being an advocate for their interests. Although there are times when the principal must assume the role of manager in setting schedules, enforcing board policies, following employment procedures, etc. these aspects of leadership, or the role requiring a high degree of initiating structure, is not the most effective method when attempting to establish a new culture or achieve a shared vision for the school. The leader high in consideration has the higher moral posture.

The second implication has to do with the principal's understanding of his faculty's mind set. Too often leaders approach a new setting with preconceived notions and biases. They tend to expect a new setting (school) to have the same characteristics, problems, atmosphere, etc. as their previous school. Or, in the case of a brand new principal, their own experience with the teacher/principal relationship will serve as a basis for developing new relationships with their new faculty. This is a mistake. The principal should – whether just beginning, or a seasoned veteran – know that his faculty desires the same outcome he desires. They want "good" results. They do not need to be motivated as in the textbook examples; they simply need to be allowed to succeed. The motivation, or energy, required to succeed is self-contained by each teacher. The principal should see himself as being a facilitator for school improvement, not a leader. His words, deeds and interactions should always show his intentions – intentions that align with the faculty's intentions naturally. Assuming such a moral posture will only ignite the energy of the faculty and carry forward each initiative they join with the principal in completing.

The final implication for principals extends to the greater community. Someone once said that success breeds success. If this is true, a successful school created by the collective spirit of the teachers and principal will be absorbed by the community and parents. It can only happen as a direct outcome of the students' success. The implications for an involved, satisfied, community with the school's performance are many, and all positive.

Conclusion

Sergiovanni (2001) sets apart the *normative rationality* from the *technical rationality* in understanding the different moral dimensions of leadership. The *normative rationality* is based upon what we deem as good and what we believe. The *technical rationality* is based upon effectiveness and efficiency. He continues by saying that principals want what is good for their schools, and to be moral is to prize the normative rationality: "Normative rationality provides the basis for moral leadership" (p.348).

Rather than relying on just authoritarian means, or psychological means to manipulate people, principals assuming a moral posture provide reasons for choosing one alternative over another (Sergiovanni, 2001). This writer would add that teachers also expect principals to act in this manner and all too often school improvement initiatives fail because the principal overlooks his moral purpose in communicating and exemplifying the reasons. If teachers and principals have the same purpose and end in sight, effective principals will work with and through their faculty.

The end result of my work shows that there exists a congruence, or alignment, with the natural tendencies of both principals and teachers to work toward student success. Each wants the "good" outcome as a direct result of being in the profession. The wise principal will know this and tap into the natural energy teachers bring to the school and their classrooms. The most intelligent way to accomplish this is by knowing that education has a higher moral purpose and leaders who assume a moral posture in all they do are more likely to bring about whatever the intended outcome.

References

Beckner, W. (2004). *Ethics for Educational Leaders*. Boston: Allyn and Bacon.

Burns, J.M. (1978). *Leadership*. Harper & Row: New York.

Chan, W.T. (1963). *A Source Book in Chinese Philosophy*. Princeton: Princeton New Jersey Press.

Chemers, M.M. (1997). *An Integrative Theory of Leadership*. Mahwah, N.J.: Erlbaum.

Corey, G. (1995). *Theory and Practice of Group Counseling*. 4ed. Brooks/Cole: Pacific Grove, CA .

Cowley, W.H. (April, 1928). Three Distinctions in the Study of Leaders. *Journal of Abnormal and Social Psychology*, 144-157.

Cunningham, W.G.,& Cordeiro, P.A. (2003). *Educational Leadership: a Problem-Based Approach,* 2ed. Boston: Allyn and Bacon.

Gibson, J.L., Ivancevich, J.H. and Donnelly, J.H., Jr. (2000) *Organizations: Behavior, Structure, Processes,* 10ed. Boston: Irwin McGraw-Hill.

Goleman, D., Boyzatis, R. and McKee, A. (2002). *Primal Leadership: Realizing the Power of Emotional Intelligence*. Boston: Harvard University Press.

Hoy, W.K. & Miskel, C.G. (2005). *Educational Administration: Theory, Research, and Practice*. 7ed. Boston: Irwin McGraw-Hill.

Hughes, R.L., Ginnett, R.C. & Curphy, G.J. (2002). *Leadership: Enhancing the Lessons of Experience*, 4ed. Boston: Irwin McGraw-Hill.

Knoll, M. K. (1987). How to Communicate Successfully: Establishing a Secure Climate. *Supervision for Better Instruction,* 191-201.

Kouzes, J.M. and Posner, B.K. (1995). *The Leadership Challenge*. San Francisco: Jossey-Bass.

Kowalski, T.J. (2003). *Contemporary School Administration: an Introduction,* 2ed. Boston: Allyn and Bacon.

Lo, S.K. (1996). *A Debate with thought* (In Chinese; Taiwan: Student Press).

Lunenburg, F.C. & Ornstein, A.C. (2004). *Educational Administration Concepts and Practices,* 4ed., Wadsworth/Thomson: Belmont,CA.

MacIntyre, A.(1966). *A short history of ethics*. New York: MacMillian.

Owens, R.G. (2004). *Organizational Behavior in Education: Adaptive Leadership and School Reform*. 8ed. Boston: Allyn and Bacon.

Rebore, R.W. (2003). *A Human Relations Approach to the Practice of Educational Leadership*. Boston: Allyn and Bacon.

Roach, C.F. & Behling, O. (1984). Functionalism: Basis for an Alternative Approach to the Study of Leadership. *Leaders and Managers: International Perspectives on Managerial Behavior and Leadership*. New York: Pergamon.

Safty, A. (2003, Fall). Moral Leadership: Beyond Management and Governance. *Harvard International Review,* 84-89.

Senge, P. M. (1994). The Fifth Discipline: *The Art and Practice of the Learning Organization*. New York: Doubleday/Currency.

Sergiovanni, T.J. (1992). *Moral Leadership: Getting to the Heart of School Improvement*. San Francisco: Jossey-Bass.

Sergiovanni, T.J. (2001). *The Principalship: a Reflective Practice Perspective*. Boston: Allyn and Bacon.

Snowden, P.E. & Gorton, R.A. (2002). *School Leadership and Administration*. Boston: Irwin McGraw-Hill.

Wong, K. (1998). Culture and Moral Leadership in Education. *Peabody Journal of Education,* 73(2), 106-125.

Wong, K. (2001). Chinese culture and leadership. *International Journal of Leadership in Education,* 4(4), 309-319.

Yukl, G.A. (1989). *Leadership in Organizations*, 2ed. Edgewood, NJ: Prentice-Hall.

Zalenick, A. (1989). The Managerial Mystique: Restoring Leadership in Business. New York: Harper-Collins.

No Child Left Behind: Four Perspectives

Steven P. Jones, Jerry Whitworth, Thomas E. Deering, and Eric Sheffield

Guiding Questions:

1. No Child Left Behind (NCLB) is intended to change education in powerful ways literally, to make sure no child fails to get a quality K-12 education. But might this legislation also bring about some changes we do *not* want to see for the children who attend our schools?

2. Does NCLB legislation mean that teachers pay more attention to test scores than they do to deep and interesting subject matter content?

3. What were some of the political reasons NCLB was passed into law in the first place?

4. How does NCLB affect students with special needs?

5. Is NCLB anti-democratic and anti-communitarian?

No Child Left Behind: Four Perspectives

Steven P. Jones, Jerry Whitworth, Thomas E. Deering, and Eric Sheffield

If the designers and proponents of The No Child Left Behind Act (NCLB) of 2001 wanted to shake up the education system and get some things changed, they have gotten their wish. NCLB demands change from all manner of educators--public school teachers, school district administrators, school board members, university teacher education faculty, and state education officials. Because state officials examine the learning progress of students in a given district (as required by NCLB), and because they have the power of severe injunctions if that progress is not deemed adequate, there is much for the personnel in that district to worry about and change. And if public school educators have new pressures and expectations, then teacher educators must adapt and provide what is needed to meet those pressures and expectations. No one asked, in this federal intervention in what is historically a state and local concern, if these educators wanted to change--it was assumed change was needed.

Educators generally laud the notion of improving public education even while they point out problems of NCLB specifically, and heavy-handed federal intervention in educational decisions generally. Because the impact of NCLB is so broad, there are many different questions to ask and criticisms to make of it, and this essay explores four such questions and criticisms. It is intended to point out to educators and teacher education students (and legislators, should they want to be an audience) some important, if unfortunate, implications of NCLB legislation. We begin with an argument about how standards-based movements such as NCLB foster negative pedagogical consequences--consequences that include taking an important hope out of teaching and learning. A second perspective suggests that beyond simply being troublesome legislation, NCLB is a political conspiracy, one supported by both sides of the political spectrum for different reasons. Our third perspective points out numerous and troubling consequences that NCLB has for special education students and teachers. Our final argument suggests some community consequences that might further erode our already weak participation in democratic/civic concerns. It is the authors' hope that these four perspectives lead to further debate as to the wisdom of holding onto a piece of educational legislation that might well do more harm than good.

Negative Pedagogical Consequences of NCLB Legislation

NCLB, passed by Congress in late 2001 and signed into law by President Bush in January 2002, is the crowning achievement of standards-based assessment. Standards-based assessments have long been used at state levels for accrediting purposes, but with the passing of NCLB we have lent to standards and standards-based assessment a wide-ranging, official, and federally sanctioned stamp of approval. For educators now imbued with the advantages of standards-based assessment, this counts as a good thing. Supporters claim that with its backbone of enforced standards-based assessments, NCLB will ensure and improve education for *all* students, especially those who are traditionally low-achieving. Making sure all students meet recognized and agreed upon standards will guarantee them a better chance at leading a successful and happy life. This is the "hope" of NCLB legislation.

But we also see reasons for "hopelessness" in this legislation tied to its reliance on standards-based assessment. We fear teachers are paralyzed by standards-based assessments and that this paralysis leads to a loss of richness and depth in student learning. What we mean by paralysis--or at least one kind of paralysis--is seen in the following example of teaching and learning. This bit of learning has to do with the Pythagorean theorem--one of those cursed proofs so many of us hated in our high school geometry classes. One of us (Steve Jones) discusses the Pythagorean theorem with teacher education students to push them to explore the richness of the subject matters they will teach. It turns out the Pythagorean theorem is not so accursed after all--that it has a beauty and importance all students should understand and appreciate. The point, here, is that this beauty will be overlooked in the press of NCLB inspired standards-based assessments. You might well remember the Pythagorean theorem from your high school geometry class:

Given: Right triangle ABC with hypotenuse length c and leg lengths a and b
Prove: $c^2 = a^2 + b^2$

What will the high school mathematics teacher, under the pressure of NCLB enforced high-stakes achievement testing, do to make sure all of his or her students can handle any test question that might be given them about the Pythagorean theorem? If the teacher is smart, the first thing he or she will do is learn how the question(s) about the theorem have appeared on past tests and teach them in that way. Given both some assurance questions about the theorem are going to be on the test and sufficient pressure to make sure students score well, any interested teacher will not only "drill and practice" the theorem, but try to make sure students actually understand it. This is "teaching to the test"--something that used to be considered a bad thing.

We do not doubt teaching to the test will ensure more students answer test questions about the Pythagorean theorem correctly than ever before. Here it is fair to say "achievement" in regard to the Pythagorean theorem is bound to improve--and this is not of negligible importance. How could it be bad if some significant percentage of students have at least some temporary working familiarity and knowledge about this most important theorem? This is, as mentioned above, the hopeful part of NCLB. But, as we also suggest, this "hopefulness" about improved achievement is not without a related "hopelessness."

This hopelessness has to do with what *might* in the teaching of the Pythagorean theorem go beyond basic understanding and mechanical competence--the typical outcomes probed by standards-based assessment. What is "beyond" in the case of the Pythagorean theorem is, we daresay, *never* examined in a standards-based assessment. And, as it turns out, this "beyond" of the Pythagorean theorem is quite compelling and astonishing and of considerable interest to students. The theorem has a beauty, majesty, and perfection--and a revolutionary importance in how we understand life in this universe. Let us briefly (indeed, too briefly) review the great lessons of the Pythagorean theorem, the kinds of lessons teachers will most likely never teach in their rush to prepare students for state examinations.

We retell the story of the Pythagorean theorem from the understanding of Jacob Bronowski in his book *The Ascent of Man.* (In a teacher education class, students read the entire section about Pythagoras, about six pages.) In Bronowski's telling, Pythagoras finds a basic relation between musical harmony and mathematics--this by recognizing that basic harmonies we recognize in music (such as the musical third, fourth, or fifth) correspond to exact divisions of the string by whole numbers. To moderns, this may not sound like much of a discovery, but it turns out Pythagoras and his followers had uncovered one of the great and important mysteries of the universe. The agreement between nature and number was so cogent for Pythagoras and his followers that they saw not only the sounds of nature, but all her characteristic dimensions as simple numbers that express harmonies. Pythagoras believed that if the world of sound is governed by exact numbers, so should the world of vision.

Now we get to the Pythagorean theorem. Bronowski reminds us there are two experiences on which our visual world is based: that gravity is vertical, and that the horizon stands at right angles to it. This conjunction of gravity and horizon fixes the nature of the right angle. And if we look around at our world with this in mind, we realize: *our fundamental visual orientation to the world comes to us as right angles.* Why right angles and not something else? It is not unreasonable to ask: Do some absolute and binding laws govern right angles? In pursuing these laws, Pythagoras discovered that if he turned this right angle of experience *exactly* four times (never any more or less) either horizontally or vertically, back we come to our starting point. What Pythagoras established, according to Bronowski, is a fundamental characterization of the space in which we move--and it was the first instance in history that this characterization of our space was translated into strict mathematical understanding, thus paving the way, eventually, for modern science. The Bronowski text then offers a visual representation of the turning of this right angle, a representation that makes clear the mathematical understanding that is the Pythagorean theorem. At the end of this brief section, one "sees" the building of the square on the hypotenuse, and how it makes sense even to speak of such a thing. One, therefore, is assisted in understanding the theorem--but, more, one begins to "see" the mathematical and theoretical mind of Pythagoras at work and what in our understanding of nature and the nature of things this mind transformed for us.

In a recent teacher education class this section of Bronowski's text was shared with future secondary-level teachers. We read it together and imagined it being shared with high school geometry students. As always, there were some students who thought such a lesson would be way above the heads of students and of no interest to them. Far more of them, however, thought it would be wonderful. As always happens when this text is presented to students, there were a number of students who reported that they had never understood the Pythagorean theorem until they read and thought about

Bronowski's presentation of it. It was as if they were achieving a brand new insight about something they had never thought seriously about before. They liked what they were learning.

Interestingly enough, the one student in the class wanting to become a mathematics teacher thought sharing Bronowski's explanation of the Pythagorean theorem with high school students was a horrible idea. Not only did she think the text difficult, but, even more, she thought it was utterly beside the point of teaching mathematics. She was much happier with the straight-ahead presentation of the theorem in the pages of the mathematics textbook given to students as a comparison. She articulated two questions: first, why teach beyond what is going to be on the test? and, second, how could she justify the time taken to "teach beyond" the Pythagorean theorem when she would need the time to cover other material? She showed herself likely to be the kind of teacher who will study past state examinations to find out how the Pythagorean theorem is tested so she could prepare accordingly. She will find no need to share with her students the kinds of understandings Bronowski offers. She will teach to the test, school mathematics scores will go up, and she will be congratulated for her efforts. End of story.

The reader may argue the story need not end this way. That is, one may want to have it both ways: the teacher can know and share with students such important reflections about the Pythagorean theorem *and* have test scores improve. One may argue that because "deep" teaching leads to deeper, more profound, and more long-lasting understanding of subject matter, raised test scores will naturally result. Indeed, we are sure that exactly this *would* happen. But the fact is nothing in today's educational climate encourages teachers to do this kind of teaching. Talk of richness and depth is sacrificed to talk about improving test scores on NCLB mandated standardized tests. Mathematics teachers are not going to take some extra time to work through Bronowski's admiration of Pythagoras when there is more mathematics to master for the upcoming test.

In this way NCLB inspired standards-based assessments paralyze teachers. Pedagogical practices that might enrich and deepen knowledge and appreciation of subject matter are sacrificed on the alter of improved test scores. Only, what really gets sacrificed is the capacity of students to know, truly, their subject matters, and to enjoy learning them.

NCLB: Educational Reform or Attack on America's Schools?

By now, all those interested in education or teacher education know the broad outline of NCLB legislation. NCLB has four major themes: 1) teacher competency; 2) student achievement; 3) assessment; and, 4) consequences of failure. The themes are at first glance admirable. Almost no one has any concern with demanding more of teachers--more in the sense that teacher education programs should be more rigorous, possibly longer, and certainly contain more theory. Almost no one in public education disagrees with more support of teachers--higher salaries, additional paraprofessionals, more respect, better working conditions, and greater say in educational matters at the school, district, state, and national levels--in short, helping educators take charge of their profession. This, however, is not what "more" means in NCLB. What "more" means in NCLB is holding teachers accountable while giving them less say in their professional lives.

Likewise, no one, it seems, is absolutely opposed to the assessment of student learning. Without assessment of some kind we have no way of knowing if anything has been taught or more importantly learned. The problem is not with the idea of assessment, but with such issues as what, how and why we assess. This second theme is far more problematic because assessment is at the heart of the legislation. The argument in the first section of this essay articulates but one of many concerns that can be raised about NCLB and assessment.

As everyone recognizes some need to assess student learning, everyone agrees students should "achieve" something as a result of their time in school. What is the purpose of education if it doesn't mean students achieving something? Skills, knowledge, dispositions, and personal development are all part of what parents, teachers, and society want students to achieve. If students were not going to achieve something at school, society would have little reason to spend billions of dollars on schools. Those billions are society's investment in its youth, in its future. Achievement matters; it is the reason schools exist. The question is not *should* students achieve, but *what, why, and how* should they achieve? NCLB is far too narrow in what it considers achievement and unrealistic in the expectation that all students will master the same material at the same pace to approximately the same level.

Politicians might find it easy to *say* all students will be proficient in English; all students will meet high academic standards; all students will graduate from high school by 2017; and that all students will be educated in a safe environment. It is, however, educators who have to deal with the realities of American society. These realities include the fact that a growing number of students are coming to school without English as their first language. Proficiency might not occur as quickly as politicians would like. Not all students are able to learn the same material at the same pace and master it simply because politicians passed a law saying students should or would. Teachers must deal with the reality that not all students want to be in school and not all schools provide for a safe environment. As standards are raised and achievement is assessed in a standardized manner more rather than fewer students will question the value of graduating from high school. So, while the authors of this essay are not "against" student achievement, we question how it is being defined in NCLB and how the definition was agreed upon. We wonder about the motivation of those who pass laws concerning public schools, but who have never taught in public school, and might never have attended one.

The fourth predominate theme of NCLB--the consequences of failure if "achievement" is deemed insufficient--forces us to confront what we believe about the efficiency and efficacy of public schools. Should schools that plainly fail to educate students be dealt serious and substantive consequences? NCLB takes a much harder line than educators are used to in this regard, insisting, for instance, that good money should not follow bad in the funding of failing schools. NCLB requires that parents be notified if their child attends a school that has been identified as at risk. The law also opens up the possibilities of school choice, a controversial policy with as many supporters as detractors. For some, these aspects of NCLB enforcement run counter to deep social and political commitments; others, however, find NCLB measures resonate with their commitments and think the measure long overdue.

For us, the bottom line is that based on this admittedly simple and quick look at each of the above issues and its flaws, the law cannot be allowed to stand--and those flaws are only an indication of a much deeper problem with NCLB. Our dismay in regard to NCLB is not just with the effects of the law, but with how and why the law was passed to begin with. People of good will can and often do disagree about important issues, such as the ones enumerated above. And while it is usually healthy to have at least a mild distrust of government, we do not mean to be an Oliver Stone who sees a conspiracy behind virtually everything the government does. However, we here suggest that NCLB is, possibly, far more insidious than it appears--more insidious an Act than would result simply if well-meaning people were in disagreement. In fact, nothing like that was the case: we note *both* parties in *both* houses of Congress voted overwhelmingly in favor of NCLB knowing full well that America's schools would never be able to live up to the standards set by the law. Eighty-five percent of the Republicans in Congress and 94% of the Democrats voted in favor of NCLB. Congress is (usually) like a university faculty: they would not vote so overwhelmingly for anything with more substance than a proclamation recognizing today is Friday. Not unless, of course, they had other considerations in mind.

We suggest that both parties, for their own, but conflicting, political reasons wanted to see this legislation made law. Republicans wanted to undermine the education establishment. Their position has been for many years that too much federal money goes to education and the system is simply not spending it wisely. Additionally, Republicans believe that teacher unions are too powerful and use their power to keep incompetent teachers in the profession. Republicans, then, see NCLB as an opportunity to demand higher standards for students, assess their progress, and hold the educational system accountable for the results. The achievement standards and the way they will be assessed will guarantee that students, and therefore, teachers and the system, fail. This failure will justify school choice, money to religious affiliated schools, and a smaller role for the federal government in education.

The Democrats, on the other hand, are convinced that virtually everything is better when government is involved in it. Democrats have enjoyed the support of teacher unions and have been instrumental in pumping billions into our nation's schools. Democrats see teacher unions as their natural allies, and they have adopted the educational establishment's position that all students should learn. If an ever-increasing budget and intrusive government is the answer, so be it. Democrats see NCLB as an opportunity to strengthen their political position by expanding government's role in education. More and more schools will need government resources to address identified weaknesses and teachers will require more professional development. The bureaucracy will grow to meet the "needs" of the system and with this growth, become more entrenched in education, and more able to enlist an increasing number of educators to the party.

If these suggestions seem a little "Oliver Stone-esque," we apologize. And we recognize their speculative nature even while we suggest that it would be in the best interest of members of both parties to deny this analysis. If, however, this analysis is wrong, we as a nation have *even larger* problems. We contend that if upwards of 90% of our elected representatives in Washington voted for NCLB after having read, understood, and agreed with its provisions, our nation is in serious jeopardy. Or, to say it differently: if our politicians voted for NCLB because they believed it was in the best interest of our nation, our nation's schools, and our children, then America truly is in trouble.

NCLB and Special Education: A Promise Unfulfilled

The promise of NCLB conveys the confidence that all children will learn and achieve to their full potential. For many children, though, that may prove to be an empty promise and one that simply is impossible to fulfill. In particular, NCLB offers only a false hope for disabled children. If federal laws and regulations were the answer, then these children would already be happy, successful students because there are laws already in place that promise to accomplish that. Contrary to its empty promise, NCLB will in fact make it even less likely that laws such as the Individuals with Disabilities Education Act (IDEA) will succeed. We suggest in what follows why this is the case.

First of all, on a number of issues, NCLB is either in direct conflict with the IDEA or fails to clarify how the two laws will work together. NCLB requires state education agencies to develop implementation plans and makes a general reference to coordinating the development of those plans with the IDEA, which also requires a state plan. But NCLB does not specify how that coordination is to take place or who is to be involved. Since Adequate Yearly Progress (AYP) must include the achievement of students with disabilities, it is important that individuals experienced with special education be included in the discussions and development of the state plans. Also, the procedures for screening students who are at risk for reading failure may interfere with the referral process designed to identify students who may be in need of special education services.

A second concern has to do with the limitations of standardized tests. NCLB requires that student progress be measured by standardized achievement tests. However, as mentioned above, such tests are very limited in terms of what they assess. For students with disabilities, standardized tests are often not capable of fully describing their level of educational achievement. Many of these tests will give false pictures of these children.

Also, while students with disabilities are to be included in state-mandated assessments, the IEPs of these students often identify accommodations that are to be made in testing them. States are currently trying to determine how these accommodations will be accomplished and still meet the requirements of NCLB. In addition, tests are normed on students who take the tests without accommodations. If accommodations are allowed for students with disabilities, it will make it difficult to compare test results.

Under NCLB, students with disabilities are expected to meet the standards of an academic curriculum. For many of these students, however, those standards alone should not drive the curriculum. The unique learning needs and abilities of special education students must also be a factor. Modifications are often necessary for these students to achieve the individual goals and objectives set forth in their IEPs. The goal of the legislation is to make the curriculum challenging for all students. Sometimes it is necessary, for students with disabilities, to change the curriculum in certain ways to make it challenging and appropriate for them.

We must, also, not forget about the "hidden curriculum" of schools. The hidden curriculum of a school is its unwritten rules and norms. These are things almost every other student quickly learns, but with which the special education student often struggles. The hidden curriculum regulates membership into peer-controlled groups and is directly related to social acceptance and self-esteem. This often has a direct bearing on academic achievement. Not knowing and understanding the hidden curriculum can interfere with a student's ability to benefit from even the most well designed curriculum.

Furthermore, aligning the curriculum for special education students requires instruction that allows students many different ways to learn. This also requires that teachers have considerable training in differentiating instruction and in strategies and techniques that are appropriate for a wide variety of learning styles and needs. Incumbent in this, also, is the importance of collaboration among teachers and other professionals in the school environment and the willingness, as well as the opportunity, for these professionals to decide how IEP's are to be developed and evaluated relative to curriculum alignment.

We also note that NCLB legislation penalizes schools with high concentrations of special education students. NCLB requires that schools must assess 95 percent of all students with standardized testing. Many special education students, though, have needs so severe that they cannot speak or see, let alone participate in standardized testing. To think that these students are able to participate and give an accurate picture of a school's achievement levels is impractical. Additionally, many schools have high concentrations of students with severe disabilities and many districts share special education services with other districts, each assuming individual responsibility for certain groups and categories of special education students. Under NCLB, these schools may well be penalized rather than rewarded for their commitment to students with special needs.

A further concern is how NCLB places an overemphasis on teaching to the test (mentioned in our first argument). Because of a focus on increasing test scores, many schools are likely to devote considerable time, effort, and resources to pushing student test performance as high as possible. We have already seen this in places where test score performance is the prime determiner of a school's success. This will mitigate against many of the gains we have made in special education that focus on making sure students learn, not simply that they can perform well on a test.

Interestingly enough, NCLB offers no help to educators for determining why children tend to be "left behind." Perhaps one of the greatest problems with NCLB is that it gives us too little information and can lead to a superficial approach to education. There are many factors as to why a child may not be learning. To obtain an accurate picture of a student's needs, factors that go beyond the school must be examined as well. NCLB does not provide a mechanism to insure this occurs.

Finally, under NCLB the definition of "highly qualified" remains unclear. NCLB specifies that a teacher must have a degree and be proficient in his/her content field. Since special education teachers are responsible for teaching all subjects to students at all grade levels, it may be impractical for them to meet the designation of "highly qualified" since they cannot obtain degrees in every content field. Thus, the law will penalize districts for hiring special education teachers. As of yet, it is unclear how this issue will be resolved.

NCLB has been touted as a law that will assure school success for all children. In reality, it does little to deliver on that promise. And, while there are many and various pitfalls to this law, its greatest failure may be its inability to insure a successful school experience to those students who need it the most--those with disabilities.

"Unintended" Community Impacts of NCLB

Historically, legally, and philosophically public education in this country is an important local community concern. Our public school history is one that holds local school districts responsible for gathering funds and deciding how those funds should be spent. Historically, the local school district has made organizational, curricular and extra-curricular decisions based on the particular needs and resources of that particular school community. This process has regularly been accomplished through local school board meetings where local citizens can participate in making decisions that directly impact their children and their tax burden. Our constitution, in fact, has left the legal responsibility for public school decisions in the hands of state and local governments as one of those issues not specifically mandated as a federal concern.

Philosophically, one only need turn to the thinking of John Dewey for an explanation of why it is important that local citizens make local decisions about the education of their children:

> In our search for aims in education, we are not concerned, therefore, with finding an end outside of the educative process to which education is subordinate. We are rather concerned with the contrast which exists when aims belong within the process in which they operate and when they are set up from without. And the latter state of affairs must obtain when social relationships are not equitably balanced. For in that case, some portions of the whole social group will find their aims determined by an external dictation; their aims will not arise from the free growth of their own experience, and their minimal aims will be means to more ulterior ends of others rather than truly their own. The aim set up must be an outgrowth of existing conditions. It must be based upon a consideration of what is already going on; upon the resources and difficulties of the situation. They (externally established aims) limit intelligence because, given ready-made, they must be imposed by some authority external to intelligence, leaving to the latter nothing but a mechanical choice of means (1916, p. 103-104)

As an activity that is constitutionally and philosophically sound, establishing educational aims should be accomplished through democratic processes that occur at the local and state level of governance. NCLB threatens to turn that process on its head.

What is surprising about NCLB is not that the present (Republican) administration preaches small government interference and champions state's rights while it gradually and only somewhat covertly appropriates an important local democratic process. What is more surprising, and what is surely more dangerous, is the relatively quiet manner that communities are accepting of the further erosion of their democratic, participatory right to establish local educational policy decisions.

On the other hand, maybe we should not be surprised at all. It is perhaps symptomatic of a generation of Americans who feel that their voice can have only a minimal impact on governmental decision-making. As Alexis de Tocqueville pointed out long ago, local association and democratic participation is a uniquely American practice that must continue else we fall to a growing democratic tyranny; and, as Robert Putnam pointed out not so long ago, Americans are now bowling alone at an alarming rate. That is, Americans are becoming more and more adept at hiding from their democratic duty to organize into interest group associations that protect our rights as citizens--particularly on issues important to a minority of citizens. Instead, we are associating through such practices as gated communities and economically segregated living situations. This is a serious problem for education particularly, but has as well some dire consequences for communities generally. This requires some explanation.

Democratic participation is eroded when educational aims are established at the state and federal level rather than locally. At a time when we hear constant cries concerning the lack of democratic participation, one must ask "why participate, when the decisions about local education policy are being determined at the federal level and then imposed upon local communities?"

NCLB not only encourages opting out of the process of making local educational decisions by making them for us; it codifies the process in law. NCLB encourages the opting out process by allowing students to leave poorly performing schools rather than demanding that poorly performing schools be fixed. As suggested above, if a local school does not meet federally mandated standards, parents can move the child to a different public (or private or charter) school.

The continuing decline and the ultimate closing of traditionally poor schools that do not meet the externally provided federal aims will continue the destruction of cities already suffering from more traditional practices of white flight and gated communities. There exists the danger of an increase in economically and racially based segregation that can result from the reporting system required by NCLB. Furthermore, the economically able can opt to move to "high-performing" schools--schools whose racial profile will be readily available to local real-estate agents. School over-crowding might occur as parents flock their children to the two or three "best" schools. This will in turn put those schools in danger of not meeting federally mandated aims as class sizes grow and the community school becomes the regional school. Flight from public to private schools, rather than to other public schools, can result in further exacerbating those community problems mentioned before and quite possibly taking public monies to private institutions where NCLB is not in play.

Not only does NCLB take the general aims and means work away from the local community, but the legislation mandates a couple of very interesting and specific guidelines that are equally frightening. One of these is requiring that phonics be the only method of teaching reading, and a second is the mandate that the boy scouts cannot be turned down for use of public school space regardless of recent Supreme Court rulings. NCLB goes so far as to suggest what should count as "character education": caring, civic virtue and citizenship, justice and fairness, respect, responsibility, trustworthiness, regardless of what a community might define as "character."

These are just a few of the community consequences, intended or not, that will result when the NCLB steps in to dictate local educational policy. Tocqueville and Putnam are correct in warning our young democracy that allowing the federal government to make local (educational and otherwise) decisions can indeed lead to further disenfranchisement and ultimately to democratic tyranny as local voices are further stifled rather than encouraged as necessary to the democratic process.

Conclusion

It is probably not quite accurate to claim, as we did at the outset of this essay, that NCLB has demanded "change" from public school people and teacher educators. We should probably say it has demanded "response" from these agents--the new word chosen to signify more of a defensive, deflective posture than the positive, constructive implication that often goes along with the word "change." In the bullied responses of teachers to NCLB legislation we find a pale, limited conception of achievement and a frenzied concern about assessment that constricts teaching and learning. For special education students we find empty promises, and for communities we find the rending of democratic processes. We, too, want to "leave no child behind" in America's schools, but instead of a sensible plan for such an ambition, we find, instead, rhetorical swirl and suspect motives. The educational stage has been besieged by NCLB, and the self-assuming rightness of the legislation and its school-killing sanctioning power drown out alternative ideas. Perhaps if the carriage that is public schools goes nowhere under the power of NCLB legislation, legislators will spit out the bit and let teachers and teachers educators pull the load as they know how best to do. But that is to wish failure with its attendant sufferings on public schools and the people in them—not a noble position. So we offer these arguments in hopes that someone with power will listen to them.

References

Bronowski, Jacob (1973). *The Ascent of Man* (Boston: Little, Brown).

Dewey, John (1961 [1916]). *Democracy and Education: An Introduction to the Philosophy of Education* (Macmillan).

Putnam, Robert (2001). *Bowling Alone*: *the collapse and revival of American Community* (New York: Simon and Schuster).

Tocqueville, Alexis de (1961). *Democracy in America* (Shocken).

A Campus Divided:
How Intercollegiate Athletics Erodes the Educational Mission of the Academy and What Teaching Faculty Should Do About It

Thomas D. Cavenagh

Introductory Questions:

1. Why operate extra-mural athletic programs at colleges and universities?

2. What role or roles should athletics play in the life of the undergraduate student?

3. To what extent should faculty be involved in the operation of athletic programs at colleges and universities?

A Campus Divided:
How Intercollegiate Athletics Erodes the Educational Mission of the Academy and What Teaching Faculty Should Do About It

Thomas D. Cavenagh

At the time of this writing, college athletics faces what would be regarded as a crisis condition in any other venue. The *National Collegiate Athletic Association* ("NCAA"), which has a total membership of 1005 active member institutions, has placed 52 athletic programs at 31 colleges and universities on probation for violations of sports related rules (NCAA, May 2004). Men's basketball programs lead the list of programs probated for misconduct with 14; men's football runs a close second with 13 programs probated. Twelve schools have more than one program on probation, and 2 schools, Howard University and Oklahoma Panhandle State University, have 5 separate athletic programs on probation each. While men's programs account for the vast majority of the programs in disciplinary difficulty with the NCAA, 11 women's programs appear on this list of shame. Southern Methodist University has accumulated the highest number of NCAA major infractions to date with 8 (NCAA, May 2004). Investigations of athletic program misconduct are normally confidential, so it is possible that further disciplinary actions have taken place since this article went to print.

The problem is not limited to so-called 'revenue sports' or large, Division I, public institutions. The most recent addition to the NCAA probation list is the powerhouse men's basketball program at the University of Michigan, which was compelled to forfeit over 100 games and placed on probation through May, 2007, for infractions that took place during the 'fab five'era. However, recruiting, unfair benefits and inducements to athletes and other violations in women's golf, not a revenue sport by any stretch of the imagination, has landed that program at Division II Oklahoma Panhandle State University on probation through December, 2007 (NCAA, December 18, 2002). Even tiny Division III Salem State couldn't follow the rules; its men's soccer team is probated through February 2005. It is also important to note that schools on the probation list ordinarily received other and/or additional punishment including, but not limited to, reduction in scholarship availability, forfeiture of games and tournaments won, limitations of coach and player travel and extensive required corrective actions.

But it is not just disciplinary difficulties with the NCAA that plague college athletics and, in turn, harm and divide college and university campuses. While the colleges and universities at which they served are penalized, coaches often reap economic benefits of enormous proportion. For example, Larry Eustachy, after leaving the head men's basketball coaching position at the Iowa State University in disgrace recently was enriched by a severance package that totaled nearly $1 million dollars; nearly twice the collective salary of all teaching faculty at the institution of which this author is a member. A story detailing checkered career of men's basketball coach Jim Harrick adorned the front page of the Wall Street Journal (2003) recently and made readers aware that Harrick resigned from the University of Georgia after the school determined that three of his star players received 'A' grades in a, and here is a delicious irony, 'basketball coaching class' that they never attended; this from a coach already fired by UCLA and presently under investigation by the University of Rhode Island for irregularities in the administration of his basketball teams at those schools.

Moreover, running a program not disciplined by the NCAA surely has its benefits: Tubby Smith, head men's basketball coach at the University of Kentucky, extended an existing contract by eight years adding a total of at least $20.5 million in salary to his already considerable personal wealth. Smith will earn a minimum of $1.75 million in the first year of the new deal in 20030-2004; by 2010 his minimum salary will be $2.4 million (University of Kentucky, 2003). Never mind that non-athletic academic budgets are shrinking across the country while tuition rises faster than the rate of inflation at scores of public and private institutions.

These problems arise in a massive and rapidly growing enterprise. Three hundred fifty-five thousand six hundred eighty-eight (355,688) men and woman participated in NCAA sponsored events in 2000-2001; this total increased from 275,305 in 1990-1991. Of the 2000-2001 participation total, over 44,500 participated in an NCAA championship, better than double the 1992-1993 championship participation total of 21,904. Average total 1999 revenues at a Division I school with a men's football team were $21.9 million. NCAA revenues in 2001-2002 year were over $357 million, three quarters of which were generated through television revenue; seven percent plus increases in revenues are projected annually through 2006-2007. The 1999-2000 estimated total of athletics scholarships awarded by NCAA member institutions was $975 million ... more than the 2001 total gross domestic products of all but eight countries (World Bank, 2001).

While this morass is shocking, the near absence of public demands to reform the system is more disturbing. One observes occasional newspaper articles or television interviews, but legislation, the best barometer of public pressure to better regulate is essentially non-existent. The collapse of Enron has resulted in significant and widespread changes to the law and practice of business in the United States. However, the love affair the American public has with college sports seems to blind it to the deleterious effects sports clearly has on the educational mission of the academy.

Some have argued that the host of problems created by athletics is most prevalent on the campuses of large public universities. Sperber (2000), for example, argues that the party-driven, alcohol-enriched atmosphere of these large institutions is a major factor in the prominence of sport in the academy and, therefore, in creating the pressures to recruit and retain athletes that cost schools eligibility and reputation. Sperber also argues that the growing importance of sport on college campuses is responsible, at least in part, for the larger and, therefore, less academically defensible classes many undergraduates take while resources for smaller instructional settings is siphoned away to support large and costly athletic programs.

It is interesting to note that Sperber's criticism of athletics in higher education and, more specifically, of the princely treatment the University of Indiana afforded problematic former men's head basketball coach Bobby Knight has resulted in considerable personal turmoil. Indeed, the following passage from a recent interview with Sperber published in *The Atlantic Monthly* (Press, 2001) illustrates both the cost of criticizing college athletics and the significance it has for those invested in it:

> ... [Sperber] awoke to a torrent of irate and obscene telephone calls and e-mails. "Shame on you for giving such a wonderful university a black eye ... You should resign!" read one e-mail, from an Indiana University alumnus. "You are a vile and pathetic little worm," another said. Anonymous callers flooded Sperber's answering machine with vituperative messages. Disparaging letters began appearing in the local paper.
>
> ... Sperber continued to speak out on the issue, and the angry missives from Indiana fans took on an increasingly threatening tone. "If you don't shut up, I'll shut you up," one caller warned. Sperber soon noticed that the schedule for his fall classes had been posted on a Web site for Indiana University basketball fans. "I see dead bodies," a heading on the site declared; it was followed by a list that included Sperber's name and those of two newspaper columnists who had also been critical of Knight.
>
> Strangers began approaching Sperber in supermarkets and coffee shops and warning him to stop talking about Knight. ... Sperber began fearing for the safety of his family. They stopped going to restaurants, tired of the icy, intimidating glares they drew from other diners. His wife stopped using her credit card after a store clerk, recognizing her last name, verbally harassed her. ... The campus police offered to post an armed guard in Sperber's lecture rooms (p. 37).

Others offer a different view of the sorts of institutions most negatively affected by intercollegiate sport. This view acknowledges, of course, the pernicious effects of athletics on large campuses, but recognizes that smaller and Ivy League schools are not immune from very similar difficulties (Schulman & Bowen, 2001). For example, the relatively larger percentage of the student body participating in athletic programs at many smaller schools may, Schulman and Bowen believe, magnify the deleterious effects on the institutional academic mission perpetrated by sports.

A detailed review of the long history of college athletics is beyond the scope of this brief essay. Instead, this essay explores the sum of the effects modern; often revenue driven college athletics programs have on college campuses. It looks, more specifically, at the divide on college campuses between academic and athletic missions and the consequences of that house deeply divided. Finally, the essay offers several approaches to improving the campus climate and integrating athletic programs more closely into the academic mission of the college or university.

It makes sense to start by asking what benefits are sought or actually gained from the present 'sport as commodity' approach to college athletics. Of course, recruiting a larger, more diverse student body is likely the first benefit that comes to mind for most, both critics and supporters alike. Indeed, it is standard practice to compel coaches to recruit and to set quotas to measure their progress at doing so. Accordingly, large college programs draw hundreds of athletes to campus; small institutions normally see very large percentages of their total student bodies engaged in some intercollegiate athletic pursuit.

"In order to assure success on their playing fields, admissions directors are setting aside specific numbers of places for recruited athletes and going lower on the academic ladder to recruit them" (Fiske, 2001, p. 22). Beyond increasing the sheer numbers of incoming students, colleges and universities use athletics to endeavor to build more diverse student bodies. Fiske quotes Phillip Smith, director of admissions at Williams, a college that has won the Sears Cup for athletic program excellence: "[a]thletic recruiting is the biggest form of affirmative action in American higher education, even at schools such as ours" (p. 22). Fiske further notes that Williams gives preferential treatment to athletes for 71 of 551 spots in its incoming class, and Amherst designates 75 of 450 spots for athletes in 27 varsity sports.

But recruiting is only important because it supports athletic programs. Absent the need to win, it is immaculately clear that coaches, and admissions officers, could spend far less time and money seeking high-profile athletes and significantly more time seeking students better matched to the educational mission and standards of the college and who are more likely to succeed. Indeed, the Schulman-Bowen study concludes that athletes enter the academy with weaker academic records and "consistently under-perform academically even after we control for standardized test scores and other variables" (p. 58). Furthermore, students themselves could be encouraged to make college choices based on more significant matters than the number of trips made by the institution to the final four.

In short, recruiting is not a benefit of athletics, it is a burden necessitated by it. The message to recruiting admissions staff and coaches is 'we must win, so we must recruit better than our athletic competitors.' Regrettably, for some, the rest of the message is: … 'so we must push the boundaries of propriety to recruit effectively even if doing so violates rules and potentially causes us to lose our athletic eligibility altogether.'

School spirit among current students is also offered as an example of the salutary effects of big-money college sports programs. But, like recruiting, school spirit is only a relative matter. Without the need to win, and to compare one's campus to that of another, student loyalty and enthusiasm for alma mater are driven by more legitimate matters, like one's personal intellectual or social experience. Furthermore, and again like recruiting, spirit is a completely artificial objective. Only in an environment where colleges themselves tell students to value a school that excels in intercollegiate athletic competition does the sort of spirit created by athletic success matter.

Sports enthusiasts also proffer alumni loyalty and continued financial contact with the institution as a reason for the continued centrality of sports on college campuses. However, there appears to be no meaningful pecuniary benefit to the institutions whose alums root for their teams after they depart. Schulman and Bowen state unequivocally that two of the most "powerful myths that circulate around college sports" are the following: "that former athletes, having become financial winners in the game of life, and having had the privilege of representing their school in competition, are disproportionately generous toward their alma mater (pp. 205-206)."

The second myth is that "winning sports programs encourage alumni/ae in general to give more money (p. 206)." In fact, anecdotal evidence cited in the Schulman & Bowen study suggests that athletes think they have already 'given' by performing for the institution on the athletic field or court (pp. 205 & 209). Sperber claims, "when scandal occurs, the sword [of publicity] swings back, drawing buckets of negative media coverage and public scorn. During times of scandal, some alumni....close their checkbooks" (p. 259). Finally, the Schulman & Bowen study provides some empirical evidence to support the proposition that athletic gifts restricted to athletic programs essentially cannibalize gifts that would otherwise go elsewhere at the institution. So, one must ask whether it really matters that an alum dons college logo gear and cheers for the alma mater at the local tavern come bowl day if there is no money in it for the college or university.

If the intangibles of school spirit and alumni financial support are not probative in defense of the college sports industry, and an industry it is, surely it is financially profitable for the institutions that field teams. Both Sperber (p. 92) and the Schulman & Bowen (p. 227) study contradict this notion suggesting that athletic programs normally cost more to run than they garner in revenues. Moreover, Honan (2001) points out that even accounting for profit and loss in college athletics is not an exact science as "methods used are inconsistent for major sports programs (p. 19)."

Finally, some athletes have become spectacularly wealthy as professional players, and as colleges and universities serve as the de facto farm systems for most professional sports, they deserve some credit for these vocational successes, even if, as we have seen, these athletes do not give back financially in any meaningful way. That said, the NCAA publishes the percentage of students moving into professional sports - and the number is simply insignificant. The most current NCAA (2004) "Fact Sheet" shows the "professional career probability" of several NCAA sanctioned sports. A men's baseball participant has the most favorable odds of earning a living as a professional player at 10.5%. This relatively modest number still dwarfs the professional prospects of the men's football participant who has 2.0% chance of 'going pro' and of men's basketball players who have just a 1.3% chance of playing in some professional league here or abroad. The only listed sport for women is basketball; these players have a 1% chance of playing professionally.

Add this to the very short list of benefits accruing as a result of college athletic programs for the scant few who achieve it, but do so aware that it is irrelevant in the grand scheme of things. This is particularly true in light of the tremendous number of students who, having failed to make a professional club in their sport of choice fall back on the stunted education they received while devoting themselves to the pursuit of a life of sport.

Let's consider who really benefits from big money athletics. Colleges may see some largely meaningless camaraderie among present and past students, but they likely see little more. And, because it is clear that athletic programs spend as fast as they collect, increasing revenues is a false promise. The real winners are the television networks that sell advertising on the backs of colleges and universities sending teams to NCAA championships. The NCAA (2002) touts vociferously news of the revenues generated by championship payouts. It should be conceded that the amounts given to colleges under this program are not insignificant. However, they trumpet these revenues without addressing in any meaningful fashion the fact that athletic programs, as we have seen, do not net a surplus, even after all of the payouts from the NCAA.

Of course, Las Vegas and the rest of the often-illicit world of sports wagering has a deep and abiding interest in college athletics. Billions of dollars are wagered each year on college athletics. Indeed, the athletes themselves are betting: a University of Cincinnati study in which 648 college athletes were polled found that 25.5 % of them admitted to placing wagers on college football games; 3.7% bet on a game or match in which they were participating and 0.5% took money to perform poorly intentionally (Beckish, 2003). Fans of college sports certainly benefit from essentially free entertainment. But, if casinos, bookies and spectators are the primary beneficiaries of the system, a system, which has profound and abiding problems, the system is obviously broken.

If these supposed benefits do not pan out, what, if any, are the additional detriments of intercollegiate athletics? We know colleges do not benefit financially from athletic programs or even from individual athletes generally speaking; we know that the individuals recruited to play are not the best equipped students; we know that betting, alcohol abuse and other harmful activity surrounds college sports. What we have not yet paid attention to is the divisions created on campus as these athletic programs function across America's campuses.

One profoundly negative effect of the current environment is a growing and deep divide between full-time, non-athletic teaching faculty and the members of the athletic staff, often possessors of faculty rank, though rarely scholars or teachers. There is a scholarship of sport, and with those engaged in it, teaching-faculty generally have no special quarrel. However, faculty who observe resources used to build spectacular athletic facilities and to pay for the people who manage the athletic activity on campus, while the academic physical plant and environment lags behind cannot possibly avoid resentment.

Faculty who are faced with unprepared and unmotivated students tired from travel and competition, interested in preserving eligibility, but not in developing habits of the mind, certainly hold the athletics machine responsible. In short, in a larger culture that is increasingly anti-intellectual, thinkers struggle with those in the academy who dilute the educational mission of the institution by bringing in students not otherwise desirable and spending resources irresponsibly to do so.

Dividing the faculty is not the only way campus schisms are created by college athletic programs. Students are certainly driven away from the faculty in significant ways by many athletic programs. Practice, weight and endurance training and a packed competition schedule consume an athlete's time year-round. As such, they are less able to pursue academics in a serious and sustained fashion. Not only is time short for the college athlete, during their busy day energy and motivation dwindles. So, the teacher of philosophy, anthropology or history is greeted with increasing frequency by the email message from the athletic department announcing that the listed group of students will not be in class on a given day and that this absence should be treated as excused because the event is a college sponsored one.

Faculty, of course, are expected to allow make-up work, to meet with students who missed lectures - course meetings are simply repeatable events, while meets and games are irreplaceable and unique - and to tolerate substandard effort. Is it any wonder that when we signal to students that class is so fungible, they act differently when they actually do appear for a scheduled class meeting? How can faculty feel connected to students when their absences from class are sanctioned despite that fact that the absences reduce class effectiveness for both those present and those absent and produces nothing of value other, perhaps, than a win for the team? Furthermore, it is not hard to imagine that plagiarism, a problem running rampant on college and university campuses today is driven in part by the demands placed on the student to compete or practice six days out of every week and still complete a full-time schedule of coursework. This pollution of the academic environment is simply unconscionable and getting worse and the hostility between students and faculty is, as a result, often palpable.

Faculty divide themselves between the athletic and the teaching, and faculty are divided from their academic wards who are pursuing athletic accomplishments to the detriment of their classroom accomplishments. A final campus division takes place when the teaching faculty are driven away from administration because they perceive that the academic interests of the institution, ones which should be absolutely central to the college or university mission, are either made secondary to or even equivalent to the athletic program. Teaching faculty cannot feel anything but alienated from administrations that pay basketball coaches an amount equivalent to that earned by whole departments or disciplines. Suggesting that this is a market necessity driven by the need to obtain the best coaching possible is simply not an argument that faculties should accept. The market pressure to overpay coaches is driven by the need to win, which, we have seen, has no tangible benefit to the institution other than as a relative matter to other colleges competing in the athletic world.

Finally, the impact of making sports the public face of higher education has eroded public confidence in the academy. While dalliances with postmodernism and other intellectually stimulating, but socially insignificant matters have marginalized higher education, a more important matter is the fact that the wider society has virtually no commerce with higher education other through payment of tuition for children and the very public face of the academy that is college athletics. And that commerce is often in the context of news stories about the latest recruiting scandal, act of violence or coaching change.

We do not suggest here that there is no place for athletics in the academy, only that there is a much more limited and differently defined role. Better than the 'commodity' model is one that focuses the energies of athletic programs on life-long health education and maintenance and social skills development - two matters not only ignored in the current milieu but also actively thwarted. As athletes are pushed to play hurt (consider how much time, effort and money is spent in training rooms at campuses around the country preparing injured athletes to compete) and to win at virtually any cost, it is difficult to imagine how they will hear the message that they should value their health over the long-term. As victorious coaches howl and athletes strut and mug for television cameras to the obvious joy of their fans, gloating and preening with each tackle or basket made, no serious observer can believe that play in ways that display character is fostered and required in college athletic program.

The Greeks saw room for physical pursuits in the service of better intellectual development. They understood that attending to the health of the body enhanced the life of the mind. It is, however, tremendously difficult to imagine them supporting the erosion of the academy as a place of learning as it has become a place of play. Closing the divide between the athletic establishment and the rest of the campus is a complex and costly matter. The deep commitment to athletics at colleges and universities has created a deeply entrenched establishment. That said there are some ways to address the problem.

Several relatively simple efforts directed at students would have a salutary effect. It has been suggested elsewhere that colleges publish academic information including, but not limited to, majors, minors and grade averages, on the students participating in their intercollegiate athletic programs (Drake Group, 2004). Doing so would establish important accountability standards and better equip faculty to address deficiencies in the academic performance of athletes at their individual institutions rather than relying on NCAA aggregate data to surmise about their programs.

Freshman athletic eligibility should be revisited with a view toward curtailing or eliminating it. Preventing the youngest and least prepared members of the academic community from competing in ways that require travel, extensive practice and the intense pressure of the media would, to be sure, allow them an opportunity to become students before they become college athletes. Reducing the amount of scholarship monies available to athletes would deflate the importance of athletics relative to learning. Of course more stringent grade requirements to maintain eligibility, vigorous policing of athlete academic work for plagiarism and prohibiting the tracking of athletes into special areas of study or athlete only coursework designed to pass them, educated or not, would also be profoundly useful.

Institution oriented change should be made as well. The NCAA is likely to be most responsive to a large group of colleges and universities demanding profound change in the athletic arena. In addition, substantially increasing funding for the less competitive, but more mission-oriented intramural alternative to intercollegiate athletics is a splendid start to refocusing the mission of athletics at the academy. Colleges and universities are responsive to accrediting bodies, so a challenging, but undoubtedly helpful additional approach could also be found in making academic accreditation in some measure contingent on the graduation rate of the athlete. Any college with an overall graduation rate of 80% for incoming freshman, but only a 50% graduation rate of incoming freshman participating in athletics should face serious accreditation difficulties.

A much more radical notion is ending the televising of college athletic events altogether or perhaps in the regular season. Doing so would transform the culture of collegiate athletics overnight - the money would disappear, and much of the corrosive influence it has on the academy would disappear with it. Doing so would also return much of the administration of sports to the colleges themselves as the NCAA has become little more than a revenue distribution entity and it would be rendered largely superfluous if there were no revenues to distribute. Finally, doing so would put into better perspective for young, unpaid, inexperienced athletes the role of sports in their lives and in society more generally.

Beyond efforts related to students and the institution, specific attention must be paid to the role and compensation of the college coach. Salary levels for coaches must be capped in the interest of overall institutional financial health. Furthermore, coaches should be more fully integrated into the academic life of the college community. Requiring coaches to teach is one significant way to accomplish that integration. Subjecting coaches to evaluation by teaching faculty is a second useful way to integrate the two groups.

Finally, the *National Collegiate Athletic Association*, the ultimate arbiter of college athletics rules must take seriously the need to solve the myriad problems of college athletics. The present system of discipline is, for example, poorly conceived and completely inconsistent with modern conceptions of justice. For example, schools may be disciplined by exclusion from post-season play many years after the infractions for which the disciplinary action is meted out took place. The men's basketball program at the University of Michigan was recently placed on probation for player infractions that took place years ago - current players are, in short, paying for the sins of past players and coaches. A far better approach, because it is at once infinitely more just and draconian is to commence probation four years after the infraction is uncovered and adjudicated so the current players are not punished, but the college or university, which would find recruiting all but impossible for the prospectively crippled program, would be punished very significantly.

We simply must move away from the 'sale of a commodity' approach to college athletics that motivates such excesses in competitive effort. It simply should not matter to the extent and in the ways that it does, who wins any of the NCAA collegiate championships - these are children at play. College spirit and pride are valuable, but the price institutions are paying to obtain them is exorbitant by any measure. If money is the root of all evil, it has sunk deep roots into our intercollegiate athletic culture.

There is a temptation to relegate this article to the dustbin, believing as one does so that the enterprise of college athletics is simply too big, too powerful, too entrenched and too important to change. It is true that making inroads into reform in this area is particularly difficult given the fabulous sums of money involved and the tremendous power of television networks and others with a financial stake in continuing the present model, perhaps most importantly, in the sports consuming public. While women's collegiate sports are rarely the object of large viewing groups, the men's basketball championship and football bowl seasons are some of the most highly rated television events of the year. Nevertheless, change is needed, and the faculties of our colleges and universities are the only groups with a genuine interest in solving the problems created and perpetuated by big-money college athletics, as well as its smaller time counterparts at Division II and Division III schools.

Then NCAA President Cedric Dempsey prefaced the NCAA 2001-2002 Membership Report by stating:

> The future of intercollegiate college athletics rests, as it always has, on achieving an exceedingly difficult balance involving education, finances and competition. The time to improve that balance is now. Those of us most intimately involved with college athletics believe totally in our ultimate goals. These priorities set forth by our Executive Committee - the principles that drive our decision-making process - are laudable: to promote student-athletes and college sports through public awareness; to protect student-athletes through standards of fairness and integrity; to prepare student-athletes for life-long leadership; and, to provide student-athletes and college sports wit the funding to help meet these goals (p. 18).

Is it any wonder that college athletics is the quagmire that it is when the President of its regulatory body seeks to balance education, finances and competition with goals that do not even mention learning? What, after all, is a "student-athlete?" This juxtaposition of often mutually inconsistent terms is freighted with important consequences. The terms cannot, even in the imaginations of those who believe deeply in the athletic mission, have equivalent importance. Indeed, why use the misleading and pernicious moniker at all? Is a student-athlete something more than a student who, along with many other things, plays a sport? Do we honestly mean to convey parity in the importance of these profoundly different roles?

Those with a stake in the athletic establishment will not solve this problem in a fashion that reasserts the prominence of learning in places of higher education without considerable outside pressure. They will continue to 'promote,' to 'protect' and to 'fund' sports, not erudition, and they will continue to do so to the profound loss to the academy. The academic community simply must resist these efforts and make meaningful efforts to thwart them.

Accreditation in Teacher Education: A Good Idea Gone Bad?
Jerry Whitworth, Steven P. Jones, and Thomas E. Deering

Guiding questions

1. Why do we need accreditation in teacher education?
2. Is accreditation of teacher education programs a good thing or a bad thing?
3. Has accreditation improved the quality of teacher education or just added to our problems?

Accreditation in Teacher Education: A Good Idea Gone Bad?
Jerry Whitworth, Steven P. Jones, and Thomas E. Deering

A story is told of a small city in Minnesota where city officials were negotiating with local firefighters. The city wanted to reduce the required five-person crew assigned to each fire truck to four. The firemen insisted that a five-person crew was necessary for the efficient operation of the fire truck. During one negotiating session a city official said, "We've been able to figure out the jobs of four of the firemen on each truck, but what does the fifth one do?" No one could answer that question, so an investigation was begun. Finally, the answer was found. The five-person crew went back to the days when fire trucks were pulled by horses. The job of the fifth fireman was to hold the horses while the other four fought the fire. Even though the purpose for the fifth person no longer existed, the historical practice of the five-person crew continued to be maintained.

There are many who would say that accreditation in teacher education has followed a similar path. Although originally a very logical and useful practice, perhaps it has outlived its usefulness. Perhaps it is an anachronism which no longer serves its original purpose. Nothing illustrates this better than the accreditation designed and maintained by the National Council for the Accreditation of Teacher Education (NCATE). Born of noble purposes, those purposes often become lost and forgotten by a byzantine bureaucracy of anxiety and even intimidation. While acknowledging the benefits of accountability in teacher education, we explore in this essay some of the anxiety and intimidation that accompanies NCATE accreditation, and we suggest the possibility that, like the fifth Minnesota fireman, teacher educators might be better off without NCATE.

Advantages of teacher education accreditation

Teacher education programs clearly need to be quality programs. And, of course, legitimate and credible teacher education programs need to be accountable—though the question of to whom they should be accountable, and of how the effort to be accountable may benefit students, teachers, administrators and the general public, is not altogether clear. Given the crushing demands on teacher education programs made by changes in NCATE standards, it is not clear that NCATE should be the guarantor of accountability.

But from the point of view of institutions hosting teacher education programs, there are some significant advantages of NCATE accreditation. Though university presidents and college deans may be loath to admit it openly, the chief benefit of NCATE accreditation is the prestige of being able to say "We are NCATE-accredited." Those who aren't are required to hang their heads a little and murmur, "No, we aren't," and then to hastily attempt to justify to their dismissive listeners why they have not attained to those lofty heights. NCATE is considered by many to be the "gold standard" of accreditation and the acronym, if not the system, is familiar to many outside of teacher education. University administrators, PR people, recruiters, all like to push out their chests a little and say to those outside the institution, "We are NCATE-accredited." The value of this to enrollment, fund-raising, and public image cannot be discounted.

There is also the issue of consistency. Accreditation by an "objective" outside body gives the public a consistent way to compare teacher education programs to one another, in a sense allowing people to compare "apples to apples." Accreditation by NCATE implies, in the minds of many, that the institution has met certain standards of quality and achievement. It has become the "Good Housekeeping Seal of Approval" to our constituencies. It also provides a simple and convenient mechanism for outside agencies, such as state teacher certification bodies, to compare and approve teacher education programs.

In addition, it is difficult to deny that the process of accreditation also provides a tool for teacher preparation programs to set and measure goals, to evaluate their progress. The self-study, contemplation, and examination involved in accreditation approval or continuing approval can assist faculty in thoughtfully and carefully formulating well-articulated, measurable goals, and to implement a mechanism for monitoring and assessing progress toward those goals. This type of structured, organized, and purposeful approach to establishing institutional vision and goals cannot be entirely bad.

But, perhaps the greatest benefit seen by many in accreditation is accountability. Calls for accountability are reaching into every aspect of our society today, with hardly any institution left untouched. From our elementary and secondary schools to our colleges and universities, and now to our financial and business institutions, the public is demanding accountability. People want to feel confident that they can have trust in the institutions that serve our society, that those institutions will deliver what they promise. While such a goal is admirable and desirable, it almost always becomes clouded and confused by political correctness and posturing. Raywid (2002) notes that it is unfortunate that accountability was not launched for reasons other than public mistrust. As a result, institutions must operate from a defensive posture in demonstrating their effectiveness and must surrender much of their control over standards and procedures for accountability to external agencies.

Nowhere is this more evident than in higher education. The insistence that our colleges and universities are held responsible for demonstrating their value has mounted in recent years (Barnett, 1992). According to the Southern Regional Education Board (2000) there are three reasons for this.

1) The public increasingly insists on accountability for state government.
2) Competition for funding forces colleges and universities to show their efficiency and effectiveness.
3) Higher education must demonstrate its value to students, to business and industry, and to the public for the support it needs.
4)

Berdahl (1990) commented on the state of ambivalence on the part of universities in being "both involved and withdrawn; both serving and criticizing; both needing and being needed." (p. 170). As such, colleges and universities often seem aloof and arrogant, distant and mysterious to the public at large, the same public on which they depend for a large bulk of their funding. The pressure for increased accountability is an attempt to force institutions to become more accessible, more open, more understandable to the public.

While standards, historically, have almost always been externally imposed (Samaras, Francis, and Holt, 1999, Eaton, 2001) there was a time when institutions of higher education were allowed to regulate themselves through rigorous peer-review processes. Increasingly, however, funding and program approval is being tied to standards and criteria imposed through the political process (Dillon, 1995). Alexander (2002) noted the increasing pressure that government agencies have placed on higher education to become more accountable, stating "governmental authorities are no longer as receptive to the traditional self-regulatory processes that have dominated university development for centuries." (p. 411)

Another factor in the accountability picture is the increased competition for tax dollars. Government and political officials find themselves pushed to get more out of less, to operate more efficiently and productively (Dill and Sporn, 1995; Eicher, 1998). A common target is often the higher education institutions, which have long been perceived as inefficient and less than fully productive. The pressure has mounted to push colleges and universities to serve more students and to produce higher quality graduates. Cowen (1996) notes that this pressure has evolved into the development and implementation of government imposed evaluation systems to monitor productivity and efficiency.

Wellman (2001) defines accountability as "state-level indicators of institutional performance, designed to reach public audiences, using quantitative and qualitative measures that allow comparisons among institutions." And, they "are geared to legislative or gubernatorial audiences rather than individual governing boards." (p. 46) As such, there are a number of benefits to rigorous accountability procedures in higher education. Wellman observes that higher education must improve its capacity to demonstrate that it can meet the expectations of society. She insists this is so because higher education serves broad social purposes, is heavily subsidized with public funds and serves as a gateway to social opportunity and economic productivity for society in general.

Increasingly, the public wants some evidence of the value of the benefits of their tax dollars going to higher education. Accountability systems provide a mechanism to do this in a way that is quantifiable and understandable to the public at large. They allow for legislators and critics to gauge the success of colleges and universities and for comparing institutions to one another. On the part of the institutions themselves accountability can provide both a platform for public relations campaigns, and a roadmap for program improvement and a way to establish their legitimacy. According to Boland (1999) legitimacy is important because it can improve an institution's ability to command resources and increase its organizational autonomy. It can also be argued that accountability data can be manipulated and massaged, to some extent, to create opportunities and avenues for desired institutional changes, improvements and expansions.

Disadvantages of teacher education accreditation

Those involved closely, and for some hopelessly, in the throes of NCATE accreditation; however, see many disadvantages with the system. It often appears to promote a "master-servant" relationship with NCATE as masters. This is often manifested in the hysteria promoted to meet NCATE demands. Those who have worked in a college or university desperate, for one reason or another, to attain, retain, or reacquire NCATE accreditation often find them miserable places to work. They can become places where hysteria is always "in the air," if it isn't in the university's bloodstream, causing all kinds of nasty symptoms. Those faculty members who become "keepers of the NCATE flame" suffer from this illness and inflict it on those around them. "If we don't do this, we won't get NCATE." "If our assessment plan isn't done like this and finished by this date, we won't get NCATE." Disapproval of the NCATE committee is tantamount to the apocalypse or some dreaded plague that threatens to descend upon the entire university.

The hysteria often created by NCATE accreditation can be measured by the tremendous amount of time, money, and effort put into pleasing the NCATE master. Institutions must start years before the NCATE visit amassing vast amounts of data. Every practice, policy, and activity must be examined and analyzed in terms of how it will please the NCATE masters. It often seems that the accreditation process, rather than sound pedagogy and institutional mission, drives programs and practices. This can be seen in an examination of several features of NCATE's accreditation system.

Assessment

One of the major changes in the new NCATE Standards comes in the assessment and documentation process. A significant feature of the NCATE 2000 Standards is that program change must be a consequence of thorough and ongoing assessment. Program change must also be thoroughly documented and demonstrated to have a connection with program assessment. The NCATE 2000 Standards also bring a larger number of programs into the assessment process. No longer confined to teacher education programs within colleges of education, the new Standards expect other programs to participate as fully as those within colleges of education. Among others, NCATE expects history, chemistry, languages, agriculture, and every other academic program that leads to teacher certification, to meet its Standards.

Working through the NCATE process for documentation preparation and team visitation requires the quantification of teacher education. Beans and books; people and placements are all subjected to counting. The books in a library collection are counted. The courses applied to a student's major, or to general studies, or to teacher education are counted. People are counted when the goal ought to be that people are valued--that they count. The people of color are enumerated, including students, faculty and administrators.

The number of hours future teachers spend in school field placements are tallied. A number used to describe hours of "field time" does little to create a meaningful portrait of students' pre-professional experiences in schools.

NCATE is interested in counting the number of texts with publication dates more than two years old listed on faculty syllabi. Is it any wonder the words of John Dewey remain largely unknown to students unless summarized in a few paragraphs--possibly even with a single sentence--in brand new textbooks? NCATE also counts the dollars invested in a program; the dollars in endowment ready to support future work; and the sources for grants and research.

We do not argue that a college can function with one book on the library shelf or a treasury that will dissolve before the academic year ends. Nor do we argue for privacy or secrecy about the details NCATE counts. We do, however, question the intensity of counting that takes place under the guise of program description. As Cecelia Traugh says, "Education is a very human endeavor." We believe that to be true. Counting is a reductionist activity used by NCATE under the guise of being a description of experience.

Assessment hysteria can also be measured in terms of time; especially the time faculty must give over to the process. It becomes difficult to even count the personnel hours given to the accreditation process, countless hours which can compromise classroom time for faculty. Time devoted by faculty to research, reading, writing, and service is now shared or compromised by documentation and assessment committees.

This focus, some would say over-focus, on assessment also has other side affects. The talk of the university itself is changed. Faculty are forced into conversation about documentation and accreditation review preparation--forced, even, to make their students share in the conversation because their products, in the form of their now mandated "portfolios," have become a primary assessment tool for accrediting bodies. Portfolios must have "this" and "that" in them. Students must show how products are aligned to and meet certain Standards. Faculty must give time to insure that each portfolio has the necessary shine and image to match the expectation of evaluators who will look at random samples of student portfolios.

Meeting the Standards

Many find a number of the Standards NCATE has established for accreditation to be troubling. Each are accompanied by "conceptual frameworks" and "rubrics" that expand them a great deal and add to the burden of paperwork and interpretation foisted on the institution. Standard Five, for instance, insists faculty in teacher education programs must be qualified in the professional practice of scholarship, service, teaching, self-assessment, and in collaboration with colleagues, and that faculty must model these practices for their students.

No faculty member or university administrator would disagree with the tenets of this Standard. However, the way the Standard is worded raises many issues that are not well resolved. For instance, does scholarship include classroom lectures, refereed publications, "on-line" publications, invited lectures, pre-publication book reviews, supervising student teaching interns, etc.? And, who evaluates scholarship? Who determines its quality and appropriateness, and what are the standards used to make that determination? In a similar vein, what is service and teaching, and who evaluates it and by what standards?

Along with Standard Five are rubrics designed by NCATE and intended to assist institutions with the assessment of their progress in meeting the Standard. Yet, these rubrics themselves raise serious questions. Phrases such as "limited understanding of their fields," "thorough understanding of the content they teach," and "an in-depth understanding of their fields" are difficult to distinguish from one another. Who makes this determination? How much documentation is sufficient? The Standard also discusses "intellectual vitality." Is this phrase supposed to point to something more than "enthusiasm," and by means of what will it found, described, and assessed? These are just some of the many questions and issues raised by this troubling standard that are not adequately addressed by NCATE.

Equally troubling is Standard Four, "The Diversity Standard." For many this Standard is a major barrier, making impossible demands that their institutions are incapable of meeting for reasons far beyond their control. The acceptable level for this Standard states,

> "Candidates interact and work with candidates from diverse ethnic racial, gender and socioeconomic groups in professional education courses on campus and in schools. Candidates from diverse ethnic, racial, gender and socioeconomic groups work together on committees and education projects related to education and the content areas. The affirmation of the values of diversity is shown through good-faith efforts made to increase or maintain candidate diversity."

Many institutions find the issue of Diversity to be a major obstacle due to many factors including geography, history, purpose, and programs. In addition, the wording raises many questions regarding how precisely a teacher education program may be evaluated under this Standard. Diversity is, of course, a very important and necessary goal to pursue and the vast majority of institutions that struggle with this Standard have many programs, plans and efforts in place to increase their diversity among students, staff and faculty. But, many face far greater obstacles than others in achieving high levels of diversity and, yet, the implementation of Standard Four often paints all institutions with the same brush.

Resources

The new NCATE Standards require a great deal from institutions that seek to maintain accreditation. All of the details about the demands of the new Standards cannot be given here. For many teacher educators the new Standards are demanding to such a degree that they must seriously consider whether NCATE accreditation is a feasible goal, given their current resources. Preparation for accreditation or reaccredidation must begin years in advance as data is collected, aggregated and disaggregated, summarized and analyzed to demonstrate the performance of teacher candidates. In addition, faculties must prepare assessment instruments to collect needed data, as well as develop these instruments from a conceptual base upon which each teacher education faculty member has agreed.

Often it is necessary to employ the equivalent of one fulltime faculty person and at least part of the workload of a support staff person in order to coordinate and insure the successful completion of the accreditation or reaccredidation process. Some programs also add the professional services of others, such as the services of a graduate assistant or two.

The need for a faculty person to direct the NCATE preparation comes from the volume of effort that NCATE accreditation requires. The faculty person who directs NCATE preparation coordinates and assembles the work of all teacher education faculties. More specifically, all faculty persons who teach, advise, or otherwise offer academic services to teacher education candidates must be involved in several ways, including ongoing self assessment of their teaching, contributing to the development and maintenance of Web sites, documentation of all advising sessions, active participation in the development of conceptual frameworks, and much more. The volume of work that is involved in these things, and others, places extraordinary demands on faculty and staff that were not nearly as large under the old NCATE Standards.

Whether one person or two or more persons direct(s) the NCATE accrediting preparation, it is not a one-person enterprise. NCATE requires the participation of many individuals on every campus. Virtually every program professional who has a role in teacher education is expected to participate in the ongoing NCATE accreditation preparation. These include educators in colleges of education, along with educators in the content fields.

Homogenization (Standardization) of Teacher Education

Historically, NCATE has been politically powerful as the sole voice and face of accreditation in teacher education. This has produced a sameness, a blandness, to teacher education programs that has limited creativity and flexibility. As a reaction to this the Teacher Education Accreditation Council (TEAC) was launched as a fledgling alternative some five years or so years ago. TEAC was instituted as a response to many of NCATE's policies and practices, proposing a different approach to accreditation. NCATE's historical power ushered in almost immediate alterations to TEAC's plan. Each is now more like the other, and there no longer exists a clearly differentiated alternative. The similarities that now exist reinforce the quality of homogenization. While TEAC proposes that teacher education programs may tell who they are and present themselves in context, the call to document, assess and quantify the picture has produced specifications that are now remarkably like NCATE's.

Conclusion

Many teacher education programs have found they lack the resources to meet NCATE's accreditation standards without draining resources from, and thus damaging, ongoing programs. This puts many institutions in a kind of "Catch 22." The drain on resources can negatively impact existing programs and services, yet the loss of NCATE accreditation can cause the institution to suffer great harm in reputation, and it can hurt the recruitment and retention of students. Loss of NCATE accreditation can also hurt in other ways:

- Recruiting faculty would be measurably more difficult.
- Applying for and receiving grant funds for teacher education research and service or for professional education in general would become virtually impossible.
- Graduates of teacher education programs would face obstacles to securing employment as teachers.
- Collaboration with teacher education programs that have NCATE accreditation would be more difficult.
- Participation in major, influential professional associations would be lost.
- Graduates would face unique obstacles in being admitted to graduate programs.

No one questions that teacher education programs need to be quality programs or that it is difficult to determine what a "quality program" really is. No one questions that states, through their designated state agencies, have a right to investigate teacher education programs to ensure they are, in fact, "quality programs." And no one doubts that the process by which teacher education programs are evaluated requires some careful consideration of "assessment"—a consideration that automatically entails creating some vision or understanding of what a "quality teacher education program" looks like.

There is, however, some room for debate about whether or not it is good that so many teacher education programs—and now so many states—look to NCATE for the measure of whether or not their teacher education programs are, indeed, "quality programs." Likewise, there is no room for debate about how teacher educators and a whole mass of university personnel can become hysterical, or nearly hysterical, when faced with preparing for an NCATE visit. Flexibility in standards and how those standards are met must be a key feature of any accreditation system. A 'one-size fits all" approach is not fair to teacher education programs and does not accurately reflect the unique and individual features of those programs that allow them to meet the needs of their constituents.

Moderation must also be practiced in terms of the types and quantity of data required to document compliance with NCATE Standards, and how those data are reported. The process of obtaining and maintaining data is obscuring the original purpose of the accountability process. That purpose, at one time, was a noble one, to provide teacher education programs with a mechanism to evaluate and monitor their own quality and effectiveness and to document that quality for their public. Now, however, this noble purpose is at risk of becoming a good idea gone bad.

References

Alexander, F. (2000). The changing face of accountability. *The Journal of Higher* Education, 71, (4), 411-431.

Barnet, R. (1992). *Improving higher education: Total quality care.* London: The Society For Research into Higher Education and the Open University.

Berdahl, R. (1990). Academic freedom, autonomy, and accountability in British Universities. *Studies In Higher Education, 15,* 169-180.

Boland, H. (1999). Creating CHEA: Building a new national organization on Accrediting. The Journal of Higher Education, 70(4), 357-388.

Cowen, R. (1996). *The evaluation of higher education systems.* London, England: Kogan Page.

Dill, D. & Sporn, B. (1995). *Emerging patterns of social demand and university reform: Through a glass darkly.* Oxford, England: International Association of Universities and Pergamon Press.

Dillon, T. (1995). Coming after U. Why colleges should fear the accrediting cartel. *Policy* Review, 72, 39-42.

Eaton, J. (2001). Regional accreditation reform: Who is served? *Change, 33,*(2), 38-45.

Eicher, J. (1998). The cost of financing higher education in Europe, *European Journal of Education, 33,* 31-33.

Raywid, M. (2002). Accountability: What's worth measuring? *Phi Delta Kappan, 83*(6), 433-436.

Samaras, A., Francis, S., & Holt, Y. (1999). Lived experiences and reflections of joint NCATE-state reviews. *The Teacher Educator, 35*(1), 68-83.

Southern Regional Education Board. (2000, February). *Linking higher education performance to goals.* Atlanta, GA.

Wellman, J. (2001). Assessing state accountability systems. *Change, 33*(2), 46-52.

Professors in K–12 Classrooms:
Rewards, Risks, and Recommendations
John D. Hoge and Charles Jenks

Guiding questions:

1. What motivates professors to reimmerse themselves is school classrooms?
2. What are the advantages and disadvantages of professors' reimmersion in school classrooms.

Professors in K–12 Classrooms:
Rewards, Risks, and Recommendations
John D. Hoge and Charles Jenks

Context of K–12 Teaching Reimmersion

Since the mid 1980s there has been a "... vigorous and expanding literature that fortifies the already robust consensus about the negative influence of education schools" (Labaree, 1996, p.28). One approach to addressing the attack on schools of education was the formation of the Holmes Group, which promoted teacher education reform in three major areas—the professionalization of teaching, the development of school-university partnerships, and the transformation of schools of education (Lanier, et al. 1995). The university-school partnership model has been adopted in many colleges of education across the country, most often taking the form of Professional Development Schools (PDS) (Bullough, Hobbs, Kauchak, Crow, & Stokes, 1997; Darling-Hammond, 1994; Levine & Trachman, 1997). Another approach to collaboration is represented by the growing numbers of college of education professors who are individually negotiating the teaching of a single class, a semester, or a yearlong exchange in a public school (Baumann 1995b; Collins, 1997; Cuban, 1990; Elliott, 1993 Manera & Cropper, 1980; Morris, 1978). The first author voluntarily initiated a yearlong employment exchange with an experienced 5th grade teacher. He taught her heterogeneous class of 24 5th grade students in a suburban P-5 elementary school for an entire year, while she assumed his undergraduate teacher education duties. The second author experienced a classroom teaching reimmersion due to his university's PDS agreement. His experience included teaching field-based elementary social studies methods classes in two elementary schools. His pre-service teachers left the methods class and spent three hours a day in an intensive, hands-on field experience, where they were expected to apply the ideas and teaching strategies. To lend credibility to his work, the second author frequently taught demonstration lessons in the schools' elementary and secondary classrooms.

We believe that the essence of any authentic K–12 classroom teaching reimmersion experience, regardless of its context or duration, resides in taking full responsibility for the learning of a group of students under the natural, real-world conditions experienced by practicing teachers. Consequently, we restrict our discussion to experiences where the education professor essentially stands in for a K-12 classroom teacher, a situation that was the case for both authors. Such reimmersion experiences might be limited in time to as little as two weeks of teaching and restricted in scope to a single subject or a single class of students. Reimmersions that are more extensive might last an entire year and carry the full responsibilities of a typical classroom teacher. Although our experiences essentially laid at both ends of this continuum, we discovered that the rewards and risks associated with our efforts differed more in degree than in type.

This article summarizes the rewards and risks to professors that result from a K–12 classroom teaching experience. It concludes with a set of three practical recommendations for professors who are considering or being urged to take part in any type of K–12 classroom teaching reimmersion.

Rewards of Reimmersion

Successfully completing any form of K-12 classroom teaching reimmersion proves that you still have what it takes to teach young people using the content and methods employed by most teachers. Simply knowing that you made it through the experience may be enough to bolster your self-concept and enhance your image as a professor who is proficient in the real world classroom. In addition, a professor who has recently succeeded in a K–12 teaching reimmersion gains greater ability to exercise the professional educator's right and responsibility to advance criticisms of the systems of which he or she has recently been a successful part.

Of course, your stature as a capable, classroom-savvy teacher educator may be increased in your K-12 teacher colleague's eyes, too. As a result, these practicing professionals may be more receptive to receiving your future student teachers and collaborating on future writing and research projects. Their approval of your teaching performance may also translate into positive comments in front of other teachers and thus help to elevate the status of the entire teacher preparation program and the university as a whole. Some of these teachers may decide that they would like pursue advanced degrees, and, in a few years, it may be possible that the students you taught in your reimmersion experience will show up in your college's teacher education program. Such rewards are difficult to quantify, but we believe they are substantial since a high value is often attached to such webs of association with the local education community. In the end, successfully completing a K–12 teaching reimmersion will doubtlessly engender the respect of your present college students and many of your university colleagues.

Beyond such purely intrinsic rewards lies a goldmine of freshly acquired, first-hand anecdotes that may be used to illustrate your future teacher training instruction. Anecdote-based story telling is a stock and trade of virtually all teacher educators. Stories, however, age in their cultural and technological contexts. The important details that bring anecdotes to life also fade along with our other memories, making them less compelling as the years go by. Thus, gaining first-hand, thoroughly modern anecdotes is a significant benefit to any teacher educator.

It is entirely possible, of course, that your reimmersion experience will provide data for the investigation of questions related to your ongoing research interests (see, for example, Ball & Rundquist, 1993; Hudson-Ross, & McWorter, 1997). Illustrating for students the importance of theory and research is one of the most difficult tasks for all teacher educators. A reimmersion experience provides an excellent venue for pursuing research interests while obtaining practical examples of how students' learning is related to the ongoing professional dialog regarding popular educational trends and realities. Reducing the schism between theory, research, and practice is one of the most important potential benefits of reimmersion. Indeed, the potential for collaborative research was an often-discussed purpose of the PDS model (Holms Group 1986; Book, 1996) though it is clear that substantial difficulties surround the achievement of this outcome (Bullough, et. al., 1999; Book, 1996; Higgins & Merickel, 1997). Research based on a professor's classroom reimmersion experiences will carry the strength of having been a participant observer whose work in close association with classroom teachers holds a great potential for improving our understanding of education and effecting change in our schools.

Risks of Reimmersion

While the rewards of a reimmersion experience are varied and significant, the risks associated with these experiences may prove to be substantial. The risks associated with a K-12 classroom teaching reimmersion fall into three broad categories; instructional failure, loss of involvement in the department/college, and decreased professional productivity. We focus mainly on the shared elements of risk associated with both short- and long-term reimmersions but include comments about unique risks that come from different types of K-12 classroom teaching experiences.

Perhaps the most threatening risk of reimmersion is the very real prospect of instructional failure during your K-12 classroom teaching experience. Instructional failures involve such things as worksheets that are too difficult, directions and demonstrations that prove to be inadequate, and not assiduously monitoring your students' classroom behavior. At a more threatening level, are you, for example, prepared to deal with a classroom fight that results in an injury or an arrest? Are you willing to take responsibility for the absent student you failed to report who is caught cutting class? And, can you defend yourself against charges that a student's low test scores were due to your poor teaching practices? Clearly, these are just a few of the many threatening instructional failure risks you are exposed to as a stand-in classroom teacher. If it has been more than a few years since you've been in the K–12 classroom, these risks are increased if you have trouble in reactivating your hard-won grade-level-specific teaching skills and adjusting to the demands of today's students (Ciscell, 1993). If your presence in the K–12 classroom is the result of a PDS collaboration and your instructional difficulties are observed by your methods students, the consequences of such failures could be far reaching indeed. In the end, you must realistically consider the possibility of a variety of instructional failures and balance this risk against your level of public and professional exposure.

Of course if you have committed to a long-term teaching reimmersion and you manage to last only weeks or just barely make it through the first grading period, how will you explain this failure to colleagues, students, and others? If your premature departure is the result of parents' complaints, school administrators' decisions, or some particularly egregious incident, the embarrassment could be difficult to professionally survive. Plans that have been made to cover your university responsibilities will have to be abruptly changed. The school system will have to quickly move to find a more competent K–12 classroom teacher for the students you have left behind. Whether true or not, the stories and gossip surrounding such a failure will potentially do great harm.

Related to the topic of substantial instructional failures is the increased exposure you will have to lawsuits. Today's classroom teachers and public school administrators are keenly aware of this threat and do many things to reduce their exposure to lawsuits. The fact that you are a university professor, instead of inspiring confidence, may increase parents' sensitivity to instructional anomalies or any other departure from their commonplace conceptions of normal school procedures. In fact, your doctor's degree and membership in the teacher training profession makes you substantially more suspect of malfeasance than any other teacher. This is so not only because the teacher education profession is widely blamed in the popular press for a variety of K–12 educational fads and failures (Labaree, 1996), but also because your motives for undertaking an active role in a school classroom are, bluntly put, questionable. Parents may develop a number of suspicions ranging from the belief that you are teaching in the K–12 classroom because you couldn't make it in the college classroom, to the unpleasant sensation that their children are being put under a microscope for hidden research purposes, to fears that you are a pedophile. Needless to say, such veiled--and sometimes not so veiled--suspicions are unnerving. In the end, a necessary defense against groundless allegations and false complaints may significantly disrupt your work and eventually jeopardize your job.

The second area of risk related to a K-12 teaching reimmersion reflects the old adage "out of sight, out of mind." That is, when you are essentially out of the department/college for a good part of the normal 8 to 5 workday it is easy to be unintentionally excluded from day-to-day decisions. This is especially the case when your colleagues are not similarly involved in field-based activities. Unavoidable or unintentional exclusions may result from your inability to attend department or college/university level committee meetings, and they include such things as staying up-to-date with changes in the codes for the copy machine and building security system, meeting deadlines for ordering next semester's textbooks, putting materials on reserve, scheduling computer labs, and staying up to date with changes in computer resources. Related to these problems is the fact that a long-term reimmersion may still, despite ongoing efforts to infuse modern technology into K–12 classrooms, incur a dramatic reduction in access to a private, unrestricted telephone use and convenient e-mail service. As a result, communication with university colleagues and departmental staff may become infrequent and predominately characterized by episodes of "phone tag" answering machine messages.

A third and significant area of risk associated with reimmersion centers around its potential to decrease your productivity in research activity and professional writing. This is so because the time and energy required for these tasks are likely to be in extremely short supply during an intensive K–12 teaching reimmersion. The strain on your time and energy may make it difficult to adequately prepare for previously-scheduled conference presentations. Similar difficulties may arise in meeting your obligations to doctoral students, university committees, activities associated with research grants, and on-going publication commitments.

Recommendations

Based on our own work and a careful reading of the emerging literature on the risks and rewards of reimmersion experiences (see, for example, Baumann 1995a 1995b;

Kochan, 1996; Tom, 1998), we believe that professors who are considering a K–12 reimmersion teaching experience should carefully consider a number of issues that arise from this type of endeavor. Working through the following recommendations will help ensure that they receive the best pay off from their investment of time and effort.

Recommendation #1: Negotiate the terms of your experience. Without doubt, the most important recommendation we can make is that you negotiate the terms of your K–12 teaching experience with your department head and other faculty. Negotiations with the department head should include a realistic and explicit delineation of the expected outcomes to be gained from your reimmersion. The value you and your department head attach to these outcomes should be clearly stated and perhaps even equated to other typical products and outcomes of professor's on-campus work. For example, if you specify that your reimmersion will result in a collection of anecdotes suitable for teacher training use, will these be considered equivalent to some other form of course improvement work such as adding a new collection of journal articles to augment the reading lists for your classes? This negotiation of expected credit for clearly defined outcomes helps protect you against having your experience undervalued in decisions regarding raises, promotion, and tenure. Shive (1988) was among the first to sound this alarm when he noted, "Given the demands on professors to conduct research, innovative teaching practices [performed in a field-based PDS methods course] may not have brought rewards commensurate with the time and effort invested" (p. 76). More recently, Tassell (1999) reported research that substantially corroborates this problem.

Another aspect of negotiation with your department head may be a reduction of your existing departmental duties. In negotiating this aspect of your reimmersion experience it is critical that you make provisions to retain those parts of your professional practice you consider being keys to your maintenance of status in the department, college, and among professional colleagues. For example, it may be better to be given a release from an undergraduate course that you have taught for many years as opposed to giving up a recently-acquired doctoral level seminar or some very important committee assignments. Generally speaking, your internal guidelines for promotion, tenure, and annual review can inform your decisions regarding what to forego and what you should seek to maintain during your K–12 reimmersion.

Negotiations with colleagues may be important, too. For example, you may need to clarify access to instructional materials such as videotapes that you need to use while teaching out in the K–12 school. Will the materials temporarily be located in the K–12 school, or can they be carried about in your vehicle? Will colleagues be invited into your classes in the K–12 school for collaborative research purposes, and, if so, how will such access be controlled? When the products of this collaboration reach their audience, will you be appropriately credited? Finally, is there an expectation that your work in the K–12 school will result in materials that all of your colleagues may use? If so, what tradeoffs are being made by these individuals? Are they contributing anything to help in your reimmersion experience?

Depending upon the duration and depth of your reimmersion experience, it will also be essential to negotiate, no doubt more gently, your duties in the K–12 classroom. Will your teaching assignment require you to call parents, attend PTA/O, participate in staff meetings, contribute to holiday program activities, stay after school with students, go on a senior trip, or make other contributions of time that go beyond the classroom? Being clear about all aspects of your reimmersion may help you avoid time-draining tasks that hold little pay off for the outcomes you negotiated with your department head.

A final but no less essential aspect of pre-experience negotiations for a long term K–12 teaching experience is reconciling potential conflicts over sick leave, vacations, teacher planning days, compensation for substitutes, and what will happen if you become unable to carry out the terms of your reimmersion. What happens, for example, if you get the flu and simply cannot function for several days? What happens if your university's spring break fails to coincide with the school's? Will you work through both weeks? Negotiations over these matters are obviously more important for broad-scope, long-term reimmersion experiences and especially in cases where the K–12 teacher and the professor exchange work assignments for a substantial amount of time. Failure to consider these potentials can result in strained relationships and many other negative consequences.

Recommendation #2: Limit the depth and duration of your experience. Unless teaching K–12 classes is your special cup of tea, we believe it is wise to limit your experience to the minimum necessary to achieve your negotiated goals. For example, if teaching one class for a six week grading period is sufficient to produce many of the outcomes you seek, you should teach no more. Teaching more can only reduce your productivity at the university and it will most certainly increase your exposure to the risks that go with all reimmersion experiences. Obviously, being clear about your goals and objectives for the reimmersion experience is essential to deciding how much K–12 teaching is enough, but our recommendation is to do only the amount that is essential to your negotiated outcomes. Doing more only makes sense if you are unable to achieve the intended outcomes in the originally defined scope of the reimmersion experience or, alternatively, if you are able to successfully negotiate a mutually valued expanded set of outcomes that requires more instructional time in the K–12 classroom.

Recommendation #3: Secure written university and school district approvals for your specific reimmersion experience. This recommendation includes obtaining the necessary university Institutional Review Board research with human subjects clearances and the district's research approval process as well as waivers and releases for disclosure of students' voices, images, and work products as they will be used in presentations, publications, or other contexts such as future university classes. It is prudent to assume that parents, fellow K–12 teachers, and building level administrators will be highly interested in knowing exactly how they will be represented in any anecdote, video-vignette, workshop, article, or other outcome product you envision. Professional ethics and prevailing practices surrounding copyright laws will impinge on your ability to use the first-hand material you gather as a result of your experience. In this regard it is clear that everyone involved in your reimmersion experience will object to and resist being portrayed in a negative way--even when that portrayal is entirely accurate and completely forgivable. Imagine, for example, that you are videotaping a class when, unexpectedly, a student is caught misbehaving. From a purely detached instructional standpoint such material may be extremely useful in your teacher education classes. However, can you ethically and legally use it? Have the individuals signed releases for the use of their voices, images, and other representations? This is an especially significant issue if you plan to use materials that could potentially allow others to establish the identities of those who are portrayed.

Conclusion

Our experiences demonstrated that the rewards and risks of a K–12 teaching reimmersion are potentially substantial. The intrinsic rewards of reimmersion are vitally important and they may be substantially augmented by the many potentials reimmersions hold for improved teacher education within your department and college. The risks of reimmersion may be controlled or reduced by limiting the scope and duration of the K–12 teaching experience and by taking the steps needed to secure proper approval for your activities. Negotiating the value of your activities and the products that come from them are essential to securing adequate rewards from your reimmersion experience.

References:

Ball, D. L. & Rundquist, S. S. (1993). Collaboration as a context for joining teacher learning with learning about teaching. In D. K. Cohen, M. W. McLaughlin, & J. E. Talbert (Eds.), *Teaching for understanding: Challenges for policy and practice.* (pp. 13 42). San Francisco: Jossey-Bass.

Baumann, J. F. (1995a). 180 days in second grade: Knowing and growing together. NRRC News. September. 1-3Baumann, J. F. (1995b). Sabbatical in second grade: Reflecting on the lived experience. In C. K. Kinzer, K. Hinchman, & D. J. Leu (Eds.), *Forty-fourth yearbook of the National Reading Conference.* Chicago: National Reading Conference.

Book, C. L. (1996). Professional development schools. In T. Buttery & E. Guyton (Eds.) 2nd ed. *Handbook of research on teacher education.* 194-210.

Bullough, R. V., Jr., Birrell, J. R., Young, J., Clark, D. C., Erickson, L., Earle, R. S., Campbell, J. F., Hansen, L., Egan, M. W. (1999). Paradise unrealized: Teacher educators and the costs and benefits of school/university partnerships. *Journal of Teacher Education.* 50, 381-390.

Bullough, R.V., Jr., Hobbs, S. F., Kauchak, D. P., Crow, N. A., & Stokes, D. (1997). Long-term PDS development in research universities and the clinicalization of teacher education. *Journal of Teacher Education*, 48, 85-95.

Ciscell, R. (1993). Who's teaching America's teachers? *Educational Leadership*, 50 (6) 14-15.

Collins, M. L. (1997). Imperatives for teacher education faculty in higher education. *Action in Teacher Education*, 19, 47-54.

Cuban, L. (1990). What I learned from what I had forgotten about teaching: Notes from a professor. *Phi Delta Kappan*, 71, 479-482.

Darling-Hammond, L. (ed.) (1994). *Professional development schools. Schools for a developing profession.* New York: Teachers College Press.

Elliott, T. J. (1993). Back in the classroom. *Educational Leadership*, 51, 28-30.

Higgins, K. M. & Merickel, M. L. (1997). The promise and the promises: Partnerships from a university perspective. *Teacher Educator.* 32, 165-184.

Hudson-Ross, S., & McWorter, P. (1997). *Findings from a yearlong job exchange: A mentor teacher's bill of rights in teacher education.* Reading Research Report No. 74. (ERIC Document: ED402559)

Kochan, F. K. (1996). *Problems, solutions, and benefits of professional development schools as perceived by university faculty.* ERIC Document: ED404937.

Labaree, D. F. (1996). The trouble with ed schools. *Educational Foundations.* 10 (3), 27 - 45.

Lanier, J. T; Maeroff, G. I.; Brown, C. E.; Sykes, G.; Murray, F. B.; Barnes, H.; Judge, H.; & Wagstaff, L. (1995). *Tomorrow's schools of education.* (A report of the Holmes Group.) 201 Erickson Hall, East Lansing, Michigan, 48824-1034.

Levine, M. & Trachtman, R. (1997). *Making professional development schools work: Politics, practice and policy.* New York: Teachers College Press.

Manera, E. S. & Cropper, A. P. (1980). Back to the classroom: An invitation to professional renewal. *The NASSP Bulletin* 64 (433) 20 - 24.

Morris, J. E. (1978). Hey, man! Who you is? Conflicts between the sanctuary and the marketplace. *The Clearing House*, 51 375 - 379.

Shive, R. J. (1988). An experimental model for clinical experiences. A social studies preservice preparation program. *The Social Studies*, 79 (2) 74 - 77.

Tassell, F. V. (1999). Policy impact on professional development schools when faculty and administrator views conflict regarding the university reward system. *Action in Teacher Education*. 21(2), 1-7.

Tom, A. R. (1998). *Professional development schools and the destabilization of faculty work*. ERIC Document. ED420297.

One Size Does Not Fit All: Designing Classrooms for All Students
Jerry Whitworth

Guiding Questions

1. Why is curriculum modification so essential in the inclusive classroom?

2. Why do so many general education teachers have such a difficult time with curriculum modification?

3. What is the most important element in the success of curriculum modification?

One Size Does Not Fit All: Designing Classrooms for All Students
Jerry Whitworth

Within the last decade the numbers of students with disabilities in the general education classroom has escalated dramatically. There are many reasons for this escalation. Increasing emphasis on the least restrictive environment provisions of the Individuals with Disabilities Act (IDEA), along with mounting litigation by parents and advocates, have been pointed out as leading factors (Oberti v. Board of Education of Clementon School District; Holland v. Sacramento City Unified School District; Mavis ex rel. Mavis v. Sobol; Daniel R.R. v. El Paso; Osborne and Dimattia, 1994). There is also a growing body of research demonstrating the ineffectiveness of the old pull-out model for special education, as well as the development of effective instructional strategies for teaching students with disabilities in the regular classroom disabilities (Will, 1986; Affleck, Madge, Adams, and Lowenbraum, 1988; Semmel, Gottlieb, and Robinson, 1979; Banerji and Daily, 1995; Bishop, 1995; Davis, 1995). At any rate, this trend to serve students with special needs in general education classrooms along side their non-disabled peers has become part of the fabric of our current system of public education.

This change in how and where we teach children with special needs is requiring close planning and collaboration among and between general education and special education teachers and support personnel. Yet, regardless of the amount of time spent planning, or the degree of collaboration among school personnel, inclusion will not be successful for individual students unless teachers and support staff master the skills of curriculum and instructional modification.

This is something with which not all teachers feel comfortable. General education teachers, in particular, may have difficulties in adapting curriculum for special needs learners, as this is not a skill often taught in preservice teacher preparation programs. Since the traditional model of mainstreaming is based on the premise that students with disabilities must "earn" their way into a classroom to receive instruction largely without adaptations and support, teachers may have a limited understanding of how to work with other professionals to adapt instruction. This inexperience may cause teachers to doubt their own abilities to work with diverse students and result in initial negative feelings toward including children with disabilities in the general education classroom.

There are various ways that school personnel can adapt the classroom, as well as their curriculum, for special needs students. Teachers report rearranging rooms so that all activities are accessible to students in wheelchairs, redeploying therapists so that they all deliver their instruction in the general classroom, and making things that are "visual" tactile for students who are blind. Early childhood and elementary teachers report setting aside a half hour each day to work on IEP objectives that aren't addressed in other classroom activities. Middle school and high school teachers report setting aside one afternoon a week for lab time when students can come for extra help.

An important aspect of curriculum modification is careful planning beforehand, keeping in mind the IEP's of the individual students who will be in the general education classroom. There are some basic steps that might be useful in guiding this process. Write lesson plans and then ask the following questions:

1. What is the class expected to do?
2. What can the students with disabilities do?
3. Can the students do the lesson as is?
4. Can the students do the lesson with different materials?
5. What level of adaptation is needed for students with disabilities?

There are several reasons why curriculum modification can be problematic for some teachers and some classrooms. The need for training is certainly a big issue. So is the educational paradigm of many teachers that says all students in a classroom must be working on the same thing, at the same time, in the same way, for the same reason. It is important that teachers and support staff change that paradigm. There are actually a number of levels on which students can be working in the same classroom. They can:

- Work on the same task with the same materials (no adaptations needed);
- Work on the same task, but an easier step;
- Work on the same task, but with different materials;
- Work on the same theme (objective), but a different task;
- Work on a different theme, and a different task.

Remember: School personnel should focus on what the student CAN do, not what he/she can't do. Also, modify, adapt, and accommodate before changing the activity. Use the least obtrusive support first, and always use age-appropriate materials, goals and activities.

A teacher attempting to modify and adapt curriculum and/or instruction for a student with special needs may find it useful to ask the following questions as part of the planning process.

1. Can the student do the same activity at the same level as peers? e.g. Spelling

IF NOT

2. Can the student do the same activity but with adapted expectations? e.g. Less words.

IF NOT

3. Can the student do the same activity but with adapted expectations and materials? e.g. Matching the words to pictures.

IF NOT

4. Can the student do a similar activity but with adapted expectations? e.g. Words that are functional and in the student's daily environment.

IF NOT

5. Can the student do a similar activity but with adapted materials? e.g. Computer spelling program.

IF NOT

6. Can the student do a different, parallel activity? e.g. Learn a computer typing program, learn word processing with a spell checker, write or put pictures in a journal.

IF NOT

7. Can the student do a different activity in a different section of the room? e.g. Water the plants, file for the teacher.

IF NOT

8. Can the student do a functional activity in another part of the school? e.g., Help the librarian, office staff, coach, kitchen workers to perform duties.

Remember that not all students learn the same thing, in the same way, at the same time, and that is OK. The emphasis should be on the student's IEP goals and how those goals could be addressed within the general education setting. The following scenario may help to clarify this.

Kathy is in an eighth grade math class in which she works on the goals in her IEP while participating with classmates in activities within the general education classroom. Her learning objectives in math are addressed through a variety of activities. She counts out the papers her teacher needs for the class and then hands them out when requested. This addresses the IEP goal of improving her ability to use numbers. Kathy is also the timekeeper for the class, reminding her classmates when activities are to be completed and helping keep them on task. In small problem-solving groups, Kathy participates, and her responsibility is addition and subtraction facts under ten. She often uses a calculator to check her classmates' computations on class projects. While other students are working independently at their desks, Kathy works on the classroom computer using software selected by her special education teacher. Kathy also works on the goal of reading her classmates' names since it is her responsibility to hand back papers once they are graded.

When planning how to address the goals of a student such as Karen in the general education classroom consider using the following adaptations:

- Same task, same materials (no adaptations needed)
- Same task, easier step
- Same task, different materials
- Same theme, different task
- Different theme, different task (maximum adaptation; parallel activity)

There are many ways that a classroom teacher can modify and adaptive curriculum and instruction for the special needs student as illustrated by the diagram below.

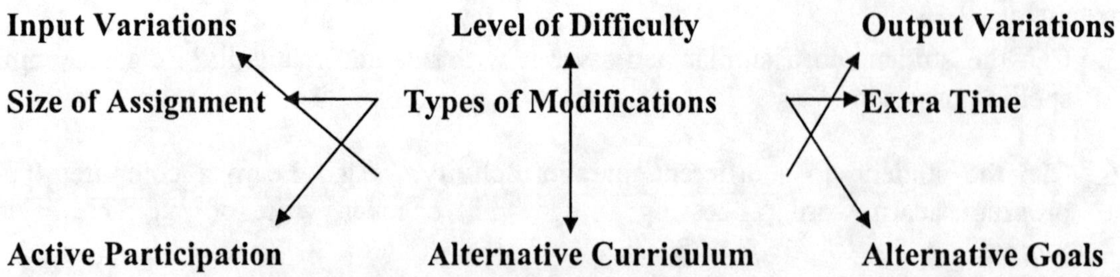

An important aspect of planning for students with disabilities involves the integration of services. In the past, various services to students (i.e. speech, physical, and occupational therapies, counseling, social skills training, etc.) were fragmented, and provided in isolation. These professionals would develop their own goals and objectives for a student with little attempt at coordination or collaboration.

When planning a student's program in the general education setting remember to integrate all of the services being provided toward the same objectives. Instead of the speech therapist having his/her objectives, the physical therapist having his or her objectives, and the teacher having his/her objectives, remember that the objectives are the student's. The job of the professionals is to help the student achieve those objectives.

Hence, one of a student's objectives might be "to use the computer to complete English assignments for class." In this situation every professional might have a role in helping the student achieve this objective; the special education teacher, the general education teacher, the language therapist, and the physical and/or occupational therapist.

Instructional and Curricular Adaptations

Below are some suggestions to use when adapting classroom curriculum and instruction for a student with disabilities. Not all of these would be appropriate to use with all students, of course. However, they will help provide some ideas as your team works through this process for an individual student. Keep these suggestions in mind as you plan for your students with special needs.

I. Adapting Instruction
   A. Modify Expectations/Goals
      1. Target fewer objectives
      2. Change objectives
      3. Modify mastery levels
   B. Modify Lesson/Unit - Partial Participation, student is involved in relevant part of instructional process
      1. Adapt materials
      2. Multilevel curriculum
      3. Curriculum overlapping
      4. Substitute curriculum
   C. Change the classroom environment or lesson location to facilitate participation.
      1. Environmental/Physical

2. Social
3. Lesson location (move the lesson for all students to another location that will allow the special needs student(s) to participate)

D. Provide for Community-Based Instruction Plan Parallel Experiences (a trip to the Public Library where one student practices bus skills while another student completes research assignment)

E. Create learning experiences that teach a diversity of skills to all students

II. ADAPTING THE INSTRUCTION

A. Providing People Supports
1. Special Education teacher/Aide
2. Peers

B. Providing Adaptive Materials & Devices
1. Modified objectives
2. Modified materials (e.g., pictorial vs. written instructions)
3. Assistive devices (e.g., calculators, tape recorders)
4. Computers (hardware and software)

C. Providing instructional support
1. Partner activities
2. Cooperative groups
3. Writing workshops
4. Whole Language
5. Individualized math & writing folders
6. Rotating groups - decentralize teacher - Centers/Stations
7. Individualized task completion schedule
8. Computer remediation - computer assisted instruction
9. Whole language - listening, verbal or augmentative expression, writing, & reading (words, pictures, other symbols)
10. Games
11. Cues & directions (e.g., pictorial)

D. Modifying Instructional Presentations
1. Skill sequence
2. Motivation/reinforcement
3. Adjust pacing
4. Same content, but less complex
5. Schedule related subjects (e.g., money at math time) and include peers
6. Rotating groups
7. Use small time blocks - 1 hour can be four 15 minute time blocks
8. Supportive seating arrangements
9. Supportive environmental design
10. Bring a friend or peer in the community

<u>Typical Methods for Modifying an Academic Task</u>

There are a number of strategies that the classroom teachers (general and special education) can use to modify academic tasks for students with mild disabilities. A number of these are listed below. However, it is important to remember that this list is not intended to be exhaustive and teachers should continually be searching for additional methods and approaches for helping students with special needs succeed in the regular classroom.

- Reduce the number of problems/sentences.
- Tape record material for students to listen to as they read along.
- Read tests aloud to the student.
- Make a bright construction paper border for the student to place around reading material in order to maintain his/her attention to the task.
- Make a reading window from construction paper which the student places over sentences or paragraphs in order to maintain attention.
- Provide manipulative objects for the student.
- Provide assistive devices - calculators, tape recorder, computers.
- Use graph paper for math problems, handwriting.
- Have peers deliver directions or explanations.
- Allow more time to take tests or quizzes.
- Use one-on-one tutorials.
- Use classroom aides and note takers.

Study Guides

Study guides are tools teachers can use to lead students through a reading assignment. A typical study guide is a series of questions or activities that students complete while they read a selection. As Wood, Lapp, and Flood (1992) noted, study guides should accompany reading, not follow it. Study guides help direct students to the key points to be learned. They also provide structure for students to reflect about what they are reading and to engage in higher-order thinking. In short, study guides can help "tutor" a student through a chapter.

Commercially prepared study guides can be purchased as supplements to some textbooks. The advantage of commercially prepared study guides is that they are already done. These can be real time savers. The disadvantage is that the publisher does not know your style of teaching, your emphasis, or your school district's requirements. Moreover, the publisher does not know your students. Many teachers elect to construct their own study guides.

Many types of study guides exist. Some are designed to help students activate prior knowledge, others to help students understand literal or inferential information in the textbook, others to foster peer interaction and discussion, and still others to help students recognize meaning patterns in text (e.g., cause and effect, compare and contrast). Following are some general suggestions for developing study guides.

Decide whether a guide is needed. Is textbook information particularly dense? Are there few considerate features? Will students with special needs require support and guidance to get through the chapter and to grasp the most important ideas?

Analyze the chapter. Can some parts be omitted? Are some parts easier to understand than others? What skills will your students need to read and understand this material? *Decide how you want to structure your study guide.* Create one that includes the following:

- Specific information about the reading assignment (page numbers, title)
- Learning objectives of the assignment
- Purpose statement for the assignment
- Introduction of key terms or vocabulary
- Activities for students to complete
- Questions for students to answer as they read

Adapting Textbooks

Research indicates that students at all achievement levels feel that they need textbook adaptations and are not getting the adaptations they need:
Substitute the Textbook for students who have severe word-recognition problems:

- Audiotape textbook content.
- Read textbook aloud to students.
- Pair students to master textbook content.
- Use direct experiences, films, videotapes, recorders, and computer programs as substitutes for textbook reading.
- Work with students individually or in small groups to master textbook material.

Simplify the Textbook for students whose reading level is far below that of the textbook used in class:

- Construct abridged versions of the textbook content or use the publisher's abridged version.
- Provide students with chapter outlines or summaries.
- Use a multilevel, multimaterial approach.

Highlight Key Concepts for students with difficulty comprehending text material:

- Preview reading assignments with students to orient them to the topic and provide guidelines for budgeting reading and study time.
- Provide students with a purpose for reading.
- Provide an overview of an assignment before reading.
- Structure opportunities for students to activate prior knowledge before starting a reading assignment.
- Introduce key vocabulary before assigning reading.
- Develop a study guide to direct learning.
- Summarize or reduce textbook information to guide classroom discussions and independent reading.
- Color-code or highlight textbooks.
- Reduce length of assignments.
- Slow down the pace of reading assignments.
- Provide assistance in answering text-based questions.

- Demonstrate or model effective reading strategies.
- Place students in cooperative learning groups to master textbook content.
- Teach comprehension-monitoring techniques to improve ongoing understanding of text material.
- Teach students to use graphic aids to understand textbook information.
- Increase idea retention for students who have difficulty with long-term memory.
- Structure postreading activities to increase retention of content.
- Teach reading strategies to improve retention.
- Teach students to record key concepts and terms for study purposes.
- Teach memory strategies to improve retention of text material.

Text Highlighting

Students with comprehension problems have difficulty sifting out important information. Underlining or highlighting key points in the textbooks can help students attend to the most salient information (Wood and Wooley, 1986). In reading the textbook, highlight the information you think is most important. Then student or adult volunteers can use your book as a guide to highlight the same information in books for students with reading and learning disabilities. Keep in mind that you will also want to teach students this and other textbook study skills.

Using Alternative Reading Materials

For students with very low reading skills who are able to learn by listening:
Audio-tape textbook chapters. Adult and student volunteers can read the chapters on audiotape. Students can then listen to the tapes at home or in their resource classes.
Read text aloud to students. Encourage students to follow along, reading silently. Pause frequently to assess student learning from the reading.

Pair a good reader with a poor reader. The good reader reads the textbook material aloud and, together, the two students learn the content.

Sometimes you will find it necessary to use alternative materials that present similar content. Films, videotapes, and trade books provide good sources. Computer software programs in which the text can be read by the computer, such as encyclopedias on CD-ROM, are other resources.

Developing Listener-Friendly Lectures

Since the popularity of personal computers, people have discussed software programs in terms of their "user friendliness." In other words, is the program easy to understand? Does the program use familiar language or at least define unfamiliar terms? Does the program give you cue words to signal the important ideas and processes? If you don't understand something, does the program allow you to ask questions? Does the program have more than one way to explain a difficult concept or process? If the program has these features, then it's "user friendly."

A well-organized lecture makes the students' work easier in that it assists them in seeing relationships among concepts and in distinguishing important from supplementary information. It also helps them relate new information to old. Well-designed lectures seem particularly beneficial for second language learners and for listeners with relatively limited language skills and little prior knowledge of the content because of the reduced processing burdens.

As you plan your teaching, the following guidelines can make your lectures *"listener-friendly"*:

- Use advance organizers.
- Use cue words or phrases to let students know what information is important (e.g., "It is important that you know ...," "The key information to remember is ...," "In summary").
- Repeat important information.
- Write important information on board, transparency, and handout.
- Stress key points by varying the tone and quality of your voice.
- Number ideas or points (e.g., first, second, next, then, finally).
- Write technical words or words that are difficult to spell.
- Use a study guide that lists the major concepts, with space for students to add other information.
- Use pictures, diagrams, and semantic maps to show relationships among ideas.
- Provide examples and nonexamples of the concepts you are discussing.
- Ask questions or encourage discussion that requires students to relate the new information to ideas they already know (from their own background or your previous lectures).
- Stop frequently and have students work with partners and discuss what they have learned.
- Allow time at the end of a lecture for students to look over their notes, summarize, and ask questions.

<u>Cues to Listen and Watch for in Lectures</u>

By using these guidelines as you lecture, you will naturally incorporate cues that indicate what information is important.
Organizational Cues
Today, we will be discussing...
There are (number) points I want you to be sure to learn...
The important relationship is...
The main point of this discussion is...
Any statement that signals a position (first, last, next, then)...
To review/summarize/recap ....
Emphasis Cues
<u>Verbal</u>
You need to know/understand/remember...
This is important/key/basic/critical ...

Let me repeat this ...
Let me check, now do you understand ...
Any statement is repeated...
Words or terms are emphasized...
Teacher speaks more slowly, loudly, or with more emphasis...
Teacher stresses certain words...
Teacher spells words...
Teacher asks rhetorical question...

Nonverbal
Information written on overhead/board...
Information handed out in study guide…
Teacher emphasizes point using gestures...

Audiotaping Content Area Textbooks

Students who have low reading skills or vision impairments can listen to chapters that have been audiotaped by classmates or volunteers. Students can listen to the tapes in a listening center in elementary classrooms, resource rooms, school libraries, or at home. Here are some suggestions for audiotaping reading assignments:

- Instead of recording an entire chapter verbatim, read the key sections and paraphrase the less important sections;
- Code the text so that readers or listeners will know whether the person on the tape is reading or paraphrasing;
- Provide an advanced organizer on the tape to get students ready to read & listen;
- Insert questions that readers or listeners can stop and think about;
- Remind readers/listeners to stop periodically and think about what they've read;
- Use a natural tone of voice and a comfortable rate;
- Have students experiment with taped texts to see whether they comprehend better with or without the text.

Along with books on tape the use of digitized books and text to voice software is becoming more easily available, flexible and inexpensive. Software such as the Kurzweill Reader (www.kurzweill.com) and sources such as Books for the Blind and Dyslexic (bfbd.org) can be of assistance.

Using the Pause Procedure

One technique that has demonstrated its effectiveness for students with learning and behavior problems in enhancing the understanding and recall of information presented through lectures is the pause procedure (e.g., DiVesta and Smith 1979; Ruhl, Hughes, and Schloss, 1987; Ruhl, Hughes, and Gajar, 1990). The procedure consists of pausing during natural breaks in the lectures and having students work in partners for about two minutes to discuss what they are learning and review their notes. At the end of the two minutes, ask students if they have any questions or concepts that need discussion or clarification, then resume lecturing. Using this procedure, college students with and without learning disabilities did better than listening to lectures without the pauses for discussion on both multiple-choice tests and on free recalls of the information presented (Ruhl et al., 1990).

Adapting Class Assignments and Homework

In a survey of students with and without learning disabilities in grades 1-8, the students with learning disabilities had greater difficulty completing homework assignments because of problems with attention, motivation, and study skills (Gajria and Salend, 1995). After conducting a comprehensive review of the literature, Cooper and Nye (1994) concluded that homework assignments for students with disabilities should be brief, focused on reinforcement rather than new material, monitored carefully, and supported through parental involvement.

The most important aspect of making assignments is to give complete information. Students need to know why the assignment is important, when it is due, what support they will have for completing the task, and steps necessary for getting the job done. Having complete information helps motivate students.

Class assignments and homework can be adapted for special learners so that they can experience success without undue attention being brought to their learning difficulties. The key to success is to make assignments appropriate in content, length, time required to complete, and skill level needed to accomplish the task. It is also important to explain the assignments, model several problems if appropriate, and check for understanding (Sawyer, Nelson, Jayanthi, Bursuck, and Epstein, 1996). Students should know how and where to get help when they get stuck.

Tips for Giving Assignments

1. Explain the purpose of the assignment. Stress what you expect students to learn and why learning the skill or concept is important. Connect the skill or concept to real-life applications.
2. Explain in detail the procedures for completing the assignment. Ask one or two students to summarize the procedures to check for understanding.
3. Get students started by modeling a problem or by providing an example.
4. Describe the equipment and materials needed to complete the assignment.
5. Anticipate trouble spots and ask students how they might tackle difficult parts in the assignment.
6. Explain when the assignment is due.
7. Explain how the assignment will be graded and how it will impact grades.
8. Describe appropriate ways to get help or support in completing the assignment.
9. For an in-class assignment, explain your expectations for student behavior while they complete the assignment, and what students who finish early should do.
10. Address student questions.

A Final Word

As we continue to move through the 21st Century we must insure that all of our children are well prepared to meet the challenges of a new world. One of the greatest challenges teachers will face in accomplishing this objective will be the increasing diversity we will encounter in the strengths, needs, abilities and learning styles of our students. The teachers of today, and tomorrow, must have the tools to adapt, adjust, modify and design both their curriculum and their instruction to make sure that all students succeed. That will take sound knowledge of how children learn, along with skill in many types of instructional techniques and practices. But, it will also take creativity, vision, and persistence to build inclusive classrooms for ourselves and for our students.

References

Affleck, M., Adams, and Lowenbraun. (1988). Integrated classroom versus resource model: Academic viability and effectiveness. *Exceptional Children*, 339-348.

Banerji, M. and Daily, R.A. (1995). A study of the effects of an inclusion model on students with specific learning disabilities, *Journal of Learning Disabilities*, 28(8), 511.

Bilken, D. and Zollers, N. (1986). The focus of advocacy in the LD field. *Journal of Learning Disabilities*, 19 579-586.

Davis, S. (1995). Report card on inclusion in the education of students with mental retardation, The ARC: Arlington, TX.

Daniel R.R. v. El Paso, 874 F. 2d 1036 (5th Cir. 1989).

Divesta, F. J., and Smith, D. A. (1979). The pausing principle: Increasing the efficiency of memory for ongoing events. *Contemporary Educational Psychology*, 4, 288-296.

Gajria, M. and Salend, S.J. (1995). Homework practices of students with and without learning disabilities: A comparison. In W. Bursuck (Ed.), Homework: Issues and practices for students with learning disabilities (pp.97-106). Austin, TX: Pro-Ed.

Gartner, A. and Lipsky, D.K. (1987). Beyond special education: Toward a quality system for all students. *Harvard Educational Review*, 57, 367-385.

Gartner, A. and Lipsky, D.K. (1989). The yoke of special education: How to break it. Rochester, NY: National Center on Education and the Economy.

Giangreco, M. and Putnam, J. (1991). Supporting the education of students with severe disabilities in regular education environments. In L.H. Meyer, C. Peck, and L. Brown (Eds.), *Critical issues in the lives of people with severe disabilities* (pp. 245-270). Baltimore: Paul H. Brookes.

Holland v. Sacramento City Unified School District, 18 IDLER 761, 786 F.Supp. 874 (E.D. CA, 1992).

Lilly, M.S. (1987). Lack of focus on special education in literature on educational reform. *Exceptional Children*, 53, 325-26.

Lilly, M.S. (1988). The regular education initiative: A force for change in general and special education. *Education and Training in Mental Retardation*, 23, 253-60.

Mavis ex rel. Mavis v. Sobol, 1 ECLPR 373 (N.D.N.Y. 1994).

Oberti v. Board of Education of Clementon School District 19 IDLER 423 (original) and (appeal) 19 IDLER 908 (1993) (N.N.J., 1992).

Osborne, A.G. and Dimattia, P. (1994). The IDEA's least restrictive environment mandate: Legal implications. *Exceptional Children*, 61(1), 6-14.

Ruhl, K. L., Hughes, C. A., and Gajar, A. H. (1990). Efficacy of the pause procedure for enhancing learning disabled and nondisabled college students' long- and short-term recall of facts presented through lecture. *Learning Disability Quarterly*, 13, 55-64.

Ruhl, K. L., Hughes, C.A., and Scholss, P. F. (1987). Using the pause procedure to enhance lecture recall. *Teacher Education and Special Education*, 10, 14-18.

Will, M. (1986). Educatihildren with learning problems: A shared responsibility. *Exceptional Children*, 52, 411-415.

Wood, J. W. and Wooley, J. A. (1986). Adapting textbooks. *The Clearing House*, 59, 332-335.

York-Barr, J., Schultz, T., Doyle, M.B., Kronberg, R., and Crossett, S. (1996). Inclusive schooling in St. Cloud: Perspectives on the process and people, *Remedial and Special Education*. 17(2), 92-105.

Resiliency: Helping Children to Beat the Odds
Barry Thompson and Gwen McAlpine

Guiding Questions:

1. Why is it important to use the term "Resiliency" when referring to our students?

2. What are some ideas for fostering resiliency in a student?

3. Why are the needs for "belonging and power" so difficult to meet for the marginalized student?

Resiliency: Helping Children to Beat the Odds
Barry R. Thompson and Gwen McAlpine

Americans who spend a great deal of time in the public schools are treated to seeing many wonderful and engaging learning activities taking place. Our graduates are among the best educated citizens in the world, and their resulting inventions and accomplishments continue to improve our way of life. Unfortunately, not all children succeed despite the best intentions of their teachers. Historically these children have been termed "at risk" (Haberman, 1995). Today the term marginalized is preferred as that term places the responsibility on society instead of blaming and stigmatizing the child. Marginalized children usually have at least one of these characteristics:

- They have low achievement scores
- They are frequently absent
- Their families move often
- Their families are dysfunctional
- Their parents are not involved in their school work or school event
- They are living in poverty
- They are frequently disciplined or suspended by the school
- They have a disability
- They are victims of crime or abuse
- They have language barriers
- They are teenage parents
- They drop out or are sent to alternative schools
- They are ethnic minorities
- They are English language learners (Haberman, 1995, p. 48).

Life is full of hardships and some children seem to cope better than others. These students are considered to be "resilient" (Berk, L.E., 2004). This chapter deals with the qualities of resilient and non-resilient children and ways to identify and better educate these students.

To begin, resiliency must be defined. Resiliency is the ability to adapt effectively in the face of threats to development (Berk, L.E., 2004; Garmezy & Masten, 1991). In a slightly different interpretation, Jaffe defines resiliency as "personal qualities and situational factors that allow individuals to adapt to difficult life circumstances" (1998, p. 498). These difficulties can manifest themselves in a variety of ways, e.g., through socio-economic, cultural, and familial circumstances (Haberman, 1995). According to Werner, resilient children develop coping mechanisms to overcome both biological and social risk factors (1993). Most teachers researched by the Center for Research on Education, Diversity & Excellence (CREDE) state that they can identify those students in their classes who are resilient (Padron, 2000). According to Reed et. al., resilient students display these six major traits (1995, pp. 3-10):

1. They make effective use of time
2. They create clear, long-term goals
3. They have an internal locus of control

4. They have positive role models at school, people who believe they can succeed
5. They have at least one adult role model who actively helps them succeed
6. They come from dysfunctional homes but do not attribute failure to them.

This chapter will examine these traits in terms of school success, including examples from a case study and implications for school reform. Furthermore, this chapter will consider best practice in teaching marginalized students with an emphasis on instruction in science and language arts. Best practice in other content areas, taught in an interdisciplinary and multicultural manner, will form an important feature of this chapter, too. Most instructional strategies will involve grades elementary through high school, but several strategies in this chapter will also be germane to higher education.

Basic qualities of resilient students are innate or external, according to Berk (2004). The innate characteristics include--but are not limited to--genetics, intellectual capability, and temperament. When addressing temperament, such personality traits as being flexible, sociable, and easygoing help students to deal with adversity. Usually having this temperament causes them to be popular. It also helps students to establish a social support network outside their immediate family. For example, establishing strong community ties through extracurricular activities or community organizations eliminates the need for these young people to become totally self-reliant (Berk, 2004).

There are other qualities which help eliminate the need for self-reliance. A very important trait is a warm parental relationship with at least one parent. Societal norms have shifted to a point whereby young people are often thought of as adults. Recent research indicates_that portions of the frontal lobe of the brain deal with response inhibition (Luna, et. al., 2004), and adult-level, mature performance begins in the mid teens. Because of this, teenagers may look like adults but often do not act like adults. They sometimes make decisions to do things that adults would not even consider doing. For this reason they need constant guidance, but high school teachers usually only see their students once a day for approximately one hour. It is important for the parents to fill that void by guiding their children in the decision-making process. If the students feel comfortable with at least one of their parents, they are more likely to ask for advice before making a potentially harmful choice.

There are other avenues for seeking advice outside of the family which can be beneficial and would classify as a quality of a resilient student. Resilient students tend to have strong school or community ties (Berk L.E., 2004). Often elementary teachers make the first strong connections between school and home. Typical initiatives include holding conferences with parents and family workshops (usually teaching content in math or science), language tutoring for parents, and newsletters sent home with student work and a report on school curricula. Especially effective with families of English language learners is the use of book packages in which classroom texts are translated into the family's first language and sent home (Gregory, 1996). Family members read the book together, act out the story with puppets, and play games with the words to strengthen the child's comprehension. These activities improve communication throughout the school community while bolstering children's opportunities to become resilient. At the high school level, many parents comment during parent-teacher conferences that teachers know their child better than they do. Students who have strong school ties are often involved with clubs or sports chaperoned by teachers. They are, therefore, less likely to be influenced by dangerous elements such as gangs. The school-related activities provide a support network where children can be positively influenced during the decision-making process. Furthermore, these activities provide a measure of cultural congruence between home and school, a vital element to success for learners who are culturally diverse, according to Ladson-Billings (1994). An added benefit for the schools themselves is that resilient students are much less likely to create dangerous situations in schools. In his book *Creating Safe Schools for All Children*, Duke recommends that educators investigate the situations that give rise to resiliency in order to support safe schools (2002).

Marginalized students share the same basic needs as everyone else, according to Glasser. As described in his Choice Theory, everyone is born with the same five basic needs: survival, love, power, fun, and freedom (1998, p. 46). Children enter school excited to learn and expecting to have their needs met. In primary grades, many students do have these needs met. However, by middle school, many students are having so few of their needs met that they are actually antagonistic toward their teachers, according to Glasser (1998). Slavin's assessment is bleaker still. In his view many students perceive schools as "punishing and demeaning" by the end of first grade (Slavin et. al., 1992). To change schools from an atmosphere of hostility, Glasser recommends that teachers daily seek students' input on lessons and that they manage students through competence and caring, not through coercion (1998). At the school level, he recommends involving students in extracurricular activities, meeting students' needs for fun, freedom, and power. The use of extracurricular activities to mentor and coach students, as well as the use of group work, seems effective in assisting students to become resilient, according to Reed et. al. (1995) and Haberman (1995). Glasser would agree. He has discovered that creating small learning teams throughout the school enhances the sense of power and belonging among students (1998).

Developing a caring-centered school is an important element for assisting all students to develop academic success, according to Noddings (1992) and Pang (2001). Studying middle school students in high-risk situations, Reed et. al. concluded that the creation of a supportive school environment with high expectations and caring relationships assists marginalized students to improve their academic skills (Reed et. al., 1995). Similarly, in Noddings' ethic of care philosophy, schools emphasize the formation of a caring and trusting community (1992). Pang's approach to caring-centered multicultural education begins with Noddings' ethic of care and develops it into a student-centered, democratic pedagogy. Within Pang's democratic school, students learn to treat everyone in society equitably. In addition, students receive instruction in social justice about inequalities that have existed for centuries (Pang, 2001). Teaching them social justice may help marginalized students to come to terms with their own sense of disempowerment, according to Nieto (2002). This teaching approach may also assist all students to understand the issues with the deficit model used to stigmatize minorities. As Nieto explains it, the deficit model means that marginalized groups are pitied and scorned (Nieto, 2002). This negative (deficit) attitude creates one more burden that resilient people must fight.

Clearly teachers shoulder much of the responsibility for assisting students to develop resiliency. Ladson-Billings and Haberman have conducted extensive research into the qualities of effective teachers who aid students who are culturally diverse to become successful academically. Ladson-Billings' *dreamkeeper* teachers are excellent teachers of African American children. Teaching well, according to Ladson-Billings, entails "making sure that students achieve, develop a positive sense of themselves, and develop a commitment to larger social and community concerns" (2001, p. 3). These teachers also employ anti-racist instructional strategies, assisting students to un-learn racist beliefs (2002). Haberman's *star* teachers of children in poverty have at least five years of teaching experience and consistently demonstrate excellence in problem solving and organizational skills. They also possess enough humility and humor to view themselves as fallible, qualities that make them good role models (Haberman, 1995). To Ladson-Billings and Haberman's frameworks, Au adds the concept of cultural congruence in which the school strives to create an environment that uses the knowledge and practices of the culture in which the students live (Au & Kawakami, 1994). For example, Au instructs teachers to conduct discussions by means of the same communication patterns that students are familiar with in their homes. Working with Hawaiian children, Au ran a literature discussion with overlapping conversation in which students were permitted to speak spontaneously, often speaking at the same time as other students (Au, 1993). This practice, which Hawaiians call "talk story," led students to remain on task in their learning while developing more logical responses to the assigned reading. According to CREDE, marginalized students learn more effectively in this kind of school environment. The best schools for meeting students' needs connect school materials to students' lives using a seminar approach (Echevarria, 1998). In reporting on such culturally congruent practices, Ladson-Billings noted that these schools draw on Vygotsky's theory of social constructivism in meeting academic learning goals. Hence, school environments designed to reach all students by incorporating cultural practices seem to increase all students' learning.

Conversely, students are often heard asking their teachers why they have to know certain content. This is much less likely to occur in a school that follows Glasser's Choice Theory and includes student input in determining how to meet instructional goals. Again, an effective teacher links school material to students' lives. Teachers must guide their students in making the connections between their everyday lives and the content covered in class. As Zemelman et. al. note, reports of national standards have consistently called for best practice that includes experiential learning with student choice (e.g., in their materials, teammates, or assessments) to meet students' affective needs (1998).

Moreover, P-12 students have not had enough of life's experiences in order to see the relevancy of the subject matter being addressed in most classes. One of the classic exercises in calculus is determining the volume of a shape rotated around the "X" axis. That is a very abstract concept: students only see a piece of paper, a graph, and a difficult assignment. The shape is never a rectangle, and it is not intuitive for most students to determine why this volume would be needed. A simple connection is to start with a practical application, such as asking the students how much water it would take to fill a swimming pool. This is an object with a strange shape that many of the students can picture in their minds. This is just one example of how to make a connection between abstract content and the real world. Students in every class at every age need to know why class content is relevant to their lives. More to the point, marginalized students appear to learn more effectively in these classrooms, which bring in the real world.

While considering the nature of resiliency, keep in mind that it is not a final stage in development or a static state. Most children in P-12 classrooms show some qualities of being resilient but also demonstrate areas for concern. For example, many children have at least one adult role model in their community but also have a language barrier and poor academic performance (e.g., speak a language other than English and/or have difficulty reading). A child may seem non-resilient and marginalized at age seven (diagnosed with a severe learning disability)--and struggle to the head of his class by high school graduation. The authors have drawn on several decades of public school and university P-12 teaching experience to reach this conclusion.

In order to fully understand resiliency, a consideration of the qualities of non-resiliency is also necessary. Hahn devised a list of common factors associated with students who drop out of school (Hahn, 1987):

1. They are older than their classmates
2. They have a history of poor academic performance
3. They are more likely to become pregnant as minors
4. They dislike school
5. They find work more attractive than school
6. They were raised in a single parent home or raised on welfare
7. They have at least one undiagnosed learning disability
8. They have a language barrier.

One illustration of these characteristics involves a young woman named Keisha [name changed] in an urban, alternative high school. As Keisha herself explained, her English teacher was her role model, inspiring her to consider becoming a teacher. Keisha's eleventh grade English class led a series of month-long events to honor African and African-American culture and history throughout the school, a major interdisciplinary project. This Celebration of Africa accomplished many of the goals noted in best practice literature: forging close relationships with teachers, improving social and academic skills, drawing on culturally relevant instruction and texts, and using a teamwork approach to an authentic project. According to Keisha and many of her classmates, this presentation was one of the most enjoyable assignments of their school lives. Keisha stated that she had never liked school until this year and this English course. However, this case study becomes more complicated. The day of her presentation, Keisha told her English teacher privately that she was pregnant and planning to drop out of school. Keisha had been raised on welfare and planned to apply for welfare payments while seeking a job in retail. Her English teacher's dreams for Keisha seemed to vanish that day. However, Keisha's English teacher had taken a similar path herself at age 17, but she had become resilient, completing a high school diploma and continuing in college, becoming a teacher while managing as a single mother.

Recent research gives us insight into some of the reasons this Celebration of Africa proved so meaningful to these eleventh grade students. CREDE publishes strategies for effective pedagogy on its web site, strategies that should meet the needs of all learners but that are especially useful with students who are ethnically or culturally diverse (Echevarria, 1998). These five strategies are as follows:

1. connecting school to students' lives
2. the creation of a "joint productive activity" by teachers and students
3. teaching through conversation
4. teaching complex thinking
5. the development of language skills through cross-curricular methods.

In considering the pedagogical approach used in this Celebration of Africa, the most prominent aspect is its interdisciplinary nature. This high school unit is one example of a larger concept of school curricula devised by James Banks (2003). In his book *Teaching Strategies for Ethnic Studies*, Banks recommends that schools develop multicultural education around key concepts, taught across disciplines (P-12). He suggests, for instance, that social studies could address these questions, probably most suited to upper middle grades and high school students: In what ways are the cultures of ethnic groups such as African Americans, Jewish Americans, and Mexican Americans similar and different? Why? These questions could act as extension activities for units such as the Celebration of Africa unit. Simultaneously, within the same unit, students could explore this question in mathematics: What is the relationship between the number system used within a society and its culture? Teachers and students could work as teams to complete this interdisciplinary unit, also involving literature, music, drama, physical education, art, language arts/communication, home economics, and science (Banks, 2003, pp. 32-34).

These focus questions on culture should lead to lively and meaningful classroom discussions. Discussions about real-world issues that matter to students can lead to the level of genuine motivation that Keisha felt in her eleventh grade class. This unit seems to meet many students' need for belonging and power, which Glasser states are the most difficult needs to meet. Additionally, with a large amount of student decision making involved in the kind of presentations to give and in developing the presentations, many students' needs for freedom and fun were also met. Grant and Sleeter had similar findings about students' needs for some sense of control and enjoyment in school (2003). From a survey of working-class students' attitudes toward classroom activities, Grant and Sleeter developed a list of activities that students said they liked; activities that also taught them subject area content. These activities included "small-group projects, whole-class discussion in which kids do most of the talking, and lab experiments" (2003, p. 5). The least popular activities were listening to lectures and watching films (2003, p. 5). Thus these students confirmed that they found hands-on projects entailing teamwork to be fun and informative. It is easy to generalize these study results. Grant and Sleeter reached the same conclusions as did Echevarria (1998) and Ladson-Billings (2001) in studies which were described earlier in this chapter.

Almost any topic can be addressed through the use of an educated debate, which is one way to ensure that all students participate. Students can be assigned to research controversial topics and then defend a pro or con stance. A great deal of content can be covered and the students are actively involved in their own learning. An example from science is cloning (for high school and college-level courses). All biology classes cover DNA structure but usually in a lecture or laboratory format. In contrast, students will learn the basic structure of DNA during preparation for a debate and may even learn more details than they would by just watching their teacher write on the board in the front of the class.

Another strategy for actively involving the students in the classroom involves mutual teaching opportunities for the instructor and the students. This practice is called reciprocal teaching (Palincsar & Brown, 1985) and, as the name implies, students and teachers share the responsibility for the teaching process. This process can include reading texts and making observations. During the reading or observing, the students summarize the material and develop questions on it. In addition students make predictions about what might occur next in the text or what the outcome of a demonstration might be. This process helps students clarify instructional content that might otherwise have not been clearly learned, read or explained. Also, in simplified, highly scaffolded form, reciprocal teaching works well with elementary students. It is an effective tool for teaching reading and higher order thinking at the middle grades, high school, and college levels. This practice is similar to the Socratic Method whereby the instructor guides the students during the discussion by answering a question with a question in round table fashion. The teacher is asking as many questions as the students, and in answering, the students are doing as much teaching as the teacher. Haberman states that "modeling is the best way to foster children's intrinsic need to learn" (1995, p. 34); this Socratic method stimulates students' desire to learn.

The observations in the aforementioned paragraph are often appropriate in science classes because some processes are either too dangerous for the students to perform, or too costly to have enough available resources for all of the students to perform the experiment. If it is not too dangerous or costly, an excellent classroom condition can be created by incorporating hands-on activities for each student. In fact all the content areas have published reports on national standards that call for an increase in hands-on activities in P-12 classrooms, as reported in Zemelman et. al. (1998). This is one example of effective hands-on instruction from a high school science classroom.

> "The teacher can explain the proper use of the scalpel, and then have the students read directions from a lab manual, but the students will not experience the proper technique for the separation of tissue until they experience it for themselves. Developing concepts and relationships from empirical experience can sometimes be accomplished through visual observation, but often in science the

> empirical experience must take the form of hands-on material manipulation" (Thompson & MacDougall, 2002, p. 45).

Students often are required to sit all day with only brief moments to move around between subjects in primary schools, and between classes in secondary schools. Many students may learn more through hands-on activities (Zemelman et. al., 1998), and in addition they may look forward to the opportunity of getting out of their seats during the learning process. A hands-on and kinesthetic classroom is especially effective with African American students, according to Sanacore (2004). With this active learning approach, students look forward to entering the classroom.

Similarly, Haberman (1995) highlights 20 strategies designed to convince children that learning is "intrinsically useful" (pp. 19-20), including these five strategies that seem especially helpful for reaching marginalized students: raising questions with no known answers to prompt student investigation; using computers; choosing topics from real events or the mass media; modeling behavior that establishes that the teacher cares about these students; and using individual student leaders and teams to perform extension activities (Haberman, 1995, pp. 19-20). One strategy needs more elaboration here, the use of computers. Research findings on the effectiveness of computers in reaching marginalized students and on achieving learning goals have been mixed (Roblyer, Dozier-Henry, & Burnette, 1996; Livingstone, 2003). In fact, Gorski states flatly, "There is virtually no evidence that across the board, computers and the Internet strengthen teaching or student achievement" (Gorski, 2004, p. 37). However, several research studies have suggested that computers provide a constructive means for stimulating the interest of students who may otherwise not find school interesting (Kozma & Comminger, 1992; Bialo & Sivin, 1989; Pask-McCartney, 1989; and Summers, 1990-1991). Two studies appeared to show that marginalized students spent more time on learning tasks that involved computers (Pask-McCartney, 1989; Summers 1990-1991). Several studies indicate that technology can be an excellent tool for engaging students in analyzing and synthesizing multicultural information (Anderson & Speck, 2001; Diamond & Moore, 1995; Snyder, 1999). Software programs that are particularly effective in teaching multiculturalism include Wiggleworks by Scholastic, Multicultural Links, and encyclopedias on disks such as Compton's and the World Atlas. Since the earliest days of computer use, students have seemed more intrinsically motivated to engage in learning tasks on computers because they felt they could control their own learning, according to Roblyer (2000). This evidence brings new insight to Glasser's Choice Theory with its focus on students' meeting their basic needs to feel free and powerful (Glasser, 1998). One important caveat, however, emerges in three studies: advanced computer tasks involving hypertext and interactive videodiscs can be too difficult for those students who are struggling academically (Kozma, 1991, 1994; McNeil & Wilson, 1991). These students may still learn to use these complex computer tools, but they need the teacher to guide them through structured learning activities (Kozma, 1991, 1994; McNeil & Wilson, 1991).

For several years, the educational community has been concerned with the effects of the digital divide, defined by Gorski as a divide between households who have computers and those that do not (2001, p. 14). For instance, families comprised of African Americans and Latinos are much less likely to own a computer than are families of white Americans, Asians, and Asian Americans. Analyzed by income and educational level, a significant and growing divide occurs between people with the highest level of education and income and those at the lowest level (Gorski, 2001, pp. 14-15). Schools have been expected to assist those students who do not own computers to reach a level of literacy equal to that of their more advantaged peers. This is an onerous task. In order to accomplish this task, teachers may turn to books such as Roblyer's *Integrating Educational Technology into Teaching* (2000) and Gorski's *Multicultural Education and the Internet: Intersections and Integrations* (2001), which describe K-12 best practice techniques using technology. These books also contain sections that specifically address the needs of marginalized (at risk) students and feature dozens of useful software programs and web sites.

Another important strategy for best practice involves relating the students' culture and/or ethnicity to one's teaching. Teaching a culturally relevant curriculum can also help to create a positive atmosphere in which students are less likely to drop out. The culturally relevant curriculum is vital for ethnic minorities with its focus on students' own culture, addressing their concerns and background (Au, 1993; Delpit, 1995; Diamond & Moore, 1995). Ladson-Billings describes the effect on African American students of implementing a culturally relevant curriculum. This curriculum aims to counteract the negative effects of curricula, texts, and hidden political agendas that have historically rendered ethnic minorities invisible in many schools. In so doing, it assists African American students to develop an ethnic identity and to pursue academic excellence without losing their identity (Ladson-Billings, 1995, pp. 11 & 17). To name just one example, Keisha's alternative high school engaged in a culturally relevant curriculum in its African program. This African high school curriculum also matches Sanacore's requirements for effectively teaching African American students. The whole school was the classroom, creating myriad opportunities for interaction and physical movement in a structured but not rigid environment. Projects and presentations involved students in high-order thinking tasks that activated their prior knowledge of lessons learned in other high school courses about Africa. Additionally, culturally relevant instruction used storytelling activities as the oral tradition plays a major role in the African American community. (Sanacore, J., 2004, pp. 749-751). All of these instructional strategies should strengthen marginalized students' academic skills, thus increasing their resiliency.

The use of storytelling is another valuable instructional tool that is especially effective with minority students. Storytelling works well in any classroom, P-12 through college level, with homogeneous or heterogeneous groups. Elementary students always enjoy story time, but this practice does not need to be limited to a certain age group. Any content can be learned and discussed through stories and metaphors. One example that could apply to both the middle school and high school levels involves cell division. The assignment could designate that students give the cell a name and create an anthropomorphic situation, complete with a personality. As an example the cell named Jamal is feeling funny inside as though butterflies are fluttering around in his stomach, a metaphor for the chromosomes becoming visible instead of their being dispersed throughout the cytoplasm, and thus not dense enough to be seen during other times in the life of a cell. This metaphor activity lends itself well to oral instruction and requires the students to stretch themselves cognitively, thus enhancing their use of higher-level thinking skills.

Storytelling with a link to writing is also a valuable tool in instruction. Students who are English Language Learners (ELL) obviously need more instruction in the use of the English language than do students with English as their native tongue (Echevarria, 1998). Instructors can teach comprehension through literature across the curriculum. A science example could be to use literature such as Mowat's *Never Cry Wolf,* a novel about interactions in Alaska between humans, wolves, and caribou, to aid in the instruction dealing with ecosystems and niches. This gives the students an incentive to better learn the language because the reading is interesting and in novel form instead of textbook form. The content can then be addressed through guided discussions with students using elaborated responses, and encouraging higher-order thinking skills.

Similarly, ELL students at all grade levels need thorough training in vocabulary, involving multiple encounters with words in different genres, content areas, and contexts, according to a recent study (Droop & Verhoeven, 2003). Another recent study reminds educators that an important tool for strengthening reading comprehension for ELL students is to reread a text, a useful strategy for primary classrooms in general and for ELL students at all grade levels (Samuels, 2002). Also vital in teaching primary grades and ELL students is the shared reading technique in which the teacher reads a book aloud while talking students through the book with questions and predictions (Lenters, 2005). Shared reading seems to assist students in building comprehension skills (Lenters, 2005). According to two studies (Lenters, 2005; Anderson & Roit, 1996), graded readers also look as if they assist students to develop vocabulary skills, but Lenters cautions that these graded readers must be "somewhat reflective of natural speech" (2005, p. 331) to be effective. Thus, a storytelling approach to classroom texts may work well when selecting texts for meeting the needs for vocabulary acquisition of ELL students.

A crucial method for implementing culturally relevant instruction is to find materials that relate to students' lives and cultures (Ladson-Billings, 2001; Echevarria, 1998). One series of books that features stories from many nationalities and cultures, the American Girl series titled Girls of Many Lands, gives middle grades students opportunities to glimpse societies new to them, such as India prior to its independence (i.e., Divakaruni's book *Neela*). For P-12 trade books and videotapes that appeal to diverse students, educators should see the annotated bibliography in Pang's book *Multicultural education: A Caring-centered, Reflective Approach* (2001) and reviews in the journal *Multicultural Perspectives*, published by the National Association for Multicultural Education. An excellent source of nonfiction (elementary through high school) books on ethnic minorities is the Carter G. Woodson Book Award winners, an annual prize, with full information found at this web site: www.socialstudies.org/awards/woodson. These texts and films focus on societies throughout the world, including historical depictions.

Similarly, culturally relevant books that are routinely required by schools become important to allowing students from culturally diverse backgrounds to see themselves represented in the school curricula. It is important to note, too, that a culturally relevant curriculum also benefits mainstream students from a white, middle class background (Nieto, 2002). White students who only experience Eurocentric K-12 curricula may never develop respect for other cultural groups, according to Ayers (1993) and Boutte (1999). More importantly, white students may develop a superior attitude toward other cultures, forming a barrier to communication and cooperation in an increasingly diverse world, Boutte concludes after a review of relevant research (1999). *Anne Frank: The Diary of a Young Girl*, one of the most frequently assigned books in public schools at the middle school and high school levels, is the classic story of a Jewish family's struggle to survive in Nazi Germany. A related and contemporary story, *Zlata's Diary: A Child's Life in Sarajevo,* is a diary written by an eleven-year-old girl in Sarajevo during the war of the 1990s. Assigning these books as a pair gives students historical perspective, especially helpful in studying social justice. One can usually find a novel, textbook, or magazine with material relating to the background of ELL students. These students will be more likely to read such material than they would material with which they have trouble identifying. This will help with the language skills and make learning more enjoyable to the students.

A popular reading-writing technique that strengthens the language acquisition skills of primary students and ELL students is the language experience approach (LEA). According to Tompkins, LEA is a teaching technique in which students dictate an account to their teacher, who records it. Then the teacher uses this newly created text for reading instruction (Tompkins, 2003, p. 398). Lenters notes the advantages of LEA to young language learner students in that it permits them to "understand the encoding of oral language into written language" in a lesson that is meaningful (Lenters, 2004-2005, p. 333). This is a strategy that primary teachers have used for years with all ability levels, a strategy that fits easily into a culturally relevant curriculum.

Cultural relevance of a subject may be influenced by biases, unbeknownst to the students present in the classroom. Chambers (1983) conducted a study with a sample size of 4807 students ranging in age from kindergarten to the fifth grade. He asked them to formulate their respective images of a scientist and only 28 women scientists were drawn (p. 261). In the years since that study was completed, one might assume that the stereotypical image of a scientist may have changed. However, Newton and Newton (1998) researched the effectiveness of a national curriculum at altering the stereotypes which existed regarding scientists, and their results re-confirmed the prevalence of gender-biased stereotypes. The most significant consequence of this faulty thinking is that students with pre-existing stereotypes regarding scientists may be less positive about science if they do not fit the stereotypical mold. Modifying pre-existing beliefs about a subject or career path should be attempted if effective instruction is to take place.

Fortunately, reversing or modifying stereotypes has been tried and found to be effective by Edwards (1999) through the use of multimedia software. This study was conducted with community college students as the participants and with minorities being the target population. The software included graphic images with occupation and background information about ethnic groups which were considered counter-stereotypic. The results indicated that the participants exhibited less negative stereotypic attitudes than did the students who did not participate in the multimedia software. Clearly, teaching strategies can be effective in helping to change scientific stereotypes which exist among minority populations.

A strategy which can be employed in the science classroom involves materials that may be contributing to these stereotypes. Science textbooks often have drawings or pictures accompanying the content that includes a person involved in the field being covered. A valuable teachable moment appears every time one of these pictures is present because the teacher can lead the class in a discussion regarding the person(s) present in the diagram or picture. Are they all of one color, gender, age? These discussions can result in the students' discovery that anybody could be depicted regardless of their backgrounds.

An intriguing extension activity for this lesson would involve engaging students (from middle grades level through graduate school) in a Socratic discussion about race. This extension delves into science, social studies, and multiculturalism. Ideally this lesson would begin with a consideration of students' own race, culture, nationality, and background with individual journal writing leading to discussion in pairs. Then students who felt comfortable volunteering their own information or the information of a classmate would report orally to the whole class. A general discussion on the influence of one's background and race would lead to students writing a series of questions about the effects of factors such as race on one's perceptions and one's teaching. The next step is to view the film series *Race: The Power of Illusion* by Newsreel, stopping periodically to review the film material and the students' questions (Adelman, 2003). This film series deals with the history of race and racism in the United States of America, beginning with the scientific premise that there is no genetic basis for race. Most students are surprised and shocked at the film's revelations. Following this film, the teacher could lead students into a consideration of the answers to their own questions, guide them through the film content (key questions appear on the web site for Newsreel), and conclude by talking and writing about the effect this new information will have on students' teaching dispositions.

Teachers' attitudes toward students are a major factor in creating a caring-centered school. Although two research studies suggest that most teachers unconsciously prefer students from the same race, class, and set of values as themselves, Ladson-Billings urges teachers to work consciously to overcome this tendency. Thus, teachers can assure their students that they genuinely care for them (1995, p.66). In contrast, many teachers hold a cultural deficit perspective on their students from cultures or races that differ from their own, according to Pang (2001) and Zemelman et. al. (1998). In this point of view, "disadvantaged" students, their families, and their culture are blamed for these students not fully meeting the expectations of public schooling. In this perspective, the ELL child and the child's family and culture are to blame when the child performs poorly on a standardized test administered in English (Pang, 2001, p. 57). Zemelman (1998) reminds us that this same ELL child may be approaching fluency in his/her first language, an intellectual accomplishment not taken into account by those who label ELL children as illiterate. This child has many literacy skills to build on and can be as successful in school and life as other children, given adults' guidance and care, as Zemelman makes clear (1998).

A vital component of a resilient school is an instructional leader who promotes strategies such as those discussed in this chapter. Such a caring-centered school would help marginalized students by providing a structured environment to develop qualities of resiliency: e.g., long-term goals, an internal locus of control, and a positive relationship with a mentor at school (Reed et. al., 1995, pp. 3-10). Certain students need more help than others, but all students will benefit from the practices described in this chapter. Enjoyable educational experiences can help to foster resiliency in children. Information from this manuscript can be used in order to help to identify qualities of children and schools that promote resiliency characteristics. Certain populations, such as African Americans and English Language Learners, may require additional support in order to gain the characteristics needed to remain in school. CREDE's research indicates that most teachers are skilled in identifying resilient and non-resilient students and in finding the best strategies to use in order to address their needs. Unfortunately, many teachers never adapt their teaching techniques accordingly (Padron et al, 3).

As resiliency is not a fixed state, it would be a mistake for educators to dismiss any child, saying that he or she is non-resilient. The authors' reflections on resiliency presented in this chapter derive from case studies and professional literature in education and psychology, which demonstrate that resiliency is complex condition involving multiple facets. Educators need to view resiliency as a dynamic state that causes many students to succeed in school despite all odds. Accordingly, educators should teach employing approaches that strengthen resiliency. Keep in mind the consequences of not helping students to attain resiliency, the cost in drop outs, and the implication for an increase in substance abuse and crime. Using best practice and adopting a caring-centered ethic will improve schools. Educators can improve the favorable odds for resilient children while helping non-resilient children to recognize the odds against them and beat these odds.

Recommended Readings in Children's Literature

Divakaruni, C. B. (2002). *Neela: Victory song*. Middleton, WI: Pleasant Company.
Filipovic, Z. (1995). *Zlata's diary: A child's life in Sarajevo*. Penguin Books: New York.
Frank, A. (1993). *The diary of a young girl*. NY: Bantam.
Mowat, F. (2001). *Never cry wolf*. Boston: Back Bay Books.

Recommended Readings for Further Study

Barton, P. (2003). *Parsing the achievement gap: Baselines for tracking progress*. Princeton, NJ: Educational Testing Service.

Barton, P. E. (2004). Why does the gap persist? *Educational Leadership, 62*, 8-13.

Brooks, J. G. & Brooks, M. G. (1993). *In search of understanding: The case for constructivist classrooms.* Alexandria, VA: Association for Supervision and Curriculum Development.

Burt, M., & Aron, L. (2000). *America's homeless II: Populations and services.* Washington, D.C.: The Urban Institute.

Comer, J. P. (2004). *Leave no child behind: Preparing today's youth for tomorrow's world.* New Haven, CT: Yale University Press.

Derman-Sparks, L. & Phillips, C. B. (1997). *Teaching/learning anti-racism: A developmental approach.* NY: Teachers College Press.

Duffield, B. (2001). The educational rights of homeless children: Policies and practices. *Educational Studies, 32*, 323-336.

Hall, J.A., & Maza, P.L. (1990). No fixed address: The effects of homelessness on families and children. *Child and Youth Services, 14*, 35-47.

Hickman, P., S. Pollard-Durodola, S. Vaughan. (2004). Storybook reading: Improving vocabulary and comprehension for English-language learners. *The Reading Teacher, 57*, 720-730.

Jaffe, M. L. (1998). *Adolescence.* NY: John Wiley & Sons.

Ladson-Billings, G. (2001). *Crossing over to Canaan: The journey of new teachers in diverse classrooms.* San Francisco: Josey-Bass.

Noll, E. & Watkins, R. (2003). The impact of homelessness on children's literacy experiences. *The Reading Teacher, 57*, 363-371.

Rothstein, R. (2004). A wider lens on the black-white achievement gap, *Phi Delta Kappan, 86,* 105-100.

Rutter, M. (1985). Resilience in the face of adversity: Protective factors and resistance to psychiatric disorder. *British Journal of Psychiatry, 147*, 598-611.

Rutter, M. (1987). Psychosocial resilience and protective mechanisms. *American Journal of Orthopsychiatry, 57*, 316-331.

Spring, J. (2004). *Deculturalization and the struggle for equality: A brief history of dominated cultures in the United States*. 4th ed. Boston: McGraw Hill.

Zimmerman, M.A. & Arunkumar, R. (1994). Resiliency research: Implications for schools and policy. *Social Policy Report*, Society for Research in Child Development. Ann Arbor, MI, 1-18.

References

Adelman, L. (Director). *Race: The Power of Illusion.* Motion picture. California Newsreel.

Anderson, R., & Speck, B. (2001). *Using technology in K-8 literacy classrooms.* Upper Saddle River, NJ: Merrill Prentice Hall.

Anderson, V., & Roit, M. (1996). Linking reading comprehension instruction to language development for language-minority students. *Elementary School Journal, 96,* 295-310.

Au, K. (1993). *Literacy instruction in multicultural settings.* Fort Worth, TX: Harcourt Brace Jovanovich College Publishers.

Au, K. A. & Kawakami, A. J. (1994). Cultural congruence in instruction. In E.R. Hollins, J. E. King, & W.C. Hayman (Eds.) *Teaching diverse populations: Formulating a knowledge base* (pp. 5-24). Albany: State University of New York Press.

Ayers, W. (1993). *To teach: The journey of a teacher.* NY: Teachers College Press.

Banks, J. A. (2003). *Teaching strategies for ethnic studies.* 7th ed. Boston: Allyn & Bacon.

Bialo, E. & Sivin, J. (1989). Computers and at-risk youth: Software and hardware that can help. *Classroom Computer Learning, 9,* 48-55.

Berk, L. E. (2004). *Development through the lifespan.* 3rd ed. Boston: Allyn & Bacon.

Boutte, G. (1999). *Multicultural education: Raising consciousness.* Boston: Wadsworth Publishing Company.

California Newsreel, retrieved on January 30, 2005, at www.newsreel.org.

Chambers, D. W. (1983). Stereotypic images of the scientist: The draw-a-scientist test. *Science Education,* 67, 255-265.

CREDE, the Center for Research on Education, Diversity, and Excellence, retrieved on January 17, 2005, at http://www.crede.org.

Delpit, L. (1995). *Other people's children: Cultural conflict in the classroom.* NY: The New Press.

Diamond, B., & Moore, M. (1995). *Multicultural literacy: Mirroring the reality of the classroom.* NY: Longman.

Droop, M. & Verhoeven, L. (2003). Language proficiency and reading ability in first- and second-language learners. *Reading Research Quarterly, 35,* 520-523.

Duke, D. L. (2002). *Creating safe schools for all children.* Boston, MA: Allyn & Bacon.

Echevarria, J. (Ed.). (1998). Teaching language minority students in elementary schools. Report for the Center for Research on Education, Diversity & Excellence. Retrieved 6/7/04 at www.cal.org/creded/pubs/ResBrief1.html.

Edwards, L. D. (1999, February). *Using multimedia to counter stereotypes in science classrooms: New perceptions of who becomes a scientist.* Paper presented at the National Convention of the Association for Educational Communications and Technology, Houston, TX.

Garmezy, N. (1991). Resilience and vulnerability to adverse developmental outcomes associated with poverty. *American Behavioral Scientist, 34,* 416-430.

Glasser, W. (1998). *The quality school: Managing students without coercion.* New York: HarperPerennial.

Gorski, P. (2001). *Multicultural education and the Internet: Intersections and integrations*. NY: McGraw Hill.

Gorski, P. (2004). Multicultural education and progressive pedagogy in the online information age. *Multicultural perspectives 6*, 37-48.

Grant, C. A. & Sleeter, C. E. (2003). *Turning on learning: Five approaches for multicultural teaching plans for race, class, gender, and disability*. NY: John Wiley & Sons.

Gregory, E. (1996). *Making sense of a new world: Learning to read in a second language.* London: Paul Chapman.

Haberman, M. (1995). *Star teachers of children in poverty*. West Lafayette, IN: Kappa Delta Pi.

Hahn, A., (1987). Reaching out to America's dropouts: What to do? *Phi Delta Kappan, 69*, 258-260.

Kozma, R. (1991). Listening with media. *Review of Educational Research, 61*(2), 179-211.

Kozma, R. (1994). Will media influence learning? Reframing the debate. *Educational Technology Research and Development, 61*(2), 179-211.

Kozma, R. & Croninger, R. (1992). Technology and the fate of at-risk students. *Education and Urban Society, 24*(4), 440-453.

Ladson-Billings, G. (1994). *The dreamkeepers: Successful teachers of African American children.* San Francisco, CA: Jossey-Bass.

Ladson-Billings, G. (2002). Fighting for our lives. *Journal of Teacher Education, 51*, 206-220.

Ladson-Billings, G. (2001). Teaching and cultural competence: What does it take to be a successful teacher in a diverse classroom? *Rethinking Schools, 14*. Retrieved 12/14/04 at www.rethinkingschools.org/archive/15_04/Glb154.html

Lenters, K. (2004/2005). No half measures: Reading instruction for young second-language learners. *The Reading Teacher, 58*, 328-336.

Livingstone, S. (2003). Children's use of the Internet: Reflections on the emerging research agenda. *New Media Society 5*, 147-166.

Luna, B., Garver, K. E., Urban, T. A., Lazar, N. A., & Sweeney, J. A. (2004) Maturation of cognitive processes from late childhood to adulthood. *Child Development* 75 (Sep/Oct.), 1357-1373.

McNeil, B. & Wilson, K. (1991). Meta-analysis of interactive video instruction: A 10-year review of achievement effects. *Journal of Computer-Based Instruction, 18*(1), 1-6.

Newton, Lynn D. & Newton, Douglas P. (1998). Primary children's conceptions of science and the scientist: Is the impact of a national curriculum breaking down the stereotype. *International Journal of Science Education,* 20(9), 1137-1149.

Nieto, S. (2002). *Language, culture, and teaching: Critical perspectives for a new century*. Mahwah, N.J.: Lawrence Erlbaum Associates.

Noddings, N. (1992). *The challenge to care in schools: An alternative approach to education*. N.Y.: Teachers College Press.

Padron, Y. N., Waxman, H., Brown, A. P., & Powers, R. A. (2000). Improving classroom instruction and silent learning for resilient and non-resilient English language learners. Center for Research on Education, Diversity & Excellence, 2.

Palincsar, A. & Brown, A. (1985). *Reciprocal teaching: Activities to promote reading in your mind.* Ed. T. Harris & E. Cooper. NY: The College Board.

Pang, V. O. (2001). *Multicultural education: A caring-centered, reflective approach.* NY: McGraw Hill.

Pask-McCartney, C. (1989). A discussion about motivation. Proceedings of Selected Research Presentations at the Annual Convention of the AECT (ERIC Document Reproduction No. ED 308 816).

Reed, D.F., McMillan, J.H., & McBee, R.H. (1995). Defying the Odds: Middle schoolers in high risk circumstances who succeed. *Middle School Journal, 27*, 3-10.

Roblyer, M.D., Dozier-Henry, O., & Burnette, A. (1996). Technology and multicultural education: The "uneasy alliance." *Educational Technology 35*(3), 5-12.

Roblyer, M.D. & Edwards, J. (2000). *Integrating educational technology into teaching.* 2nd ed. Upper Saddle River, NJ: Merrill Prentice Hall.

Samuels, S. J. (2002). Reading fluency: Its development and assessment. In A.E. Farstrup & S.J. Samuels (Eds.), *What research has to say about reading instruction* (pp. 166-183). Newark, DR: International Reading Association.

Sanacore, J. (2004). Genuine caring and literacy learning for African American children. *The Reading Teacher, 57*, 744-753.

Slavin, R., Karweit, N.L., & Wasik, B.A. (1992-1993). Preventing early school failure: What works? *Educational Leadership, 50, 10-18.* Retrieved 6/7/04 at www.ascd.org/publications/ed_lead/199212/slavin.html.

Snyder, J. (1999). Using information technology in language and literacy education: An introduction. In J. Hancock (Ed.), *Teaching literacy using information technology* (pp. 1-10). Newark, DE: International Reading Association.

Summers, J. (1990-1991). Effect of interactivity upon student achievement, completion intervals, and affective perceptions. *Journal of Educational Technology Systems, 19*(1), 53-57.

Thompson, B. R. & MacDougall, G. D. (2002). Intelligent teaching. *The Science Teacher*, 69, 44-48.

Tompkins, G. E. (2003). *Literacy for the 21st century: Teaching reading and writing in pre-kindergarten through grade 4.* Upper Saddle River, NJ: Merrill Prentice Hall.

Werner, E.E. (1993). Risk, resilience, and recovery: Perspectives from the Kauai Longitudinal Study. *Development and Psychopathology, 5*, 503-515.

Zemelman, S., Daniels, H., & Hyde, A. (1998). *Best practice for teaching and learning in America's schools.* 2nd ed. Portsmouth, NH: Heinemann.

Acknowledgements: Thank you to Monica Allmond and Angeleen McDonnell for their assistance in developing this chapter.